Affluence with Abundance

'An insightful and well-written book, describing the hard transition of foraging communities in Namibia from relative affluence during the Stone Age to contemporary poverty and misery. Avoiding both modern conceits and romantic fantasies, Suzman chronicles how economics and politics have finally conquered some of the last outposts of hunter-gatherers, and how much humankind can still learn from the disappearing way of life of the most marginalised communities on earth' Yuval Noah Harari, internationally bestselling author of *Sapiens* and *Homo Deus*

'Suzman deftly weaves his experiences and observations with lessons on human evolution, the history of human migration and the fate of African communities since the arrival of Europeans. The overarching aim of the book is more ambitious still: to challenge the reader's ideas about both hunter-gatherer life and human nature' *Economist*

'A vivid and compassionate portrait . . . An elegant and absorbing contribution to our knowledge of the hunting and gathering way of life, both in the present and in the recent past . . . The story Suzman tells is complex, addressing the divergent fates of several Khoisan-speaking groups over a long period of time. He tells it with aplomb. *Affluence without Abundance* is a book in the high tradition of anthropological writing' *Financial Times*

'[An] honest and sharp account . . . As much personal memoir as anthropological survey . . . Suzman's talent for evoking the region's vast and haunting landscapes, his elegiac account of a passing covenant with nature, and his warm and compassionate character sketches of individual Ju/'hoansi, make this a fascinating and at times profoundly moving work of literary non-fiction' *Irish Times*

'Suzman's descriptive prose and affection for his subjects generate the reader's genuine empathy. This fascinating glimpse into a disappearing way of life lead   re wealth and possessi   ccount of the

lives of Bushmen, past and present, offers plenty of fuel for thought'
Washington Post

'This book has truth on every page' Elizabeth Marshall Thomas, author
of *The Harmless People* and *The Old Way*

'This beautiful book – part memoir, part ethnography – offers a window
into the lives of one of the most enduring of human cultures . . . If you
have ever wondered how it might be to measure wealth not by material
possessions but by the strength of social relations between people, read
this book' Wade Davis, author of *The Wayfinders* and *Into the Silence*

'[A] beautiful, heartfelt paean. *Affluence without Abundance* is learned
without being condescending, tender yet unsentimental. It is both a celebration of an ancient way of life and a lament for all that has been lost in
our own headlong pursuit of the material' Peter Godwin, author of *Mukiwa*
and *When a Crocodile Eats the Sun*

'Through neglect, abuse and misunderstanding, an ancient way of life is
being finally extinguished. Yet, Suzman argues, even now the Bushmen
have much to teach us about a social order that, in many ways, offered a
freer, fairer existence and a non-invasive adaption to ecology' *New Scientist*

'[Suzman creates] a feeling for the landscape, the difficulties encountered by
the Bushmen, and the pleasures of their simple, if rapidly changing, way
of life . . . This is a delightful book, full of perceptiveness and understanding' *Science*

A Note on the Author

Midway through an anthropology degree at St. Andrews University in Scotland – and with a head full of adventure – South African James Suzman left home and hitched a ride into Botswana's eastern Kalahari in June 1991. After a few months he returned to university and completed his undergraduate degree a year later. By the time he was twenty-five, he was awarded his doctorate in social anthropology from Edinburgh University. Since then he has lived and worked with every major Bushman group in the Kalahari Desert in Botswana and Namibia. Better known in the Kalahari by his !Kung name, /Kunta, Suzman remains locked into the Bushman universe.

He was awarded the Smuts Commonwealth Fellowship in African Studies at Cambridge University for the period 2001 to 2004. In 2007 he joined the De Beers Group of Companies where he was global head of public affairs.

Since 2013, Suzman has worked full-time on Kalahari issues and he founded the anthropological think tank Anthropos, based in Cambridge.

AFFLUENCE
WITHOUT
ABUNDANCE

WHAT WE CAN LEARN FROM
THE WORLD'S MOST
SUCCESSFUL CIVILISATION

JAMES SUZMAN

BLOOMSBURY PUBLISHING
LONDON • OXFORD • NEW YORK • NEW DELHI • SYDNEY

BLOOMSBURY PUBLISHING
Bloomsbury Publishing Plc
50 Bedford Square, London, WC1B 3DP, UK

BLOOMSBURY, BLOOMSBURY PUBLISHING and the Diana logo are
trademarks of Bloomsbury Publishing Plc

First published in Great Britain 2017
This edition published 2019

ISBN: PB: 978-1-5266-0931-1; eBook: 978-1-5266-1550-3

2 4 6 8 10 9 7 5 3 1

Typeset by Westchester Publishing Services
Printed and bound in Great Britain by CPI Group (UK) Ltd, Croydon CR0 4YY

To find out more about our authors and books visit www.bloomsbury.com
and sign up for our newsletters

CONTENTS

Author's Note

This book is the result of nearly a quarter of a century working among southern Africa's San peoples. It is the product of many close friendships forged over this period as well as many interviews with and incidents involving people I know less well. In some instances, I have changed people's names or disguised them in other ways to protect their privacy.

There are many other people whose thoughts and lives have shaped this book but whose individual stories are largely absent. None more so than my friend and mentor !A/ae "Frederik" Langman, who in 1994 eased me gently into the then unfamiliar and sometimes terrifying reality of the Omaheke Ju/'hoansi. !A/ae is now the government-recognized chief of the Omaheke Ju/'hoansi. I am proud to say that we still consider each other family. This book is dedicated to him and my many friends at Skoonheid Resettlement Camp in Namibia's Omaheke Region.

On Names and Clicks

NAMES

In spring of 1904 the German zoologist, linguist, anatomist, and philosopher Leonard Schultze was having the adventure of a lifetime. He had spent several months traveling to German South-West Africa (now Namibia). In addition to evaluating the fishing potential of Namibian coasted waters on behalf of the German colonial office, he hoped to collect a range of zoological specimens to take back to Germany. But his plans were upset by the outbreak of war that year as the German colonial authorities sought at first to subdue and then exterminate the two most powerful peoples in central Namibia, the Nama and the Herero. The Nama were descendants of indigenous cattle- and sheep-herding populations in the Cape of Good Hope on Africa's southern tip. By 1904, they had adopted Western dress, weapons, and religion. The Herero were a pastoralist people who had dominated much of central Namibia from the eighteenth century onward. Determined not to let what became the most brutal colonial genocide of the twentieth century ruin his trip, Schultze reported cheerfully that instead of collecting zoological specimens while battle raged he would instead "make use of the victims of the war to take parts from fresh native corpses" for the "study of the living body."

Schultze noted two distinct "races" of people in southern Africa. He differentiated the smaller-statured, lighter-skinned, click-language-speaking people like Nama and Bushmen from taller, darker-skinned, central-African-language-speaking people like Herero. For the former, Schultze coined the term "Khoisan," which has now been widely adopted to describe the indigenous people who lived in southern Africa long before the arrival of both white colonials and other African farming peoples.

The term "Khoisan" is a compound of the words "Khoi" (meaning person) and "San" (meaning hunter-gatherer or vagabond) in the largest of the modern Khoisan language groups referred to by linguists as "Khoi." The Khoi (sometimes also spelled "Khoe") refers to the small number of Khoisan, mainly concentrated in what is now South Africa's Northern Cape Province, who had adopted herding by the time of European colonialism. "San" refers to Bushmen: people who still made a living from hunting and gathering.

Khoisan have been referred to by many different labels in the past, most of them derogatory. The most widely used have been "Bushman"—referring to Khoisan who hunted and gathered—and "Hottentot"—referring to those who made a living from livestock herding. Both of these terms were coined by others and both carry a burden. The Dutch term *boschjesman*, from which "Bushman" originated, was the same word used to describe orangutans in the Dutch East India Company's possessions in Malaysia. The term "Hottentot" is a crude onomatopoeia intended to invoke the clicking that makes Khoisan languages so distinctive.

Now, as in the past, Khoisan peoples speak many different languages. And each surviving language community has its own name for itself. Names like "Ju/'hoansi," "G/wikhoe," and "Hai//om." The term "Khoisan" resonates little with them.

Beyond a few San individuals who have cut their political teeth in various UN forums or under the tutelage of indigenous rights organizations, I have met few who care a great deal about what terms others use to refer to them. As far as they are concerned, the problem is not how others refer to them but rather how others treat them.

And, as with hunting and gathering populations the world over, Bushmen have encountered monumental prejudice from pretty much every other people they have encountered. The term for Bushmen in the Tswana language, "Basarwa," invokes a broad set of crude racial stereotypes and is considered by most Bushmen there to be pejorative. In rural Namibia, most refer to themselves as "Bushmen" or by the Afrikaans term "Boesman." They see little stigma attached to it and some view it as positive, because it implicitly reaffirms their status as a "first people" with a special connection to their environments. Internationally, the term "Bushman" is seen as broadly positive, invoking as it does a set of positive if romantic stereotypes. It is for this reason that international NGOs still use the label "Bushmen" and that it remains the most widely used term for them in international literature. It is for this reason that I use the term "Bushmen" here.

It is worth noting, though, that some Khoisan political and community organizations have taken the view that "San" is the most appropriate term to refer to them collectively. As a result, "San" is gradually supplanting "Bushmen" in everyday and official use in much of southern Africa and is generally accepted as the most appropriate term by means of which to refer to speakers of Khoisan languages who are descended from populations that hunted and gathered until very recently.

CLICKS

Khoisan languages are distinguished by many things, from their distinctive use of tone to their phonemic complexity. But they are best known for their frequent and expressive use of clicks. The four basic clicks in Khoisan languages are represented by the symbols ≠, !, //, and /. The Ju/'hoansi, who are the primary subject of the book, have adopted these symbols into the conventional alphabet to represent major click consonants. For most readers it is simplest to ignore them or substitute them with a hard consonant as many people in Namibia and Botswana who aren't comfortable clicking do. Many Namibians refer to the Hai//om Bushmen as "Haikom" and the Ju/'hoansi as "Jukwasi."

/ **Dental click.** This click is made by bringing the tongue softly down from behind the front teeth while sucking in as a mother might in scolding a child with "tsk, tsk, tsk."

≠ **Alveolar-palatal click.** This plosive click is made by bringing the tip of the tongue sharply down the alveolar ridge to the front of the mouth.

! **Palatal click.** This robust click is made by pushing the tongue into the upper palate and bringing it sharply forward and down to make a popping sound like a cork being pulled from a wine bottle.

// **Lateral click.** This click is produced by putting the tongue on the hard palate and drawing breath inward over it. It is a sound familiar to many horsemen when egging their horses on.

To hear how the clicks and names are pronounced, please see the website for the book: www.fromthebush.com.

Southern Africa and the Kalahari Basin

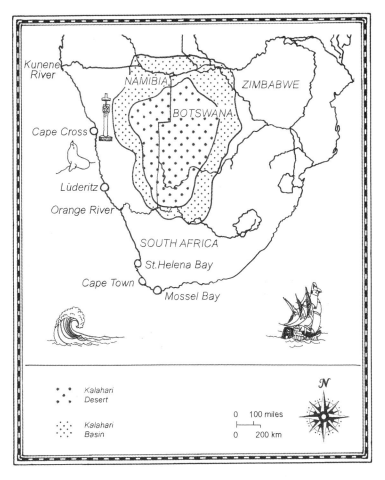

Khoisan Peoples and Language Groups of Southern Africa

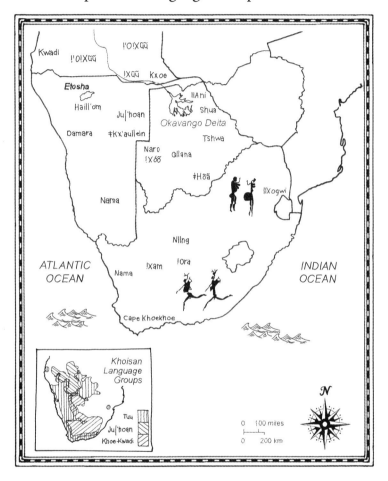

Key Archaeological Sites in Khoisan History

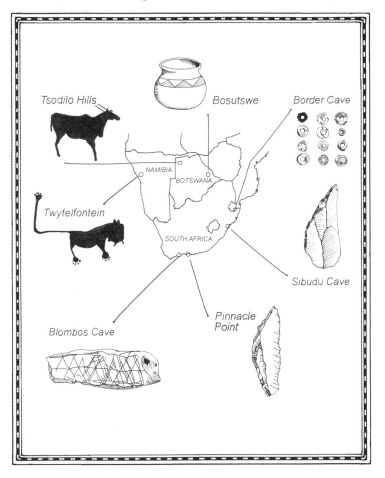

Tsodilo Hills

Bosutswe

Border Cave

NAMIBIA

BOTSWANA

Twyfelfontein

SOUTH AFRICA

Sibudu Cave

Pinnacle
Point

Blombos Cave

Eastern and Central Namibia

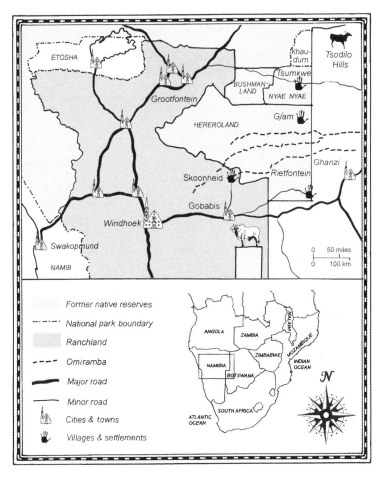

The Bantu Expansion

Congo River

Zambezi River

Kalahari
Desert

Rainforest

Bantu home area
2000 B.C.

Bantu expansion
1000 B.C.

Bantu expansion
A.D. 500

Kingdom of Mapungubwe
founded A.D. 1075

Kingdom of Zimbabwe
founded A.D. 1220

0   250 miles

0   500 km

N

"True happiness is to enjoy the present, without anxious dependence upon the future, not to amuse ourselves with either hopes or fears but to rest satisfied with what we have, which is sufficient, for he that is so wants nothing."

—Seneca

PART ONE

OLD TIMES

I

The Rewards of Hard Work

Skoonheid Resettlement Camp, Namibia, Spring 1995

//Eng had busy hands. When she was not knitting, she fashioned intricately patterned jewelry from ostrich eggshells to sell to the white farmers, or ferreted around in the small garden she had planted in the sand behind her hut. If anyone here was going to persuade the desert to yield up a few vegetables despite the drought, it was //Eng.

Sometimes, when it was too hot to do anything but snooze in the shade, I would imagine what my Ju/'hoan Bushman neighbors like //Eng would have become had they been born into my world. In these moments //Eng would be transformed into a snappily dressed entrepreneur, celebrated and envied in equal measure for her energy and success.

But instead she lived on a resettlement farm in eastern Kalahari, expended her energy on survival, and dressed herself in a patchwork of carefully reworked rags. She was one of thousands of Ju/'hoansi whose ancestors had hunted and gathered in this part of the world from soon after the evolution of modern humans two hundred thousand years ago until the white soldiers, farmers, and magistrates appeared two generations ago—with their guns, borehole pumps, barbed wire, and herds of cattle—and claimed this desert for themselves. After this the Ju/'hoansi and other Bushmen in this part of the Kalahari had no option but to work for white farmers if they wanted to survive. Now //Eng, along with around two hundred other Ju/'hoansi who had been deemed superfluous by the white farmers, had been moved by the government to a newly established resettlement area on what until recently was a Kalahari cattle ranch.

Why did she work so much harder than the others in the resettlement camp? I wondered aloud when sitting with her one afternoon. And why was she always busy when most of the others were content to sit around waiting for the food aid, which we all knew was never enough and never arrived on time?

"/Kunta, my boy," she said, addressing me by my Ju/'hoan name, "do you not know why? I thought that you were supposed to be clever."

I reminded her that she had spent most of the preceding year pointing out her surprise at my stupidity and so asked her to explain.

//Eng spoke fast. She fired out clicks and consonants like a Gatling gun. While at that time I had managed to master the basic clicks of !Kung, the language spoken by the Ju/'hoansi Bushmen, I still struggled to speak it competently. The breathy aspiration, the shifting tones, the growly pharyngealization, the nasalization, and the glottal stops that made this one of the most phonemically sophisticated languages in the world contorted my tongue and teased my ear, so I asked her to explain in Afrikaans, a language that she and most other Ju/'hoansi in this part of the Kalahari were fluent in by the time I started to work there in the early 1990s.

"They are lazy!" she exclaimed. "They do not yet know that to live you now must work hard."

//Eng had the virtues of hard work drummed into her from an early age. Her parents struggled to adjust to farm life and parted ways when //Eng was a toddler, and her headstrong mother took her and her brother to stay on another farm. But soon after arriving there her mother died suddenly and inexplicably. //Eng and her brother were then sent to another farm to be playmates for a white farmer's two children, who led lonely lives when not away in the capital at school. The farmer was kind but intolerant of idleness. This didn't bother //Eng. She had plenty of energy and, when not playing with the children, performed various chores around the house.

"I was very neat. Very organized," she explained. "I cleaned, polished the floors and furniture, dusted, washed clothes, and did sewing and ironing. And because I worked so hard and so well, I was given old clothes and shoes and never went hungry. /Kunta, it was there that I learned to work and to understand how white people lived.

"But these *Bushmen* here still think like the old people who were happy to wait for the manketti nuts to fall from the trees or for a hunter to have good luck and kill a big kudu or an oryx." She laughed at the thought of a belly full of game meat before grabbing the half-smoked cigarette from my outstretched hand.

She sucked down what was left of the cigarette in a single sustained drag, spat, and, with smoke streaming out of her nose, continued. "But people here are happy to wait. They think the new government will look after them. That there will always be food. Yet they complain, complain, complain about being hungry today and fight each other and complain more even when the food comes because it is not enough. But still they do nothing because they think that those food trucks will come again. But the trucks won't always come, /Kunta. One day they will all die from hunger. You will see. But I will work to live, /Kunta. This is what I learned from the whites."

I thought //Eng's characterization of her neighbors was unfair. Not all sat around waiting indigently for the government to deliver emergency food rations. Like people everywhere, the Ju/'hoansi at Skoonheid couldn't abide boredom or the sense of powerlessness that came from being dependent on others. For many, alcohol—when available—provided some respite. It made them forget their pain and their hunger even if it was just as likely to unleash violence as give them pleasure. Some snuck onto the white farms to hunt warthogs, small fowl, springhares, and larger antelope if they were lucky. Some became accomplished stock thieves. Others, nervous of the farmers' guns and dogs, diligently traipsed the wide gravel roads that cut through the desert offering their labor as cattle minders or fence builders. But there were few opportunities for them. They had little option but to sit and wait.

//Eng would have scolded me for thinking it, but I also had a different view of why her "lazy" neighbors were seemingly content to sit and wait while their stomachs rumbled. To me their apparent indigence was neither a consequence of laziness nor even entirely a consequence of their ill fortunes. Instead I saw in their behavior a trace of how their parents and grandparents had lived before the white settlers came, a way of life that shines a new light on an ever more urgent and perplexing problem that was first raised by the economist John Maynard Keynes at the height of the Great Depression, a time when in this part of the Kalahari manketti nuts still fell from the trees and kudu bearing their giant spiral horns walked gamely into hunters' paths.

———

In the winter of 1930, Keynes was understandably preoccupied with the depression that was strangling the life out of European and American economies and the collapse of his personal fortune in the stock market crash the preceding year. Perhaps to persuade himself of the ephemeral nature of the crisis, he published an optimistic essay titled "The Economic Possibilities for our Grandchildren."[1]

"My purpose in this essay . . . is not to examine the present or the near future, but to disembarrass myself of short views and take wings into the future," explained Keynes in its introductory paragraphs.

The future to which Keynes's wings flew him was an economic Canaan: a promised land in which technological innovation, improvements in productivity, and long-term capital growth had ushered in an age of "economic bliss." An era in which we are all able to satisfy our material needs by working no more than fifteen hours in a week and in which we are liberated to focus on more profound joys than money and wealth accumulation. Things like art, philosophy, music, religion, and family.

While Keynes was uncertain as to whether humanity would be able to easily adjust to a life of leisure, he was convinced that, save for war or cataclysm, this reality would come to pass in the time of his grandchildren. "I would predict," he wrote, "that the standard of life in progressive countries one hundred years hence will be between four and eight times as high as it is today."

Keynes was right about improvements in technology and productivity. Nuclear power, cheap plastics, the communications and digital revolutions, and all manner of life-changing innovations bear testimony to his foresight. The U.S. Bureau of Labor Statistics tells us that labor productivity in the United States saw a fourfold increase between 1945 and 2005. But Keynes was wrong about the fifteen-hour week. While average working hours have declined from around forty hours per week in Europe and America to between thirty and thirty-five hours per week in the last fifty years, the drop has been much slower than the rise in individual productivity.

Given the increases in labor productivity in the United States, the modern American worker should be able to enjoy the same standard of living as a 1950s worker on the basis of a mere eleven hours of productive effort a week.

But Keynes was prescient about this too. He anticipated that there would be a lag between improvements in productivity and technology and its translation into fewer working hours. For him, the biggest obstacle to overcome was our instinct to work hard and to create new wealth.

"The struggle for subsistence . . . always has been hitherto the primary, most pressing problem of the human race . . . We have been expressly evolved by nature—with all our impulses and deepest instincts—for the purpose of solving the economic problem," he lamented. "I think with dread of the readjustment of the habits and instincts of the ordinary man, bred into him for countless generations, which he may be asked to discard within a few decades." "Dread" was perhaps too weak a word to use in the circumstances.

Keynes's personal fortunes would soon be restored, thanks to some savvy investments. But he was scathing about those who sought wealth for wealth's sake. As far as he was concerned, the abandonment of avarice was key to ensuring the realization of this economic Utopia. "The love of money as a possession . . . will be recognized for what it is," he opined: "a somewhat disgusting morbidity, one of those semi-criminal, semi-pathological propensities which one hands over with a shudder to the specialists in mental disease."

Keynes was right to worry about this. But I suspect that if he were alive today he would accept that he was overly optimistic about our ability to overcome it. He failed to anticipate our capacity to consume whatever new things our increased productivity enabled us to create. He also underestimated quite how far people would go to create work when—in material terms, at least—there was none to do. But he believed economics to be a rational science, and people, on the whole, to be capable of making rational choices when presented with them. So he took the view that, save the odd aberration in the form of a few "purposeful money-makers," we would "be able to enjoy the abundance when it comes." Keynes was also unable to predict the environmental costs of humankind's obsession with work or, for that matter, his own inadvertent role in ensuring the ascendance of a global economic model focused myopically on capital growth and the ever-quickening cycle of production, consumption, and disposal that it spawned.

Perhaps Keynes would have had a better sense of the scale of this problem—and of its genesis—had he realized that hunter-gatherers, the least economically developed of all the world's peoples, had already found the economic promised land that he dreamed of and that the fifteen-hour working week was probably the norm for most of the estimated two-hundred-thousand-year history of biologically modern Homo sapiens.

But Keynes was a creature of his time. He could not have known something that would only be revealed some thirty years after his death. To him, the idea that primitive people with no interest whatsoever in labor productivity or capital accumulation and with only simple technologies at their disposal had already solved the "economic problem" would have seemed preposterous.

———

The notion that hunter-gatherers might not endure a constant struggle to survive was first proposed at the University of Chicago in 1966—home, ironically, to Keynes's fiercest critics and the most enthusiastic advocates of unbridled, free-market economics.

But this time it wasn't the Chicago School economists who would be pouring cold water on Keynesian doctrine. It was a group of anthropologists, specialists in an obscure branch of the discipline, the study of hunter-gatherers. They had gathered at the university for a conference during an unseasonably cold April to share data they had collected among the few remaining groups of autonomous hunter-gatherers scattered across the globe. Despite the withering wind that rattled the windows, animated chatter filled the hallways.[2]

This conference was one of the few in anthropology's history where its findings would resonate far beyond the academy and be enthusiastically embraced by a broader public that was hungry for inspiration in a seemingly monochrome world shaped by a cold war and the even colder ice cream that had become emblematic of America's postwar economic boom.

For most of the twentieth century, hunter-gatherers had been of special interest only to anthropologists looking for insights into how our earliest ancestors lived before the widespread adoption of agriculture. By the late 1960s most ordinary people's interest in hunter-gatherers did not extend further than the television show *The Flintstones*, or the contents of Raquel Welch's fur bikini in the stone-age epic *One Million Years B.C.*

At the time, most anthropologists considered the last few remaining hunter-gatherer populations to be "living fossils." They took the view that hunter-gatherers endured an unremitting struggle against material scarcity, and if a handful of people continued to hunt and gather into the twentieth century, they did so only because they had been isolated from the transformative wonders of agriculture and industry by impenetrable rain forests, waterless deserts, vast oceans, or mile upon mile of ice and tundra.

The conveners of the conference set out to challenge this view. Over the preceding few years they had gathered field data from across the globe that suggested hunter-gatherer life was not nearly as treacherous as had previously been believed. In fact, their data suggested the opposite.

The most important presentation was made by a young American anthropologist, Richard Borshay Lee, one of the conference organizers. He had recently returned from a period of fieldwork among the Ju/'hoansi Bushmen of the Kalahari who lived in the border area between Namibia and Botswana. At the time, they were thought to be the most pristine exemplars of the hunting and gathering way of life, as a result of having lived in the "splendid isolation" of the Kalahari Desert for untold millennia. In a paper titled "What Hunters Do for a Living, or, How to Make Out on Scarce Resources," Lee set out to challenge the accepted wisdom that Ju/'hoansi in the Kalahari—and by implication hunter-gatherers elsewhere—endured a precarious existence constantly on the edge of starvation. He was emphatic that, in the case of the Ju/'hoansi Bushmen, life in a state of nature was neither nasty nor brutish and short.

Armed with a careful analysis of energy inputs and work outputs, he explained that the Ju/'hoansi he had studied made a "good" living from their environment and that they did so by gathering wild fruits, nuts, and vegetables in addition to hunting. Most importantly, he insisted that they did so with relatively little effort. He revealed that Ju/'hoansi spent only fifteen hours a week securing their nutritional requirements and only a further fifteen to twenty hours per week on domestic activities that could be loosely described as "work." Given that in 1966 the forty-hour week had only recently been introduced for federal workers in the United States, and that the average adult worked around thirty-six hours per week in addition to spending time on a long list of domestic chores like shopping, cleaning, and mowing lawns, these figures appeared extraordinary.

Although others attending the conference had reached similar conclusions about hunter-gatherers elsewhere, Lee's data was the most detailed and also by far the most compelling. This was because the Ju/'hoansi Bushmen lived in one of the least hospitable environments on earth. If Bushmen were able to conjure a good life out of this landscape, Lee reasoned, then surely other hunter-gatherers in more abundant environments must have enjoyed a similar, or greater, level of comfort.

Lee did not go to great lengths to spell out the potential implications of his findings. Perhaps at the time it was enough for him to have overturned an idea that had been unquestioningly accepted for as long as it had been talked about. But, of course, his results had ramifications that extended far beyond the academy. After all, they challenged the view that our species had progressively elevated itself from its base origins through ingenuity, innovation, and hard work.

The full implications of Lee's research were eventually spelled out by one of the symposium's other participants, Marshall Sahlins. Then a junior professor at the University of Michigan, Sahlins was the odd one out at the Chicago gathering. He was a promising theorist who had no more than a passing interest in hunting and gathering societies. But it was his taste for radical ideas and his interest in economics that had brought him to Chicago. That, and the fact that he had recently come across an interesting piece of ethnography regarding a group of Aboriginal hunters in Australia that didn't accord with the received wisdom that hunter-gatherer life was one of unremitting hardship.

Sahlins was much taken by what he had heard in Chicago, and by Lee's presentation in particular. Drawing on the conference proceedings, he set about rescuing hunter-gatherers from the clutches of the "dismal science" of classical economics. His thoughts were ultimately to crystallize around the notion that hunter-gatherers were "affluent" in their own terms and the obvious question it raised: If hunter-gatherers were affluent by their own standards, what did this mean for those who believed that affluence could only be achieved through industry, effort, and innovation?

"A good case can be made that hunters and gatherers work less than we do," Sahlins explained, "and that, rather than a continuous travail, the food quest is intermittent, leisure abundant, and there is a greater amount of sleep in the daytime per capita per year than in any other condition of society."

Sahlins was particularly interested in the fact that hunter-gatherers appeared to be content—in fact, to thrive—on mere nutritional adequacy and with a limited material culture. Their approach to well-being, he noted, was based on having few material wants, and those few wants were easily met with limited technologies and not too much effort. He reasoned that hunter-gatherers were content by the simple expedient of not desiring more than they already had. In other words, Sahlins took the view that hunter-gatherers were content because they did not hold themselves hostage to unattainable aspirations. With a knack for coming up with catchy phrases, Sahlins dubbed hunter-gatherers "the original affluent society" and referred to their economic approach as "primitive affluence."

The idea of being satisfied with what was ready to hand contrasted starkly with the American dream of the 1950s—a dream that celebrated the ability of capital, industry, and ultimately plenty of good honest hard work to narrow the gap between an individual's material aspirations and their limited means. In the idiom of the counterculture movements that were sweeping through the United States in the 1960s, Sahlins characterized hunter-gatherers as the gurus of a "Zen road to affluence" through which they were able to enjoy "unparalleled material plenty—with a low standard of living." Here, it seemed, was a people unconcerned with material wealth, living in harmony with their natural environments, who were also egalitarian, uncomplicated, and fundamentally free. There was, it appeared, a real possibility that the likes of the Bushmen, "our contemporary ancestors," would have been happy dropping out and tuning in to the Woodstock vibe.

The fact that hunter-gatherers were understood to form the base of the human evolutionary tree was also important, for it meant that they represented something essentially human. If hunting and gathering societies pursued "a way of life that was, until 10,000 years ago, a human universal,"[3] as Richard B. Lee reasoned, then there must be something of a hunter-gatherer in all of us. "If we are to understand the origin of man," gushed Sherwood Washburn, the father of modern primatology, "we must understand man the hunter and woman the gatherer."[4] Other aspects of hunter-gatherer life also chimed with other contemporary concerns, like the struggle for gender and racial equality, the peace movement, and the antiwar lobby.

It was no surprise that the idea of primitive affluence, coming to public attention as it did during the "summer of love," was embraced beyond the academy. It formed part of a compelling narrative that, at least for a moment, challenged the idea that Europe and America were at the vanguard of humankind's journey to bigger and better things.

But, like all scientific ideas that take root in the popular imagination, primitive affluence took on a life of its own. It gave newfound energy to popular movements in the West, still active today, in support of indigenous peoples and environmental consciousness, and it offered inspiration to those seeking a radical alternative to Western consumer culture. The publication of two books on the Bushmen in the late 1950s that would later rank among the bestselling popular anthropology books of all time helped pave the way for the popular embrace of primitive affluence. The first was Laurens van der Post's *The Lost World of the Kalahari*, published in 1958, a book based on a television series of the same name first broadcast on the BBC in 1956. The second was Elizabeth Marshall Thomas's *The Harmless People*, published in 1959. Both remain in print.

Both books were lyrical testaments to a way of life that was alien and inviting, mysterious yet, strangely, accessible. To van der Post, the Bushmen were practical mystics. They were spirit hunters, rainmakers, life takers, and life givers. But his book was riddled with factual errors, outlandish pronouncements, and unadulterated fantasy. He got the names and languages of different Bushman groups hopelessly muddled and he described their cosmologies, social organization, hunting practices, and ways of living with so little regard for the truth that it is hard to understand how his work escaped critical scrutiny until he was well into his dotage. To him, the Bushmen were little more than a mute canvas onto which he could project his own ideas about the world. And he did this with consummate skill.

Elizabeth Marshall Thomas's *The Harmless People*, by contrast, was more factually grounded. Her father, Laurence K. Marshall, was a founder of the American industrial giant Raytheon Company. Having secured the contract to develop the newly invented magnetrons that powered Allied radar during the Second World War, Raytheon went on to apply the technology to a more humble device but one with much greater public appeal: the microwave oven. As a result, by the early 1950s, Marshall had amassed sufficient wealth to quit his day job and take his family on a very expensive, decade-long adventure holiday.

Their destination was Nyae Nyae, a remote part of the Kalahari Desert in what was then South West Africa, where they hoped to document the life of "wild" Bushmen rumored to live there. Over the following decade they made numerous trips to Nyae Nyae, the longest lasting over eighteen months. At the outset Laurence Marshall tried to hire an anthropologist to accompany them. But, failing to recruit one, his wife, Lorna, was assigned the anthropological duties. It was a task she was well suited to. In time she would emerge as one of the most respected ethnographers of the twentieth century. But it was their children, Elizabeth and John, who had the populist touch. John worked with film and Elizabeth had a way with words. *The Harmless People* was a huge bestseller. Unlike van der Post's lyrical fantasy, the appeal of Elizabeth Marshall's writing came from the intimacy born of experience. It also reflected the rigor of her mother's ethnographic work.

Following the success of the Marshalls' and van der Post's work and inspired by the revelations from the Chicago conference, *Time* magazine published a special feature on the Bushmen in their July 1969 issue under the title "The Original Affluent Society."

"Imagine a society in which the work week seldom exceeds 19 hours, material wealth is considered a burden, and no one is much richer than anyone else," enthused the writer. "Unemployment is high there, sometimes reaching 40%—not because the society is shiftless, but because it believes that only the able-bodied should work, and then no more than necessary. Food is abundant and easily gathered. The people are comfortable, peaceable, happy and secure.

"This elysian community actually exists."

Unsurprisingly, this publicity also inspired a resurgence of academic interest in hunter-gatherers. In the 1970s and early 1980s, neophyte anthropologists clambered over one another to find "new" hunter-gatherers to study. But with the juggernaut of modernity steaming inexorably forward, anthropologists wanting to work with "authentic" hunter-gatherers found it increasingly challenging to find any. In some ways this was the final hour of "lost world" anthropology as researchers scudded over arctic tundra, hacked paths through equatorial forests, and trekked into the sandy depths of Africa's deserts in the hope of finding isolated communities still embedded in the organic rhythms of hunter-gatherer life. Different Bushman communities across southern Africa found themselves playing host to a curious procession of academics mainly from the United States but also the United Kingdom, Canada, Germany, Portugal, South Africa, Australia, and Japan. The Harvard Kalahari Research Group alone dispatched eleven researchers to work among the Ju/'hoansi, the people studied by Richard B. Lee.

Over the next two decades almost all major Bushman groups scattered across the Kalahari enjoyed, tolerated, and endured an influx of unexpected visitors armed with cameras, notebooks, and endless questions. Much of the work they produced reaffirmed Lee's findings or explored other aspects of the Bushmen's lives, from their botanical knowledge to more traditional anthropological subjects like kinship and cosmology. Their work spoke of the effectiveness of the Bushmen's shamanic practices, of their "fierce" egalitarianism, of their apparent disdain for material possessions except as a means to reaffirm social relationships, and, later, of the challenges they encountered adapting to a rapidly changing world.

But as time progressed, the utopian vision of primitive affluence that captured the imagination of *Time* magazine's editors and readers became increasingly hard to reconcile with the ever-grimmer realities of modern Bushman life. Things were changing fast in the Kalahari, and the anthropologists working among the Ju/'hoansi and other Bushman groups struggled to mesh the reality they experienced with the elysian myth invoked by *Time*.

Novelty oils the engines of academia, a place in which there is more credibility to be gained by tearing down established ideas than by reaffirming them. By the 1980s primitive affluence had joined the canon of "established ideas" and as a result would soon fall out of favor. Some anthropologists queried the nutritional bases to the argument and suggested that hunter-gatherer life was tougher than Lee and his colleagues proposed. Others suggested that Bushmen who provided the raw data were not isolated hunter-gatherers but rather failed farmers in a mature political economy in which livestock were the principal currency and that involved all the other peoples that lived in the Kalahari and its fringes. They accused the Harvard Kalahari Research Group and other anthropologists of having failed to properly examine the Bushmen's historical relationships with other peoples over time—most notably the many pastoralist peoples that had colonized parts of southern Africa during the first and second millennia. They cited archaeological and historical evidence that pointed to the possible long-term presence of livestock herders in some parts of the Kalahari as well as the existence of nineteenth-century trade routes through areas that had been assumed to be completely isolated until the mid-twentieth century.

These criticisms cooled enthusiasm for the romantic version of primitive affluence that blossomed in popular culture. But like the popularizers, the critics of primitive affluence radically overstated their case in what soon became referred to as the "Great Kalahari Debate." They imputed links where none existed and—according to Richard B. Lee and others—fabricated data in support of their views. These criticisms also engendered a bitter and often personal feud between the lead protagonists that rumbled on for nearly a decade without clear resolution. In the end it was genetic researchers who would put the debate to bed nearly twenty years after it began. Their work demonstrated that Ju/'hoansi were, if anything, even more isolated than anyone could have imagined and hence the idea that they were impoverished pastoralists was ludicrous.

Most frustratingly, this debate distracted the anthropological community from the most important and interesting aspect of the primitive affluence hypothesis. This was not that Bushmen and other hunter-gatherers suffered occasional deprivation and hardship. They clearly did from time to time. Nor was it that some Bushmen groups, like those in the central Kalahari, weren't as isolated as was previously thought. Some, but by no means all, clearly were. What was special about the Bushman data was that it showed that they coped easily with relative scarcity and that they had mastered the art of not obsessing about whether the grass was greener on the other side, which—given that they lived in one of the world's oldest deserts—almost certainly was the case.

What was also special about primitive affluence was that it suggested that Keynes's "economic problem" was not a "permanent condition" of the human species but instead that it was a relatively recent phenomenon when viewed against the broader scope of human history. One that emerged only when some of our ancestors abandoned a life of foraging and became farmers and food producers.

———————

The story of southern Africa's Bushmen encapsulates the history of modern Homo sapiens from our species' first emergence in sub-Saharan Africa through to the agricultural revolution and beyond. It is an incomplete story, one pieced together from fragments of archaeology, anthropology, and most recently genomics. Taken together, these fragments offer a sense of how hunter-gatherers came to exemplify elements of Keynes's Utopia and how, since the invention of agriculture, our destiny has been shaped by our preoccupation with solving the "economic problem."

The glue that holds these fragments together is the story of one particular Bushman group, the Ju/'hoansi of Namibia. The words *Ju* and */hoan* translate into English as "people" and "truth." Thus "Ju/'hoan" means "Real Person" or "Proper Person" and "Ju/'hoansi" means "Real People."

There are between eight and ten thousand Ju/'hoansi alive today. Roughly two-thirds of them live in Namibia. The remainder live just on the other side of the border with Botswana that bisects the Kalahari from north to south. Even though Ju/'hoansi represent only around 10 percent of the total Bushman population in southern Africa, I focus mostly on them in this book. In part this is because they are the best documented of all the Bushman peoples and, arguably, the best documented of all twentieth-century foraging peoples. It is also because the experiences of Namibia's two Ju/'hoan communities, the northern and southern Ju/'hoansi, are idiomatic of the most important aspects of the broader encounter between hunter-gatherers and others.

The northern Ju/'hoansi live in Nyae Nyae. They were almost certainly the most isolated of all Bushman communities up until midway through the twentieth century. It was for this reason they were the focus of the Marshall expeditions, Richard B. Lee's groundbreaking work, and much other anthropological research besides. The early work by the likes of the Marshalls and Lee offers us a uniquely nuanced picture of their lives as hunter-gatherers. Subsequent research by many others offers insights into how they coped with the ever more profound changes visited upon them after the Marshall expeditions came to an end. The Nyae Nyae Ju/'hoansi are also almost unique among Namibian Bushmen in that they have retained meaningful control over at least a decent proportion of lands they traditionally occupied. As a result, they are among the few Bushman communities anywhere that still are able to hunt and gather even if not all of them do anymore.

The southern Ju/'hoansi are closely related to the Ju/'hoansi of Nyae Nyae. Sometimes referred to as ≠Kxao//eisi, they share the same language and have many intersecting kinship ties with people in Nyae Nyae. But their recent history is very different from that of their northern cousins. Here Ju/'hoansi found themselves at the sharp end of the colonial encounter from the beginning of the twentieth century. As a result, by the time the Marshalls embarked for Nyae Nyae, most of them had already been robbed of their lands and forced into an often brutal life of servitude for people who regarded them as "creatures from the bush."

The speed of the Ju/'hoansi's transformation from an isolated group of closely related hunting and gathering bands to a marginalized minority struggling to survive in a rapidly changing polyglot modern state is almost without parallel in modern history. And as bewildering as this process has been for the Ju/'hoansi, it has bestowed upon them a special, if ephemeral, double perspective on the modern world—one that comes from being in one world but of another; from being part of a modern nation-state yet simultaneously excluded from full participation in it; and from having to engage with modernity with the hands and hearts of hunter-gatherers.

This double perspective also brings the differences between foraging and production cultures—like our own—into vivid if sometimes uncomfortable relief. It reveals how our sense of time shapes and is shaped by our economic thinking; why, despite our obsession with celebrity and leadership, we take such pleasure in seeing the successful stumble and why we object so viscerally to inequality when we feel ourselves to be the victims of it. It also invites us to query how, why, and to what we ascribe value; how we understand affluence, satisfaction, and success; and how we define development, growth, and progress. Perhaps most importantly it reveals how much of our contemporary economic and cultural behavior—including the conviction that work gives structure and meaning to our lives, defines who we are, and ultimately empowers us to master our own destinies—is a legacy from our transition from hunting and gathering to farming.

My association with the Kalahari began in 1992 when I presented myself as an uninvited volunteer at a small Bushman development project in Botswana. I made a nuisance of myself there for three months. But I also made many friends and so promised to return as soon as possible—in the guise of a doctoral research student.

During the 1980s and '90s, Bushmen were looked down on by almost everybody else in Botswana. At the time, Botswana was developing economically at a meteoric rate, thanks to the discovery of the world's two richest diamond deposits and a government that was intolerant of corruption. The majority population—and primary beneficiaries of this diamond wealth—took the view that their fellow Bushman citizens were "primitive" and something of an embarrassment.

By then Botswana's Bushmen were the focus of a paternalistic government development program that involved "relocating" those who still lived "in the bush" into larger settlements where they would be provided state services like health care and schooling. The official stance was reflected by Botswana's former president Festus Mogae, who in 2002 described the Bushmen as "Stone Age creature[s]" who "must change, otherwise, like the dodo, they will perish." Sensitive to external criticism, the government took a dim view of anthropologists. So, when I applied for permission to do research there for my doctorate, my request was denied.

The obvious solution to this problem was to apply to do research in Namibia.

When I applied to do my fieldwork there in 1994, Namibia was still celebrating the end of a two-decade-long liberation war as a result of which it had won its independence from apartheid South Africa in March 1990. It felt like half the world had gathered for a five-year party to celebrate the birth of a nation, and its famously dour capital, Windhoek, jived to a cosmopolitan chorus of aid workers, diplomats, and do-gooders from across the globe. In this optimistic atmosphere I was given my research permits without any fuss.

Encouraged to find a Bushman community that no anthropologists had yet studied, I headed eastward into Namibia's Omaheke Region. I began my research at Skoonheid, a recently established "resettlement farm" built to provide a home to Bushmen deprived of their lands under apartheid. It was the only place in the Omaheke where it was possible for Ju/'hoansi to live independently of white farmers and the Herero pastoralists who between them now owned all of the land in the Omaheke.

On arrival at Skoonheid I was introduced to !A/ae "Frederik" Langman, a Ju/'hoan man who had taught himself to read and write. I set up camp at the fire he shared with his wife, Xoan//a, his four children, their spouses, and their children. Within a month of my arrival, Xoan//a renamed me /Kunta, after their firstborn son, who had died as an infant.

In the Omaheke, most Ju/'hoansi had two names: an Afrikaans name, like Frederik Langman, and a traditional Ju/'hoan name, like !A/ae or /Kunta. They were given their Afrikaans names by farmers who struggled to pronounce or learn their Ju/'hoan names. Over time Ju/'hoansi adopted these as family names. But when not dealing with farmers, government officials, and others, Ju/'hoansi referred to and addressed one another almost exclusively by their Ju/'hoan names.

Traditionally Ju/'hoansi saw no reason to give people elaborate names that told a story in the way that some other hunting peoples, like many Native American cultures, did. Instead they recycled a small pool of around 150 names with the result that in any gathering of more than ten people the chances were that there would be several who shared names with one another. Ju/'hoansi considered their names to be the most important determinant of relatedness beyond immediate biology. Having been named /Kunta, all other /Kuntas became either my grandfathers or grand-children, depending on whether they were younger or older than me; all other people named !A/ae became my fathers or sons; and all other people named Xoan//a became my mothers or daughters.

All Ju/'hoan kin and name relationships fall into one of two categories: "joking" relationships or "respect" relationships. Each category imposed a clear set of expectations and obligations. Joking relationships—grandparents, grandchildren, maternal uncles, and others—were, as the name suggests, more fun than respect relationships—fathers, mothers, most in-laws. All people who shared your name, for example, were joking relatives and were, depending on age, to be addressed as either "Grandfather" (*!U'n!a'a,* or "Big Name") or Grandchild (*!Uma,* or "Little Name"). A joking relation-ship provided an instant license for bawdy banter, chirpy insult, and the open expression of affection. Respect relationships required a little more care. They were prescribed by a clearly defined set of obligations, and flouting these was a cause of much tut-tutting.

This model of determining relatedness gave Ju/'hoan individuals the ability to move easily between bands and to find "relatives" wherever they went. Almost every anthropologist who has lived among Ju/'hoansi for any sustained period (and not been a complete asshole) has been similarly named and welcomed.

With Skoonheid as my base and a new name that helped ensure I was welcomed by Ju/'hoansi wherever I went, I traveled widely through the Omaheke and beyond to Nyae Nyae before returning to the UK to complete my doctorate in 1996.

I returned to Namibia thirteen months later. Over the following two decades I worked with almost every major Bushman language group in Botswana and Namibia, from the G/wikhoe of the Central Kalahari Game Reserve in Botswana to the Hai//om of Namibia's Etosha National Park. But even in moving from one community to another, and from one project to the next, my relationships with the Ju/'hoansi in the Omaheke and Nyae Nyae who first welcomed me in 1994 strengthened and grew.

The Mother Hill

/Kunta is a *mmoruthi*, a lay minister with no church. He does not joke when it comes to the Gospel. As a young man he subscribed to a traditional Ju/'hoan view of the cosmos, but not since he "saw and felt the Holy Spirit." So, with a shake of his head, he politely dodged my questions about *g//ausi*—the spirits of the dead—as we marched past panel after panel of the rock art for which Botswana's Tsodilo Hills are now famous. I have nagged him with similar questions many times over the years. And on each occasion he has dismissed them as patiently as he did that day. /Kunta and I share the same Ju/'hoan name. This means that we can be cheerily rude to one another without causing offense.

I suspect /Kunta's ongoing interest in the Gospel stems in part from where he lives. Even the most shriveled agnostics cannot help imagining some kind of divinity when standing in the shadow of the Tsodilo Hills, four small mountains that rise like a vast rocky cathedral complex out of the otherwise unremitting flatness of the northern Kalahari. The sheer rock walls of the two largest mountains form a giant natural canvas onto which around 4,500 individual paintings and petroglyphs have been etched and daubed over the last fifty millennia. There are also lots of caves, many of which are filled with tantalizing traces of ancient humanity. I asked /Kunta to show me to a particularly important cave, one that remained a local secret until he revealed it to a team of archaeologists conducting an "audit" of Tsodilo rock art during the 1990s.

The Rhino Cave is hidden on the northernmost ridge of the "Female" or "Mother" Hill. It is so named because on the north wall of the cave there is a picture of a rhino painted in white near a giraffe painted in red. Protruding out of the southern wall of this cave is what appears to be the head and upper body of a titanic python, forged from stone with most of its massive body trapped forever beneath the weight of the mountain above. Its diamond-shaped head rears slightly upward toward the roof of the cave and its jaw and upper mouth are separated by a long, narrow fissure that sketches out the edges of a distinctly serpentine lip. Just above and behind the mouth is another, smaller fissure. When the light catches it just right it transforms from an unremarkable cavity into what appears to be a single serene eye staring forever toward the dry grass and trees that lie just beyond the cave's mouth. Behind the rearing head and the curve of the python's neck are the first ten feet or so of its body before it disappears into the rock wall behind.

Despite its frozen posture, there is something vital about this python. Its skin dances and breathes when the sun's rays move across it, animating what looks like a thousand shimmering scales. On closer inspection, these scales reveal the hand of an artist. Each one is a cupule, a shallow oval depression two inches tall and a half inch wide that has been ground into the rock. The cupules are cool to touch and the stone is unforgiving. Each one must have taken hours if not days of patient, laborious grinding with a small hard stone. Archaeologists have recently been digging in the sand floor of this cave. Their efforts have revealed layers of delicate stone arrowheads of uniform color, some burnt, others left pristine. With some of these artifacts having been speculatively dated to around seventy thousand years ago, some archaeologists believe it to be the oldest evidence of complex ritual activity by modern humans anywhere in the world.

/Kunta agreed that the rock looked a bit like a python but was not certain. I wanted to ask him whether he thought the snake might be a giant penis. A rock art panel not far away from the cave is known as the "dancing penises" for obvious reasons and this is, after all, the "mother hill" from which all life was said to have sprung, so it is not an absurd idea. There is also another group of rocks nearby said to be shaped liked three vaginas. According to another oral history, these were created by God as a sort of three-dimensional PowerPoint to help Him demonstrate to the first people how to make love.

But for *mmoruthi*s like /Kunta, genitals are not an appropriate topic of conversation. So instead I asked him if he thought the old-time people would have danced here, in this cave. He agreed that it was possible they did. To keep discussion within the vernacular of his faith, I asked him whether he thought it possible that we were standing in the Garden of Eden and whether he thought it possible that Adam and Eve were Bushmen. He looked at me askance and I worried whether I had made myself sufficiently clear. My Ju/'hoan was very rusty, having spent the previous five years working with a different Bushman language group, and my Setswana, his other language, was almost as poor as his English, so we had been communicating in a haphazard patchwork of the three. Half the time I suspected that /Kunta's attentive nods when I spoke were being offered more in sympathy than comprehension. Unlike anthropologists who like to make sense out of everything they are told and rudely ask questions again and again until they do, Ju/'hoansi often prefer to feign understanding in the interests of politeness.

"No, /Kunta," he replied. "Adam and Eve were white. I have seen pictures of them in a Bible. I am surprised you have not."

I suggested that maybe his parents would have thought my question made sense and he agreed. Until recently most people around here spoke of the hills as the place where the "first people" were created at the beginning of time. This is why there is a male and female hill. He explained that his parents had told him that the song of the wind as it blows through the hills is the lament of the spirits of the dead—the *g//ausi*. But he reminded me that he now "knows this is not true." The Tswana *mmoruthi*s showed him the truth and the light of Holy Spirit confirmed it. The *mmoruthi*s also insisted that the god of his parents—G//aua, the trickster—was an imposter, that he was Satan in a disguise and had tempted the Ju/'hoansi away from the One True God since the beginning of time.

It was getting dark when we began the slow march back to my vehicle on the south side of the female hill. As we walked, the evening wind started to swirl and eddy through caves and over the cliffs, singing the same breathy song that has brought shivers to the spines of visitors to these hills over countless generations.

The Tsodilo Hills rise from the desert sand roughly sixty miles to the northwest of Xai-Xai where /Kunta and his family used to live—although he insists there were always Ju/'hoansi living at Tsodilo. Tsodilo is also only around thirty-five miles away from the "panhandle" of the Okavango Delta, the point where the Okavango River surges into the Kalahari before spreading out to form a massive wetland that remains a treacherous paradise for wildlife. The hills are such a prominent landmark that for hundreds of years they have been a beacon to people living near the panhandle. A group of "River Bushmen" who called themselves the N/aekhwe were still living at the Hills when /Kunta's parents arrived there. As were a community of Mbukushu, a people that migrated to the fringes of the Kalahari two centuries or so ago and have fished and farmed along the banks of the Okavango River ever since.

Over his lifetime, /Kunta has seen his small community of Ju/'hoansi bullied by their Mbukushu neighbors and forced to move off a small, manketti-nut-rich escarpment on the Mother Hill to its base and then on to where they live now, a small village of grass huts half an hour's slog through soft sand from the base of the hills. But there is no doubting /Kunta's enduring love for this place. He is adamant that it is his *n!ore*— his land—and that, as a representative of the small Ju/'hoan community there, he is one of its principal custodians. It is an obligation that he does not take lightly and one that he is certain God approves of.

I didn't badger him with more questions about gods, origins, or rock-hewn penises that afternoon. I didn't have the vocabulary to do so, and even if I did, I doubt that what I would have said would have resonated with his experience of this place.

I would have liked to have known what he thought about all the things that science was now revealing about his home and the fact that there is good reason to believe that Tsodilo's importance extends to all mankind: that this desert may have been the birthplace of modern Homo sapiens and that, even if it wasn't, there is evidence for a continuous human history here that renders the pyramids of Giza, the Parthenon, and the Colosseum novelties, icons of the hubris of the farming societies that emerged only a mere ten thousand years ago.

I also wanted to say that recent human genetics studies suggest that his direct ancestors probably lived in this broader region in an unbroken line from a time many tens of thousands of years before the first anatomically modern humans set foot in Europe, Asia, Australia, or the Americas, and that this landscape had nurtured them in such a way that they were not driven to contrive new technologies or new ways of being. I wanted to tell him that if necessity is the mother of invention, my sense is that his ancestors had found something within this place and the surrounding desert that enabled them to banish necessity from their lives. I also wanted to explain that the petroglyphs and panels around us that he knows so well— as well as similar ones in hundreds of other mountains and rocky outcrops across southern Africa—all suggest an extraordinary level of cultural continuity between the people who lived here tens of thousands of years ago and people like the Ju/'hoansi who still hunted and gathered well into the twentieth century.

I wanted to say that this is important because we are living in an era of unprecedented change, because there are so few "wild" spaces left, and because maybe there is something we can learn from understanding how his ancestors had lived. But then I realized that /Kunta knows all of this anyway. He has witnessed the game numbers around Tsodilo decline over his lifetime as more cattlemen have moved in, and he cannot but have noticed the rapid increase in the human population in this part of Botswana. He has also seen the new roads being built and waves of geologists ferreting around with their drills and magnetometers in pursuit of diamonds, iron ore, and copper. So we returned to my truck in silence, happy to surrender ourselves to the sunset as it painted the sheer rock face of the male hill first red, then purple, then mauve.

———

Compared to other famous mountains, the Tsodilo Hills are small. The entire "range" covers no more than twelve square miles, the size of an average university campus. Yet, when you see them, they are incomparably majestic, their scale amplified by the miles of unending flatness that surrounds them. When, after a rainstorm, the haze that usually hovers over the hills has been scrubbed from the sky and the fine white dust that paints every surface has been washed away, the landscape becomes saturated with color, like a ghost rediscovering a vivid corporeal form. The largest outcrop, the "male" hill, rises almost fifteen hundred feet above the surrounding flatlands. It presents a sheer rock face decorated with interwoven streaks and ribbons of ochre, purple, and rust caused by minerals leached from the rock by a million rainstorms. The male hill towers above the larger but flatter and more fertile "mother" hill, which hides within it a number of small depressions and gentle plateaus that reveal secret manketti nut groves, seasonal springs, and beehives dripping with wild honey. Farther to the west lies the smaller "child" hill, which in the mornings is embraced by the shadows of the male and female hills and in the late afternoons casts a shadow that reaches toward its parents like an outstretched hand. From the top of the male hill it is possible to see and be seen from nearly a hundred miles in every direction, and the abundance of rock art shows just how magnetic a beacon these small mountains must have been for the thousands of generations of people who lived here.

The desert sands surrounding Tsodilo, which stretch southward for nearly two thousand miles, sit on a giant rock basin that has protected it from tectonic upheaval for nearly a billion years. As a result, this landscape has aged gracefully over its recent geological lifetime, molested only by the relatively gentle forces of wind and rain. Covering nearly two million square miles, it now forms a vast plain that extends from South Africa's northern Cape, through Botswana and Namibia, and into Angola and Zambia.

The Kalahari's climate is stabilized by its subtropical position. But the influence of idiosyncratic ocean currents, rogue volcanic clouds, and occasional interference by the gods has meant that over its history parts of it fluctuated between being a desert and a wetland. Paintings of fish on some of the rock art panels at Tsodilo remind us of a time when these hills once overlooked a shallow inland lake that stretched as far south as the eye could see.

Over the last billion years, many rivers have flowed into the Kalahari Basin, but very few ever flowed out of it. Rivers need hills and mountains to form catchments and valleys, and they need gradients to enable them to flow. But the Kalahari offers none of these. So, having blundered into this vast flatland, these rivers dissipated into giant, shallow inland deltas where they deposited the sands they had swept along their course onto the rocky basin floor before evaporating in the subtropical sun. These sands, in turn, were spread by dry winds, gradually creating a 600,000-square-mile patch-work of dune fields and fine-sand plains.

During some of the wetter periods in the Kalahari's history rainwater carved channels between dunes, forming a network of shallow valleys that guided ephemeral rivers that had neither sources nor deltas and rarely flowed for more than a few hours after a storm before disappearing into the sand. These channels now form a series of shallow "fossilized" river-beds, known as *omiramba* (singular: *omuramba*), that spider across the Kala-hari and still act as localized catchments for water when the rains arrive. Nharo Bushmen, who live to the south and east of the Ju/'hoansi, have a story about the origins of these *omiramba*. They are not the products of rain, they say, but of their trickster god, G//aua. They tell of how he was bitten in the testicles by a puff adder after carelessly emptying his bowels on it. His testicles swelled to such an extraordinary size, so the story goes, that they gouged the shallow valleys out of the sand as he dragged them behind him while he ran around screaming in agony.

When the first anatomically modern humans settled in the northern Kalahari perhaps as long as two hundred thousand years ago, the Zambezi, the Okavango, and the Chobe Rivers converged into this geological sink and formed a series of shallow inland lakes. Like water spilled on a tabletop, these paleo-lakes changed shape constantly, coalescing for at least one period in their history into a single shallow mega-lake covering some forty thousand square miles and stretching from what are now the Makgadigadi salt pans in the east of Botswana all the way to the Tsodilo Hills in the west.

The first people to see this lake were almost certainly the genetic ances-tors of all modern Khoisan and, quite possibly, the genetic ancestors of all of us. It is not certain if they arrived there on the crest of an evolutionary wave as modern Homo sapiens expanded beyond eastern Africa, or whether this part of southern Africa was itself the birthplace of modern Homo sapiens. But what is certain is that sometime around a hundred and fifty thousand years ago there was a branching in the human family tree. Those who remained in southern Africa became the ancestors of modern Khoisan, and the others who expanded northward became the ancestors of everyone else. Contemporary Khoisan are now the only people who still carry some of the distinct sequences of DNA associated with African "Adam," the first small group of anatomically modern people who bind all of humankind together into one family.

Whether the early Khoisan were immigrants to this land or evolved with it, this was a place that suited them. Something about this environment helped them create a way of life that would become nearly as stable and enduring as the geology around them. Over subsequent millennia, the Khoisan slowly expanded south of these mega-lakes, colonizing much of southern Africa.

But this was a gradual expansion. With long-term success in hunting and gathering in a desert environment so dependent on knowing the land intimately, Khoisan populations succeeded because they were so spatially stable—so stable, in fact, that there is negligible evidence of substantial genetic transfer between Khoisan in the southeast Kalahari and those who lived in the north for much of the last thirty thousand years.[1] To put this in perspective, over the same period that there was barely any movement over the one hundred miles or so of desert that separated northern Khoisan from southern Khoisan, the remainder of humankind colonized eastern Asia, crossed the land bridge into the Americas, and settled across both North and South America.

The Khoisan's success relative to other lineages of humankind is supported by research that looks at genetic mutation rates. These offer insights into the levels of genetic diversity in communities. And levels of diversity in turn help us understand historical population and demographic trends. This research shows extraordinary levels of genetic diversity among modern Khoisan and suggests that while Khoisan form a tiny minority in southern Africa now—and an even tinier minority in global terms—for much of the last 150 millennia they were the largest population of biologically modern humans. It also shows that while the Khoisan population was relatively stable over the last hundred and fifty thousand years, the non-Khoisan population suffered frequent and precipitous declines to the point that it lost nearly half of its total genetic diversity.

The same data suggests that it was only during the last twenty-two thousand years that other African branches of the human family tree, including those that would later form the first human populations in Europe and Asia, began to grow significantly. The researchers analyzing this data speculate that climatic changes in central and western Africa, as well as the challenges of adapting to new and unfamiliar habitats as they expanded out of Africa, affected these declines.[2]

As genetically diverse as Khoisan were before the arrival of others in southern Africa, they shared similar cultures, similar technologies, similar views on the nature of the cosmos, and similar ways of relating both to one another and to their environments. While Khoisan peoples spoke—and continue to speak—a range of mutually unintelligible languages, these languages all share the same roots marked out most obviously by the use of a series of distinctive click consonants. In many ways the secret of their success, and the endurance of their way of life, was based on their having reached a form of dynamic equilibrium with the broader environment, a balance between its relative stability and harshness. The evolutionary success of Khoisan, in other words, was based not on their ability to continuously colonize new lands, expand and grow into new spaces, or develop new technologies, but on the fact that they mastered the art of making a living where they were.

That Khoisan remained in one region for such a long period of time may well also have helped ensure the survival of much of Africa's mega-fauna into the modern era. The expansion of modern Homo sapiens across the planet is associated with the waves of mass extinction that took place in Europe, Asia, Australia, and the Americas over the past hundred millennia. North America, South America, and Australia all witnessed the disappearance of nearly 80 percent of their large mammal species in the period following the arrival of modern Homo sapiens. Sub-Saharan Africa, by contrast, only saw the extinction of two out of forty-four large mammal genera.

There is some debate about how much of this was due to human agency. Climate change was almost certainly the most important catalyst for the disappearance of Eurasian and American megafauna. But there is little doubt that humans played an important role even if it was not by hunting megafauna to extinction. Predators exercise tremendous influence over the ecosystems in which they live, often in ways that are not at first immediately obvious. This was demonstrated clearly following the reintroduction of a small wolf population into Yellowstone National Park in the United States in 1995, which induced, often indirectly, dramatic transformations across the ecosystem, from altering the flow of rivers to restoring the health of woodlands and improving the productivity of grasses. The sudden arrival of sophisticated predators like humans into established ecosystems would almost certainly have had a similarly dramatic effect. But whereas the reintroduction of wolves in Yellowstone helped restore some balance to a declining ecosystem, the sudden arrival of hunter-gatherers in a stable environment would have had a much more transformative impact.

This is where sub-Saharan Africa, with its much longer human history, is unique. Evidence of long-term human habitation suggests that humans and other animals coevolved as parts of complex ecosystems. As a result of this, it is likely that plant and animal species within those ecosystems adapted progressively to the presence of sophisticated hominid hunters, thus helping to ensure their survival into the present. The now-imminent threat of extinction for sub-Saharan Africa's megafauna has only come about as a result of the introduction of firearms to the continent in the colonial era and the subsequent human population explosion that has massively eroded megafaunal habitats.

There are limits to what we can infer from genetics and archaeology, in particular when dealing with timescales like these. But there is no doubt that something important happened here—that somehow this environment and the people who lived there had found a formula that was sustainable. And an important part of that formula was the fact that the Khoisan were satisfied that their environment provided everything they desired without asking too much in return.

———

Around fifteen thousand years ago, the mega-lakes in the northern Kalahari disappeared, destroyed by the very rivers that created them. Along with the uncountable billions of tons of water that these rivers funneled into the Kalahari Basin, they also deposited billions of tons of silt gathered on their long journeys from central Africa. As the silt settled to the lake floor, the lake bed rose higher and higher, until eventually the water began to spill over the basin's edge. And when it did, it carved a channel into the basin's wall that grew deeper and deeper as more water flowed over it. As a result, the trillions of cubic meters of water stored in the mega-lakes escaped forging a new course for the Zambezi River that bypassed most of the Kalahari altogether. In doing so, it gave birth to one of Africa's most dazzling natural wonders, Mosi-oa-Tunya—Victoria Falls. With the Zambezi having escaped this ancient craton, the complex of lakes dried up, leaving only the Okavango Delta in the west and a series of crystalline white salt pans spread over thousands of square miles as reminders of the great wetlands that were once there.

Now the most important legacies of the ancient river systems and mega-lakes are the extraordinary subterranean water systems that lie far beneath the Kalahari soil and that are accessible if you can dig deep enough and have a pump strong enough to bring these waters to the surface. Most of these are modest networks of aquifers, but some are a little more special. The Dragon's Breath Cave in the western Kalahari acquired its name because of the humid air that condensed into wispy clouds around the cave mouth on cold mornings. When, in 1986, speleologists first managed to navigate into the cave's depths, they discovered the largest nonglacial underground lake in the world. It lies around three hundred feet below ground level and has a surface area of around five acres. But no one has yet been able to establish its depth with any certainty. More recently, hydrologists found another underground water resource by using new drilling technology that enabled them to drill hundreds of meters into the earth's surface. This complex of aquifers, which lies near Namibia's border with Angola, is thought to be large enough to meet modern Namibia's water-consumption demands for the next four hundred years. This water is also estimated to be at least ten thousand years old, suggesting it infiltrated in from the mega-lakes.

———

Not long after the lakes in the northern Kalahari dried up, humans in the Levant and elsewhere discovered agriculture and began to domesticate animals. This transformation, dubbed the Neolithic ("new stone age")

Revolution, transformed how people related to and worked with their environments and led to them developing a radically different understanding of their place in the world. By becoming farmers, our ancestors changed from foragers to producers and from hunters to makers, a process that ultimately paved the way for our transition from being the cleverest mammal to the most dominant species of any kind at any point in our planet's history.

Agriculture was much more productive than hunting and gathering and enabled populations to grow rapidly. It also created occasional surpluses, and with surpluses came hierarchies and systems of tribute. And hierarchies and tributes, in turn, nurtured an urge to gather more resources, to expand and conquer.

Like an algal bloom, agricultural civilizations spread rapidly across the planet, leaving few places untouched. Because farming required much larger, more complex forms of social organization, it enabled farming civilizations to easily overwhelm small dispersed populations of established hunter-gatherers. In Africa it gave rise first to the great Egyptian and Nubian civilizations along the Nile delta and floodplain. And then around five thousand years ago it gave birth to the great African Bantu civilizations, a network of peoples with similar customs and closely related languages that slowly expanded across western, central, and, eventually, southern Africa along with their cattle, sheep, and grains over a period of three millennia. While the precise timing of these movements is uncertain, it is likely that some pioneers of these expansion reached Angola, just north of the Kalahari Basin, as long as 2,500 years ago. Those who expanded down Africa's east coast reached the northern borders of modern South Africa around 1,500 or 1,600 years ago and came to a halt near the Great Fish River on South Africa's east coast a few centuries later.

In the process, they displaced, absorbed, assimilated, and crushed hunter-gatherer populations they encountered en route. But, just like the rain forests that blocked their expansion in central Africa, deserts formed natural barriers. And when farming peoples reached the fringes of the Kalahari, they went no farther. The open waterless expanses, while rich with grasses, offered their herds no places to water and fewer places still where they could plant crops. So they remained on its fringes, leaving many of the resident Bushmen largely undisturbed. Similarly, those that expanded down the east coast and inland ground to a halt when they hit the dry lands south of the Kalahari in the Karoo desert and the spartan gravel plains and hills of Namaqualand. This left the Khoisan living in the Kalahari Basin and in much of what is now South Africa's Northern Cape Province undisturbed. The only clear impact of these migrations on these populations was the adoption of cattle and sheep herding by some groups that by the fifteenth century were concentrated in the better-watered lands around what are now the vineyards and fruit farms of South Africa's Western Cape. It was only when European colonialism began to reshape southern Africa that the independence and autonomy of Khoisan in the vast Kalahari Basin would eventually be challenged.

3

A Beachside Brawl

The most startling thing about Cape Cross, on Namibia's storm-battered Atlantic coast, is the smell. It lingers heavy in the saline air, reaches deep into your sinuses, and then creeps down the back of your throat. It is a nasal cacophony of acrid, fishy fecal decay so strong that it reduces the view in front of you into soft focus and smothers the source of this smell— eighty thousand Cape fur seals barking, grunting, fighting, and farting— into dull white noise. It is only after some time that the urge to retch and flee passes and your senses recalibrate enough to take in your surroundings.

Cape Cross is not particularly hard to get to nowadays. Approached from Namibia's capital, Windhoek, it is reachable by road on a journey that takes you from the mountainous Khomas Hochland region that fringes the Kalahari's western border, across the rocky plains of Damaraland, and into a desert that merges gently into a vast beach before disappearing beneath the frost-fisted Atlantic waves that batter southern Africa's western coast. Approached by sea from the north, Cape Cross forms a small promontory that breaks the monotony of six hundred miles of desert coastline—now called the Skeleton Coast because of the rusting hulks of the ships that fell foul of its heaving currents and hidden sandbanks and now litter the shore.

For the Portuguese adventurer Diogo Cão, the first European to sail into the unchartered waters off the African coast south of the equator, this promontory was far enough. His fleet had been hugging the coast for several weeks and, with the desert showing no signs of receding, he instructed his crew to turn back northward toward the Congo. But not before making landfall and erecting a *padrão*, a ten-foot-tall limestone cross, to mark the southernmost point of his voyage and claim this land for his king.

Cão's embarkation at Cape Cross in 1485 marked the beginning of Portugal's domination of the southern seas during the first great age of global naval exploration, when an ever-greater thirst for trade, fame, and royal approval, combined with a desire to extend the boundaries of their known world, drove sailors to take their fleets where none had gone before. At that time cognoscenti in Lisbon lusted for news of sailors' exploits in unchartered seas, while tradesmen, merchants, and mongers hungered for cargoes of exotica. In royal courts and markets alike, people lapped up gilded tales of mythical lands, the legendary kingdom ruled by Prester John, and treasures beyond imagination.

Cão's original *padrão* is no longer there. It was purloined nearly four hundred years later by a German naval captain wanting a souvenir of his trip down the Skeleton Coast in 1893. He installed it at the German Imperial Naval Academy in Kiel. Kaiser Wilhelm II was apparently displeased by this act of vandalism. He ordered a replica *padrão* to be installed in the original spot, bearing the original inscriptions as well as some additional text in German, in case there was any doubt as to which European power held sway over this coastline.

Nobody now knows whether Cão ventured inland here or not. He was a more committed explorer than notetaker. He clearly had enough time there to erect his *padrão*, and even a short hike inland up the dry bed of the Messum River a few miles to the north of Cape Cross would have afforded him a glimpse of the peak of Namibia's tallest mountain, the Brandberg. The Brandberg lies only a two- or three-day hike inland from the coast. It is also the site of over fifty thousand rock paintings and petroglyphs. Some are relatively recent, but most date back over the last five thousand years, so it is almost certain that people were living there when Cão anchored at Cape Cross. There is also little doubt that during wet seasons the inhabitants of the Brandberg would have ranged as far as the sea, using the riverbed as a road, to hunt seals and marvel at the infinity of the ocean. So while there is no record of Cão's crew seeing any indigenous people, it is possible that Cão and his crew were seen by them.

It was Cão's friend and rival Bartolomeu Dias who would make the first documented contact between Europeans and southern Africa's indigenous people. Charged by King João II of Portugal to follow in Cão's wake, find a sea trade route to India, and establish the truth of the legend of Prester

John, Dias embarked for the southern Atlantic in August 1487. He made good progress and after several months pushed farther south than Cão's *padrão* at Cape Cross.

Dias's fleet rounded the Cape of Good Hope in January 1488. But he was too far out to sea to spot the natural harbor that lay under the majestic slopes of Table Mountain. It was only after the fleet bore northeast again that they made landfall. And when they did, his lookout spotted a small group of scantily clad natives standing on a grassy verge just north of a beach near the modern town of Mossel Bay, a hundred miles to the east of Table Mountain. The people they saw were distinctly smaller and lighter-skinned than the other Africans they had encountered in equatorial Africa. They also appeared to be minding a herd of curious-looking fat-tailed sheep. With supplies dwindling and an increasingly mutinous and scurvy-wracked crew, Dias dropped anchor and announced that he would lead a small party ashore in the hope of procuring freshwater and food.

The people on the grassy verge decided that curiosity about these strangers was no substitute for caution. They concluded that these pale and hairy apparitions emerging from the sea should be sent back to where they came from. Perhaps they were frightened because the sailors communicated with one another in a crude tongue that lacked the clicks, plosives, and glottal stops that made human languages sensible. Perhaps the cries of their descendants, crowded into ramshackle townships and hounded by white policemen five hundred years in the future reverberated back in time, warning them that these new arrivals would eventually rob them of their lands and their dignity and that they should be driven back into the sea.

As Dias's landing party stumbled into the surf, the locals, who by then had climbed a small ridge overlooking the bay, unleashed a barrage of arrows and stones onto the sailors. Dias decided that discretion was the better part of valor and ordered his crew to return to their ship. But in retreating back to his boat Dias primed his crossbow and released a bolt. In that moment southern African flesh encountered European steel for the first time as one of the natives fell to the ground.

Tales of "first encounters" like the clash between Dias's crew and the people at Mossel Bay are often moving. More often than not, this is because with the benefit of hindsight we know what miseries they portend. But this particular "first encounter" was uniquely important because Dias's arrival at Mossel Bay signaled the reunion of two branches of the Homo sapiens family tree after over a hundred millennia of separation. But with Dias and the locals only having exchanged missiles it is hard to distill anything more significant from this encounter than that it didn't set a particularly promising tone for those that would follow.

The next encounter between Europeans and southern Africa's Khoisan would take place a decade later when Vasco da Gama unlocked a sea passage from Europe to the East Indies by way of southern Africa. Having navigated the equator and countless storms in the tropics, da Gama's pilot led their small fleet to St. Helena Bay, a bleak natural harbor in the coastal dry lands a hundred miles to the northwest of the Cape of Good Hope. They anchored there for eight days to perform essential maintenance before resuming their voyage to the east. As they set about cleaning and mending their vessels, da Gama was informed that a group of "tawny-colored" people, smaller in stature and lighter in color than the West African peoples that his crew were familiar with, could be observed on the shore.

The "tawny-colored" locals were less convinced of the dangers that da Gama's crew posed to them than the people in Mossel Bay had been of Dias's. They waved to the sailors in greeting. Confident of the locals' goodwill, da Gama dispatched several shore parties to gather water and look for food, while the rest of the crew were confined to the deck and assigned maintenance duties.

Demonstrating a bizarre approach to cross-cultural communication, one of the shore parties kidnapped a native who came to welcome them. They bundled him into a rowboat and secreted him onto da Gama's flagship, the *São Gabriel*. The sailors' plan apparently was to impress upon their captive their goodwill as unambiguously as possible. Once their captive was safely on board, da Gama ordered that the bewildered prisoner be fed and pampered.

Unfazed by the indignity of the kidnapping, the prisoner enjoyed his brief spell in a floating cell. A few hours after he had been deposited back on land, the Portuguese were approached by "fourteen or fifteen natives" seemingly intent on enjoying similar hospitality. Da Gama, though, was less keen on guests than he was on trade and profit. As far as he was concerned, trade was a universal language that transcended the particularities of culture and place. But, much to his disappointment, the natives had little of value to trade with and displayed little interest in the cinnamon, cloves, seed pearls, and gold that da Gama presented to them. Only the copper that da Gama had with him piqued the natives' interest and some was exchanged for decorative shells, a "fox-tail" fly whisk, and one of the "sheaths which they [the natives] wore on their members."[1]

Discouraged by the poor prospects for commodity exchange, da Gama decided to ship out and continue his journey eastward. While his crew loaded their cargo back into their launches in preparation for their return to the other three ships of the fleet, one of his sailors decided to explore farther inland in the company of some locals.

But after walking with them for a few miles, the sailor decided to return to the beach, his escorts following behind. By the time he made it to the shoreline, the rest of the shore party was already negotiating the choppy surf and awkward currents that lay between them and the ships anchored in the bay. Terrified that he would be abandoned, the sailor shouted and waved frantically to gain his compadres' attention. It did the trick. But his shouting and waving were misinterpreted as a cry for help. Fearing for their companion's safety, the Portuguese turned their vessels around and stormed the shore to rescue him. The hunters, in turn, hurled their spears at the invaders before retreating inland. Four sailors were injured in the skirmish and da Gama, who was also hit by an arrow, ordered his men to pull anchor and move on.

History will never reveal exactly why Dias's shore party was attacked or why da Gama's initially friendly encounter provoked sufficient mistrust to end in a beachside brawl. But we do know that the people da Gama encountered on the beach at St. Helena Bay that day shared the same indifference for profitable trade shown by hunter-gatherers elsewhere in southern Africa and beyond through to the twentieth century.

Frustrated, da Gama concluded that the indigenous people of this part of the world were dangerous and not worth the effort when it came to trade. This view would later be shared by others who followed in his wake, and for whom the Cape of Good Hope would become no more than a pit stop on their voyages to trade in India and the East Indies. But da Gama could not possibly have known that the people he met on the beach had a very different relationship to the material world than his own or that they had an unyielding confidence in the providence of their environment, produced no surpluses, and, as a result, saw little point in trade. He would also not have known that their economy was one based on short-term gratification and that, while they were opportunists who would celebrate any windfalls providence might offer, their economy was premised on having few needs, which could be easily met. And he would also not have realized that they managed to do this by not having to work very hard at all, and so had as much free time as only the most indolent of the nobles back in Portugal.

———

Da Gama's voyage presaged an era of unimaginable change for Khoisan across southern Africa. For some this process began the moment the first Portuguese sails pierced the Atlantic horizon off the Cape of Good Hope. For others it was marked by the progressive expansion of European colonialism northward from the Cape. For others still, like the Nyae Nyae Ju/'hoansi, it would be heralded by the arrival of the Marshall family's convoy in 1951.

By the 1850s only those Bushmen who lived north of the Cape Colony's (modern South Africa's) borders, in the vast Kalahari Basin, still maintained their independence in any meaningful way. Protected by an arid environment that was hostile to farmers, many of these Bushmen continued to hunt and gather well into the twentieth century. But they could not hold out indefinitely.

With new technologies like borehole pumps that tapped into ancient underground water reservoirs, opening up the Kalahari to farmers, Bushmen in even the remotest parts of this vast desert region have witnessed changes over the last century that their ancestors would never have imagined possible. Now, with most of the Kalahari having been settled by others, none of southern Africa's one-hundred-thousand-strong remnant Bushman population survives by hunting and gathering alone. In 1998, I was asked by the European Commission to lead a major international research program to investigate the status of and prospects for southern Africa's

Bushman peoples at the turn of the millennium. The reports that came out of this investigation made for somber reading. They outlined in grim detail how Bushmen were by far the worst off of any population group in the region and told of how fewer than 10 percent of them retained any meaningful access to the lands they traditionally occupied or had any substantive rights to land at all. They documented how Bushmen were still subject to routine racism and prejudice; how most of them eked out a living as serfs for both modern and more traditional farmers; how they were undernourished and progressively crippled by modern diseases associated with poverty; and, ultimately, how they were caught in a death spiral of poverty and marginalization.

Dias's and da Gama's beachside skirmishes are now mere footnotes to grander narratives of exploration and economic transformation. Their voyages were, after all, instrumental in reshaping the world. In tandem with Christopher Columbus's accidental discovery of the Americas, da Gama's voyage to the Indies would later be hailed as the "big bang" of economic globalization—the moment that catalyzed the transformation of the world from a series of often discrete economic communities into a single complex and multifaceted economic system. Articulating a view that would later be reaffirmed by many others, Adam Smith, the "father of economics," declared da Gama's voyage and Columbus's "discovery" of the Americas to be "the two greatest and most important events recorded in the history of mankind."[2]

Whether this particular moment was more important than any others in the emergence of a globalized economy is debatable. But there is no debate about the reality of globalization now. And there is also no debate about the near universality of a very particular set of economic behaviors based on labor exchange, trade, and the creation, accumulation, circulation, and consumption of wealth.

But the history of anatomically modern humans stretches back nearly two hundred thousand years before da Gama imagined a sea route to the Orient and clambered aboard the *São Gabriel*. Viewed from this much grander timescale, other moments present themselves as more important in defining the historical trajectory of our species. And perhaps the most important of these was the Neolithic Revolution, the extended moment when our ancestors transitioned from being hunters and gatherers to farmers and in doing so gave birth to the "economic problem" that has preoccupied us ever since.

As profound as the transition from hunting and gathering to farming was, it is important to remember that more than nine-tenths of the two-hundred-thousand-year history of modern Homo sapiens was shaped neither by mercantile capitalism nor by agriculture. Rather, it was shaped by hunting and gathering. If the ultimate measure of sustainability is endurance over time, then hunting and gathering is by far the most sustainable economic approach developed in all of human history, and the Khoisan are the most accomplished exponents of this approach. And the success of hunting and gathering as an economic system cannot be doubted. It is as hunter-gatherers that modern Homo sapiens expanded out of Africa and occupied Asia, the Pacific Islands, Australia, and eventually the Americas.

It is hard to imagine that the globalized economy symbolized by da Gama's voyage will endure anywhere near as long as the Khoisan managed to survive by hunting and gathering. Some of the more doom-laden forecasts of climate change suggest that it is already too late—that an important threshold has already been passed and that we should all be channeling our inner Noah and building arks of one sort or another. But then again the promise of apocalypse has been built into most organized religions that evolved since the Neolithic, because while the transition to farming incrementally increased productivity and population size, it drastically reduced the quality of life for most people and introduced them to a whole range of perils unimaginable to most hunter-gatherers, like viral epidemics from livestock and mass famines when harvests failed. Or maybe our willingness to contemplate apocalypse expresses a suppressed sense that the same qualities that have enabled our species to exert such an extraordinary impact on the world around us hold within them the seeds of their own destruction.

Whether or not our continued preoccupation with apocalypse is a carry-over from our species' transition from foragers to producers, no one doubts that farming, industrialization, and economic globalization have conspired to generate a series of social, economic, and environmental challenges that can only fuel our sense of potential doom.

The environmental costs of half a millennium of progressive economic and industrial growth amplify the historical importance of da Gama's voyage as much as our sense that we are the products of the globalized world it created. Bearing this in mind, da Gama's encounter on the beach is suddenly elevated to something potentially much more important than a whimsical footnote in the history of globalization. For might the people encountered by da Gama on the beach that day offer us some "old" ideas to solve some new problems? Might we, like our hunter-gatherer forebears, learn to be satisfied with having fewer needs more easily met, embrace the economic Utopia imagined by Keynes, and in doing so break out of the destructive spiral of endless growth and development? If so much of our species' history was spent hunting and gathering, mustn't there surely still be something of the hunter-gatherer in all of us?

4

The Settlers

Dam traced a rough map of the farm he used to work on into the sand. He then used a stick to point to where the different incidents had played out. He spoke with a lisp as if to remind me of the fact that his missing front teeth were important characters in the tale.

"After the farmer tied me to the gate," he explained, "he just left me there in the sun. I thought I was going to die of thirst. I was there for a day before that girl came and untied me. I didn't even wait to drink. I just ran. But I was weak. And even though the boss was still drunk, he followed my tracks with his dogs. He caught me again here by the other gate."

He motioned to his sand map.

"I was lucky that I had fed those dogs so often," he laughed. "Otherwise those fucking things would have attacked me. Instead when they found me they wagged their tails and jumped up and down. That made the farmer crazy. Eish, he kicked those dogs."

Dam explained that he had been accused of stealing booze.

"But it was not true," he complained. "The farmer and his wife are always so drunk on weekends that they can never remember how much drink they have left. The woman always had those big boxes of red wine in the kitchen, another on the verandah, and more of them in the pantry. She liked to drink, drink, drink red wine all day long. He liked his brandy. But he'd only drink at night and on weekends. He was okay when he was working. He worked hard."

Dam described how after his failed escape he received another beating from the farmer. He explained how a single blow accounted for his missing teeth and the narrow scar that now ran from his upper lip to his nose. He also showed me his right hand, on which his thumb was ossified into a slightly crooked but eerily optimistic permanent thumbs-up.

"Look: I can't bend it," he said, waving it in front of me. "I was holding my head with my hands when he was kicking and the wife was just shouting, shouting, shouting. But when he tried kicking my head he kept kicking my hands, and now this thumb is just so."

This time none of the other workers on the farm dared help him. But early the next morning the boss, struggling with a hangover, untied him and gave him a tin cup of sweet tea as well as some bread with no butter. "You can rest today" was all he had said.

"There were only four of us working all the time on that farm. But in the end the farmer put me in the road anyway. I couldn't hold anything with this hand and so couldn't work." He showed me his ossified thumb again.

I asked Dam if he went to the police or whether he'd like to lay a complaint now. Namibia was independent, I reminded him.

"For what?" asked Dam, echoing a sentiment that was repeated to me again and again by other Bushman farmworkers. "The farmer will just say I was stealing and then I'll go to prison. Anyway, this happened before independence; that farm is now owned by other people and that farmer has trekked. I heard he had problems with money and went to stay in Windhoek."

I had heard a few stories as extreme as Dam's in the preceding months. Stories of mock hangings, beatings, and abuse that pointed to sadistic streaks among a handful of farmers. There were also whispered stories of murders in the distant past. But by then I had learned to take stories like Dam's with a pinch of salt, because every story here became incrementally more gruesome with each retelling and it was also obvious that where farmers had felt confident to act with little restraint before independence, most were very cautious about it now.

Most instances of violence on the farms in the Omaheke were much more mundane. Ju/'hoansi spoke of casual punches, slaps over an earhole, whip-wielding bosses breaking up drunken fights in workers' compounds, casual incarcerations, and occasional violent outbursts that were often regretted soon afterward by apologetic farmers. These stories pointed less to any pathological tendencies than to the extent to which physical violence was normalized here and how the casual slap or more formalized beating had simply become part of the everyday grammar of social interaction between many white farmers and Ju/'hoansi workers.

So common was this violence that the fear of flying white fists was burned into the muscle memory of most male Ju/'hoansi who grew up on the farms before independence. Whenever I thrust my hand too eagerly in someone's direction in greeting or moved to pat someone on the back or embrace them, they would instinctively flinch or duck away, a look of momentary alarm flashing in their eyes before they recovered their composure. This, I soon learned, was because in their experience when a white man moved suddenly, there was a good chance you were going to be hit.

Based on several decades of careful observation of their bosses, Ju/'hoansi concluded that most white people were violent, proud, selfish, and unreliable. They were also irrationally greedy, sly, often sexually frustrated, obsessed with work, and perversely preoccupied with being shown gratitude even when all they had to offer was a beating. But their conclusions about white farmers weren't all negative. They said that farmers could also be resourceful, brave, occasionally compassionate, loyal, caring, and very clever. They also reminded me that, while white people were broadly similar in most respects, there were nevertheless important differences between specific tribes. Afrikaners, I was told, were typically more relaxed but were far more likely to lose the plot when drunk or lovesick. They were also far more likely to fly into a rage. German farmers were obsessive about detail and order, and generally calmer, but they could be very uncompromising when you got on the wrong side of them.

The violence that gave Namibia's twentieth-century history its jagged edge was born of a series of colonial campaigns, a genocide, a popular uprising, and eventually a war of liberation. But the culture of violence that characterized the Bushmen's experience on the farms had a distinctly different tenor from the violence that characterized the relationship between the colonialists and Namibia's other oppressed peoples. The systematic atrocities committed by the Germans against the Herero and Nama in the first decade of the twentieth century, and later by the South Africans in Ovamboland and southern Angola during the war of liberation, were repressive and cruel. They were also calculated, organized, purposeful, and intended to break the spirit of people inspired by dreams of emancipation.

But on the white-owned ranches of the Omaheke, only a few Bushman farmworkers felt they had a stake in the struggle against apartheid. Isolated and marginalized, they lived beneath the fray and were largely ignored by liberation movements and state security institutions alike. Rather than being aimed at breaking the back of a movement, the violence they experienced was part of a more enduring pattern of relations, variations of which emerged wherever farmers claiming new lands encountered hunter-gatherers. For the farmers, the Bushmen were as much part of a landscape that needed to be brought under their dominion as the leopard and lion that stalked their livestock. It was reasoned that, like a dog left to go feral, Ju/'hoansi left undisciplined would inevitably revert to their old, "unpredictable" ways. Thus farmers often referred to their laborers as "tame" Bushmen and contrasted them with the "wild" Bushmen of Nyae Nyae to the north.

In this sense, the farmers considered themselves to be the inheritors of a legacy left by South Africa's eighteenth-century frontier farmers when they battled "wild" Bushmen in the dry lands of the northern Cape in the years that followed the establishment of a permanent European presence in southern Africa.

A century and a half after da Gama's fracas on Africa's southern tip, a flamboyantly wigged thirty-three-year-old Dutchman called Jan van Riebeeck disembarked from his ship *Dromedaris* at the natural harbor beneath Table Mountain. He had been instructed by the Dutch East India Company's ruling council, the Heeren XVII, to establish a permanent settlement at the Cape of Good Hope, an act that would later see him iconified by white Afrikaner nationalists and vilified by African nationalists. In the years preceding van Riebeeck's arrival in South Africa, the Heeren XVII had become increasingly convinced of the Cape of Good Hope's long-term strategic importance. While not particularly keen on the idea of being sent halfway around the world to build a new settlement in a land as savage as it was remote, van Riebeeck was in no position to argue with the Heeren XVII. He had rung up a number of bad debts with the company and his exile on company business meant he would be spared the harsh penalties routinely imposed on defaulters at the time.

Over the years that spanned Bartolomeu Dias's ill-fated landing at Mossel Bay and van Riebeeck's arrival in 1652, the Cape of Good Hope had played host to an ever-expanding volume of European shipping traffic. So, by the time van Riebeeck started to build his fort there, some of the indigenous people were already old hands at dealing with the different varieties of Europeans who frequented their shores: Portuguese, Spanish, French, English, and Dutch. But van Riebeeck's party was not just another group of scurvy-wracked seamen stopping by for a few weeks to regain their strength, repair their ships, and provision themselves with sufficient freshwater to take them to the East Indies. Within a few short months it became clear that this group of Dutchmen was there to stay.

Their previous century and half of episodic interaction with sailors en route between Europe and the Orient did little to prepare Khoisan for the extraordinary changes van Riebeeck's arrival ushered in. The fact that settlers were obviously unwilling to make any concessions to learning local languages should have been a clue. Whereas by the time van Riebeeck made landfall some natives could communicate in rudimentary Portuguese, English, and Dutch, the settlers had little or no idea who the natives were or even what they called themselves.

It was also only with the arrival of van Riebeeck that Europeans began to make a clear distinction between those locals who made a living as cattle and sheep herders—the "Hottentots," or "Khoi"—and those who lived by fishing, foraging, and hunting—the "Bushmen," or "San."

———

Van Riebeeck and other settlers were not particularly keen on their new neighbors. Where the local populations struggled to make sense of the Dutchmen's habit of entombing themselves in layers of heavy, rough cloth, the settlers sneered at the locals' habit of smearing themselves from head to toe with animal fat and adorning their heads with skullcaps fashioned from wet dung. The Dutch were equally distressed by the local culinary specialties. They struggled to accept that rotting seal meat could be delicious or that head lice was a practical and convenient snack.

The Reverend Father Marcel le Blanc, who had visited the Cape of Good Hope before van Riebeeck settled there, expressed a view that would later be widely shared among the first settlers when he concluded that Khoisan were among "the foulest and ugliest people of all the inhabited world" and, moreover, that they were "repulsive to look at and to smell." But the Dutch settlers' snobbery about the therapeutic qualities of animal fat as a skin lotion had its costs. They were constantly molested by the swarms of stinging, buzzing, biting, and burrowing insects that proliferated in the coastal pools and shrubland. As a result, while the settlers spent much of their time frantically scratching bites, welts, pustules, and boils, the fat-smeared locals breezily went about their business unmolested by insects.[1]

A small segment of settler society were quietly impressed by their new neighbors. They expressed admiration for their extraordinary knowledge of local flora and fauna and the ease with which they procured "remedies" for all sorts of different ailments from the plants around them. They observed that, in addition to dealing with wounds, ulcerations, swellings, and inflammations, "Hottentot apothecaries" could also treat the bites of "any venomous creature." Similarly they admired the skill and bravery of Bushman hunters as they gamely tackled lions and other frightening beasts with their fragile weaponry. Perhaps it was their obvious bravery that compelled one settler to note that the natives of the Cape were possessed of "member[s] surprisingly longer than that of Europeans so that it more resembles the organ of a young bull than that of a man."[2]

Some of the settlers also couldn't help notice that, despite the natives' abject poverty, they were nevertheless "always gay, always dancing and singing," and appeared to enjoy a life "without occupation or toil." This apparent contradiction induced some awkward introspection among elements of settler society. Father Guy Tachard, a French Jesuit missionary who spent time in the Cape settlement while en route to Siam, was moved to report in 1685 that from the "Hottentot's" point of view it was the Dutch settlers who were "slaves who cultivate the lands and . . . faint-hearted folk who take shelter from their enemies in forts and houses: whereas [the natives] fearlessly camp wherever they will . . . and disdain to plough the land. They maintain that this manner of life shows that they are the true owners of the land," continued Tachard, "and they are the happiest of men since they alone live in peace and freedom and in that, they say, their happiness consists."3

All of the settlers appreciated one of their neighbors' traits: the fact that they showed no interest whatsoever in stealing the settlers' stuff. One settler wrote of how "they do not steal among themselves, nor in Dutch houses, in which they are allowed without any oversight," but added, insightfully, that "their contempt for riches is in reality nothing but their hatred of work."4 Another settler noted that "avarice is no reigning passion among them and all that come to want are immediately relieved by the rest."5

But those settlers prepared to focus on positives were a minority. The prevailing opinion among the Dutch was that the Khoisan were fundamentally ill-suited to colonial life and that if they couldn't be brought to order they should be driven away. What perplexed them most was that, unlike natives from other lands, the people here seemed incapable of being pressed into labor. As a result, the Dutch East India Company shipped in boatloads of slaves from other possessions in Angola, Guinea, Madagascar, and Malaysia.

Between 1659 and 1674 a series of conflicts between the settlers and local Khoisan groups resulted in the Dutchmen establishing ever-tighter control of the areas around what is now Greater Cape Town. With a firm foothold established, the Dutch East India Company began to issue land to farmers north and east of Cape Town itself, beginning a process of piecemeal expansion into Khoisan territory that would continue for the next few hundred years.

By 1700 the Cape Colony had not expanded much farther beyond the mountains that curtain Cape Town, isolating it from the African interior. But after nearly half a century of Dutch rule, established settlers developed ambitions for their colony to be more than a mere service depot for passing shipping. The Cape had also revealed itself to be good farmland, and many former Dutch East India Company employees chose to remain there and farm when their formal terms of service expired. The colonial population was further swelled by immigrants like the French Huguenots fleeing religious persecution and who in time would, along with the Dutch, form the core of modern Afrikaner society. With almost all of these immigrants keen to make a living from the soil, the colony expanded rapidly northward and eastward.

European ambitions for land and labor could not tolerate the presence of people disinterested in trade or formalized labor exchange. By 1750 the colony had expanded several hundred miles inland. By then most of the fifteen thousand or so indigenous Khoisan living in the southern Cape at the time the Dutch arrived had been driven away or wiped out by disease, most notably a small pox epidemic that struck in 1713. The few who remained were attached to European households as slaves, herders, and domestic servants.

It is hard to know quite what Bushmen in the territories north of Cape Town made of the land-hungry settlers who pushed deeper into the interior. Hunter-gatherers typically celebrated opportunities as they arose. And European settlers with their tobacco, brandy, and easy meat were an opportunity. Presumably it was only when it became obvious the settlers were not just passing through that the Bushmen turned on them by attacking some farmsteads and killing all the farmers' livestock. This strategy worked. By the late 1700s, Bushmen attacks managed to stall the settlers' march northward. They also forced several of them to abandon their new farms. Robert Moffat, a British missionary stationed in the area, gave an account of the Bushmen's "predatory expeditions." "When they have taken a troop of cattle, their first object is to escape to a rendezvous," he explained. But "as soon as they perceive that any of the cattle are too fatigued to proceed, they stab them; and if their pursuers come within sight . . . they will thrust their spears . . . into every animal in the troop."

Moffat, who would later dedicate much of his life to spreading the Gospel among other Bushman communities in the southern Kalahari, had a far more sympathetic view of his Bushman parishioners' plight than most others. He considered their response to be understandable. "For generations past they have been hunted like partridges in the mountains," he lamented. "Deprived of what nature had made their own, they became desperate, wild, fierce, and indomitable in their habits." Moffat's sympathies for the Bushmen were dictated by his faith that all men were created by God in His image. "We can scarcely conceive of human beings descending lower in the scale of ignorance and vice; while yet there can be no question that they are the children of one common parent with ourselves," he explained.[6]

But few frontier farmers were as sympathetic as Moffat. They were convinced that Bushmen did not share a place with them at God's table. They declared the Bushmen to be an even greater danger to their herds and livelihoods than the lions. So the farmers organized themselves into a series of commando units tasked to clear the Bushmen from the land. Armed with muskets and pistols and able to move fast on horseback, where the commandos found Bushmen, they gunned them down.

Another British missionary, Reverend Kicherer from the London Missionary Society, who preached among the frontier Bushmen in 1799, shared the same low opinion of them as the farmers. Perhaps this was because he only ever managed to attract a congregation when he offered free "victuals and tobacco." After three years on the frontier he abandoned his mission, despairing at the hostility and savagery of the Bushmen. Once home he published an account of his missionary work, writing that the Bushmen's "manner of life is wretched and disgusting," scowling at how they slept close to one another "like pigs in a sty," and insisting that they lacked even the most basic of human instincts, the desire to care of their children. "The Bushmen will kill their children without remorse, on various occasions," he informed his readers, and will throw "their tender offspring to the hungry lion, which stands roaring before their cavern, refusing to depart till some peace offering be made to him."[7]

In part to prevent a genocide, the Dutch East India Company placed a bounty of fifteen rijksdollars for each live Bushman captured, a move that spawned a cottage industry in man-stealing and temporarily flooded the slave market in the Cape. The outcome of this process was described by Richard Collins, a British colonel dispatched by the new governor of the Cape Colony in 1807 to report on the frontier territories immediately after the British had wrested control of the Cape Colony from the Dutch. He reported that several frontier commando units were in operation and that a single unit "had killed or captured 3200 of these unfortunate creatures" and that another had "caused the destruction" of a further 2,700 Bushmen.

By the end of the eighteenth century, South Africa's Bushman population had largely ceased to exist, at least as hunter-gatherers. Only those living north of the colony's borders in the Kalahari Basin remained mostly untroubled by developments in the south, but even their relative isolation would not last.

Farms in Namibia's Omaheke Region are large. As a rule of thumb you need thirty-five acres of land in the Kalahari to support a single healthy adult cow or bull. You can get away with less if you happen to be interested in farming goats, but there is no real money in goat meat and little prestige in showing off a goat herd or even a well-hung trophy ram. As a result, even the smallest farms in Namibia's Omaheke are no less than fifteen square miles. The largest are five times that size.

The road that runs northward from Gobabis, the dusty capital of Namibia's Kalahari region, slices through these vast landholdings and every seven or eight miles or so you pass gates proclaiming the entrance to one farm or another. Each farm's name tells something of the experience of the first settlers that took up residence on it during the 1920s and 1930s. Some like Sonderwater ("Without Water") reflect shattered dreams. Others like Eensaamheid ("Loneliness") or Vergenoeg ("Far Enough") speak to their fears of isolation. Others are more optimistic: Mooidraai ("Pretty Corner"), Paradys ("Paradise"), Gelukwater ("Lucky Water"), and Skoonheid ("Beauty").

To the settlers, these names were important not only because by naming the land they claimed it as their own but also because they were proclaiming that in a place where, to their minds, there was "nothing," now there was something. This process was made all the more meaningful by the fact that most of farmers who settled in the Omaheke in the early twentieth century were poor by white standards of the day and were looked down upon by the snappily dressed mining magnates and entrepreneurs that lorded over South Africa at the time. Yet they knew that if they could make things work, they would become lords of private estates that often dwarfed those held by aristocrats in the old world.

Before the white farmers came, the Omaheke was home to a large and diverse Bushman population. The far east of the region, where groundwater was funneled to the surface through a limestone ridge that pushed up through the desert, was home to the Nharo Bushmen. But most of them lived on the Botswana side of the then open border. To the south were the !Xo, another group whose traditional territories would later be split almost down the middle by the erection of the border fence with Botswana. And in the north and center of the region were the Ju/'hoansi, then the most isolated of the Bushman peoples. Their traditional territories extended several hundred miles northward from what is now Gobabis all the way to the Tsodilo Hills in the northeast. They were by far the largest Bushman group in the Omaheke.

Similar to other Bushman peoples, Ju/'hoansi in the Omaheke lived in extended family groups. Each group owned and occupied loosely marked territories they called *n!ores*. These areas were roughly similar in size to the settler farms that would later dominate this landscape even if their boundaries were far more fluid. These extended family groups, referred to by anthropologists as "bands," were flexible. In dry seasons several smaller bands usually gathered together near permanent water sources, where, for a period of several months, they would form much larger communities of fifty or even sixty people. These were the occasions where young men and women from different bands would flirt with one another, forming new families, and older friends and relations would take pleasure in a change of company and exchange gifts.

Once the rains returned, the larger communities broke up and smaller bands dispersed to their core territories to make use of seasonal, rain-fed springs or the shallow depressions—pans—that filled with water after storms. Individual bands typically moved six or seven times a year. Whenever they settled on a new location, they built temporary villages comprising no more than a series of simple wood and grass shelters that they would later abandon without regret.

The Ju/'hoansi did not view their territories in the same clearly defined spatial terms that define legal ownership in Namibia today. Their *n!ores* could not be carefully surveyed and fenced nor could they be easily represented as spaces on a map. Ju/'hoansi did not see the landscape from a bird's-eye view, as those of us who have lived with maps tend to do. Rather, they thought of their territories in terms of how they experienced them: in a flat environment and from eye level. To them *n!ores* consisted of a series of intersecting, continuously improvised pathways linked by water and food resources and that were animated by the process of walking, gathering, and hunting. There were also large patches of no-man's-land, places where there were too few reliable water sources to be easily habitable.

The relative isolation of the Ju/'hoansi in this part of the Kalahari came to an end sometime before the first white settlers arrived with their wagons, guns, and grand ambitions. Since the mid-seventeenth century, strangers from other African civilizations have occasionally traversed the southern flanks of the region. Some ventured up the *omiramba* in search of grazing and water for their cattle. The expansion of white settlements in the Cape and, later, across South Africa, set off successive waves of migration into areas that previously were considered too marginal and unproductive to bother with. During this period of upheaval, Tswana-speaking herders from the east pushed deeper into the Kalahari, as did Herero and Mbanderu from the west.

At around the same time, the first white hunters and explorers arrived in the Kalahari hoping to make their fortunes from ivory and ostrich feathers. They followed a series of narrow trade routes along which their booty flowed west from the Kalahari to the coast and European goods like muskets, ironware, and textiles flowed from the coast into the interior.

But their activities were contained by the Ju/'hoansi. James Chapman, a white hunter and explorer whose legacy still looms large over the Kalahari, remarked in 1851 that "the inhabitants of these parts are a much finer race of Bushmen" than others his men had encountered. He also noted that the Bushmen here acknowledged neither chiefs nor leaders and were "in the habit of defending themselves against oppressors and intruders."[8] He concluded that, since these Bushmen were "independent," "fearless," and "rather bold," he and his party would have to exercise caution in traversing these lands.

When Germany claimed Namibia as a colony in the late nineteenth century, most of the immigrant population of the Omaheke still lived adjacent to these narrow trade routes, even though they had become moribund since the 1870s, by which time so many elephants had been killed that it was no longer worth the expense of mounting large-scale hunting expeditions. With ivory harvesting no longer an option, the German colonial authorities were persuaded that they would be able to extract value from the east of their colony only if they could transform it into farmland. And for that they needed willing settlers.

But even promises of vast landholdings were not enough to persuade the poorest citizens from mainland Germany to sail for Africa and settle in Namibia's Omaheke. The Reichskolonialamt (Imperial Colonial Office) portrayed the Omaheke as a land ripe for exploitation by racially superior Europeans and reminded prospective settlers of the protection offered by a platoon of well-equipped and well-provisioned *Schutztruppe* ("protection troops") garrisoned in a sparkly new fort in Gobabis. Despite this, the total nonmilitary white population of the Omaheke was reported to have grown to just twelve by 1904.

It was only once the Germans were ousted from South-West Africa during the First World War that white settlements in the Omaheke took off. Two substantial waves of white southern African immigrants, the first in the early 1920s and the second in 1929, resulted in much of the central Omaheke being carved up into farms and allocated to aspirant ranchers under favorable terms.

Many of the immigrants underestimated quite how hard it would be to make a good living out of a desert that had resisted the advances of other agriculturalists for over a thousand years. With the added pressure of having to establish homes, kill marauding lions, find water, and develop a rudimentary infrastructure on their farms, farmers demanded the administration find affordable and reliable labor. But labor supply was a real problem throughout the colony and the farmers were forced to make do with whatever they could find locally.

The Ju/'hoansi were surprisingly welcoming at first. No Ju/'hoansi now remembers quite why their grandparents were so accommodating of the people who would soon take their land and liberty. Some speculate it was because of offers of tobacco, booze, and beefsteak. Others express the view that the old people let the farmers stay because they assumed that they were only temporary visitors and would soon move on with their wagons. Whatever their motives, the Ju/'hoansi helped the new settlers to settle with little thought about the future implications of doing so.

But it soon became clear that the new settlers had grander ambitions, and the Ju/'hoansi felt compelled to remind the farmers that they were there only at their sufferance. They did so first by attacking that which the settlers held most dear: their cattle. And then, when the settlers called for police assistance, the Ju/'hoansi, inspired by a man called Tsemkxau, mounted a brief armed rebellion during which they killed the region's white magistrate in a chaotic skirmish just beyond the northernmost white farm in the Omaheke in 1923. But this rebellion was short-lived. Where the Ju/'hoansi's poison arrows kept club-wielding pastoralists like the Herero out in the past, they were no match for the guns and horses of the mounted police patrols. The uprising was brutally suppressed and the leader and another hundred of the rebellious Ju/'hoansi were arrested. While the official inquest reported that six Bushmen were killed while the arrests were made, subsequent accounts written by police officers put the number of Bushmen killed above thirty, with a large proportion of them shot while "trying to escape." The rebellion's leader, Tsemkxau, served a few years in prison before being released a broken man.

The ferocity of this and subsequent police actions discouraged further acts of armed resistance by the Ju/'hoansi. But they were not enough to persuade the Ju/'hoansi to surrender their economic autonomy. Elsewhere in the colony, "native" laborers inevitably became economically dependent on the farmers they worked for. Robbed of their agricultural land, they had little option but to do so. But as long as the Ju/'hoansi were able to hunt and gather freely, they could survive outside of the colonial labor-based economy. So when the rains were good, farmers would sometimes wake up to find that all their Ju/'hoan laborers had disappeared eastward to hunt and forage in the as-yet-unsettled wilds of Rietfontein, an area of around ten thousand square miles adjacent to the border with Botswana. There they would meet up with other Ju/'hoansi as well as Nharo-speaking Bushmen. Only when the seasons turned again and the wild foods began to run short did they return to the farms.

Some farmers tolerated these occasional disappearances, but most found them infuriating. Farming in the Kalahari was treacherous enough without their workers disappearing with no warning. They reasoned that the Ju/'hoansi's propensity to disappear was because they were too "wild" to adapt organically to the rigors of farm life and that the Bushmen would need to be "broken" or "tamed" as if they were wild stallions. Some farmers took the view that this could be achieved by teaching them the way of the Lord, instructing them in virtues of labor, and demonstrating the obvious superiority of "white" civilization. Others believed it required the judicious use of the whip.

Over a period of around two decades, a culture of violence became entrenched on the Omaheke farms as the colonial state informally licensed farmers to run their farms more or less as independent fiefdoms. The farmers were given further legal power to manage difficult laborers by laws like the Masters and Servants Proclamation and the Vagrancy Proclamation that were enacted in 1920 and which made it a criminal offense for native workers to leave their employment without their bosses' explicit consent.

Emboldened by these laws and frustrated by their disappearing laborers, farmers assembled armed posses to drag absent workers back to their farms and teach them the consequences of disobedience. Finding a particular group of individuals in this vast desert when they didn't want to be found was tricky. So instead farmers searching for vagrant laborers pursued any Bushman whose tracks they found. One Bushman worker was likely to be as good as any another, they reasoned. While technically illegal, the administration turned a blind eye to this practice of man-stealing, and some farmers, like the notorious Boltman brothers, made a career out of it. One of the first well-publicized incidents of man-stealing involved three young Gobabis farmers in 1929. They captured fifty or so Bushmen and, after burning down their huts, drove them westward through the night, depositing them at various white farms in return for a small commission. A police constable passing through the area encountered the party, but rather than arresting the farmers he arrested the Bushmen for poaching. The bewildered Bushmen were sentenced to five days in the local jail before being allocated to white farmers.

The practice of man-stealing endured well into the second half of the twentieth century. But as time progressed, man-stealers had to head deeper into the desert to find "virgin" labor. South-West Africa's secretary to the Commission for the Preservation of the Bushmen, Claude McIntyre, reported being assailed by wailing women when he first arrived in Nyae Nyae—an area many days hard driving from the nearest farms—in 1955 and where until recently Ju/'hoansi had lived almost entirely unmolested by white settlers. In a report to the native commissioner, McIntyre described how "the Bushmen claim that their men-folk had been removed by Europeans . . . Apparently what happens is that the Europeans arrive in the area and spend a few days talking to the Bushmen, persuading them to come to work on the farms. The Bushmen steadfastly refuse and then the Europeans choose a time when a few men are present and hustle them onto their cars and drive off."

Other farmers, less keen on blundering off into the bush in pursuit of errant laborers, found it far simpler to take Bushman children hostage to ensure their parents would not abscond. Even if farmers sometimes questioned the Bushmen's humanity, they did not for a moment doubt their dedication to their children.

By the mid-1960s man-stealing more or less ceased. In 1961, Rietfontein, the last remaining part of the Omaheke occupied by independently foraging Ju/'hoansi, was formally ceded by the colonial administration to the Herero king as an extension to the already sprawling Hereroland East native reserve. This left Ju/'hoansi in the Omaheke without any legal rights to land and little option but to accept that, in this new world, it was their fate to live at the sufferance of others.

Skoonheid Resettlement Camp was the first of several halfhearted steps taken by the government after independence in 1990 to assist the six or seven thousand Bushmen in the Omaheke with no legal rights to land.

Up until the late 1980s even the toughest farmers tolerated the presence of large groups of Bushmen in their workers' compounds—just as long as they caused no trouble. But with independence looming the farmers feared new, progressive labor laws would require them to build proper housing for their farmworkers and pay them proper salaries. They also realized that in the "new Namibia" it would be much harder for them to run their farms as fiefdoms. As a result, they started to chase from their farms "surplus" Bushmen, who, with nowhere else to go, squatted in ever-growing numbers along the verges of the main gravel road that cut northward through the ranches.

So while the majority of Namibians jived and sang to celebrate the birth of a new republic and the end of apartheid, many Omaheke Bushmen spent Independence Day in 1990 sitting hungry, looking over fences marking the boundaries of vast ranches established on land that two or three generations previously had been theirs.

Similar purges occurred in other commercial farming areas in Namibia, and the new government decided that something had to be done. A new act of parliament was passed empowering the government to purchase land to provide landless Bushman farmworkers and other vulnerable groups somewhere to stay. Skoonheid was one of the first farms to be transferred to the authority of the newly established Ministry of Lands, Resettlement and Rehabilitation. It was one of three farms acquired in the Omaheke by the new government soon after independence from a prominent Gobabis rancher. Before independence the farmer was a big cheese in these parts. He had owned five big farms covering nearly a hundred square miles. His farms obviously weren't enough, because he developed a broader portfolio of other business interests, at least one of which got him in serious trouble with the authorities. In 1993 he was caught in a police sting operation in South Africa with forty-two elephant tusks and six rhino horns. In part to pay the resulting fine and manage the fallout of other business deals that went south, he sold three of his farms—Skoonheid, Rosenhof, and Rusplaas—to the new government.[9]

The Ju/'hoansi arrived at Skoonheid in 1993 to find a derelict farm with none of the amenities or utilities needed to support a sudden influx of more than two hundred people. The settlers were provided old military tents and sporadic food aid and given cement with which they were expected to make bricks for housing. They also discovered that even though the farm had been set aside for them, most of the prime land was already settled by Herero with their cattle herds.

Skoonheid was a violent and drunken place back then. The Ju/'hoansi's shared trauma of half a century of oppression was amplified by alcohol and sharpened by hunger. The volatile atmosphere wasn't helped by the fact that many of the Ju/'hoan settlers were deemed unemployable by farmers. This meant that, in addition to the old and the infirm, the settler population at Skoonheid included those with a reputation for causing trouble.

In common with many other settlers at Skoonheid, my adoptive father, !A/ae "Frederik" Langman, was considered an undesirable by most white farmers. Unlike other Ju/'hoan undesirables on this unwritten blacklist, this was not because of an extensive criminal record, a propensity to drunkenness, or a reputation for easy violence. Rather, it was because he was literate, articulate, obstinate, sober, inquiring, argumentative, and unafraid to speak his mind. That he did so quietly and with a disarming humility caused further annoyance.

Born in 1948, !A/ae only ever knew life on the farms. While his father was "an old-time man" who knew of hunting and gathering, !A/ae knew only of labor and servitude. By the time he was born his parents had abandoned hunting and gathering altogether after a brutal encounter with a man-stealing posse. Sometime in the mid-1940s, the family had left the farm where they lived and headed east to hunt and gather in Rietfontein in early autumn when the veld foods were at their best, as they had done every year. But only a few days after leaving they heard the thud of horses' hooves approaching from the west. They started to run. Gunshots shattered the morning air before a bullet slammed into his oldest brother's shoulder blade. They were tied up and marched like slaves back to the farm. After that, as !A/ae puts it, "my father decided it was safer to just stay and work under the farmers."

Ju/'hoan children on the farms like !A/ae were not offered even the rudimentary apartheid education provided to other nonwhites in Namibia in the 1950s and 1960s. Instead they were put to work on the farms from when they were "tall enough to touch the top of a fence post." Farmers and state administrators shared the view that school would be wasted on the eternally "childlike" Bushmen. !A/ae was a diligent worker and a quick learner but he was restless. In his late teens he set off on his own to take up an offer of work at another farm.

Unlike many other Ju/'hoansi who aspired to stay on the farms on which they were born, !A/ae struggled to settle into life on any single farm. On some "the farmers hit too much." On others they "cheated too much." Some made you work too hard; on others there was not enough work. But on all farms, !A/ae believed, even if the farmer was a "godly man" or a kind man, they still treated Ju/'hoansi as "dumb things that cannot look after themselves."

"Listen, /Kunta, there are Bushmen who only know life on one farm and grow old there and know nothing," he once explained. "And there are others who understand farm life and trek between farms. I know farm life."

As a young man !A/ae noted that whenever he started work at any new farm, his name would be entered into an employment ledger, documents that over the decades had assumed great mystical power among Ju/'hoansi on the farms. The secrets held by these ledgers evidently had the power to give or withhold pay, issue rations, and determine an individual's right to stay on any particular farm.

"Those ledgers!" !A/ae railed. "Look, the farmer can write that he has paid you a thousand rand for the month but you know he has only paid you ninety rand and even taken money for rations. But you cannot complain and you will put just your thumbprint there or make a cross even though you do not know what it is saying. And you cannot go to the magistrate. The book doesn't lie. No. Even when it does not tell the truth, *the book doesn't lie*."

The employment ledger was a form of magic !A/ae was determined to unlock. The key to doing so was to learn to read and write. Literacy had further appeal to !A/ae because it might reveal to him the contents of another powerful book whose words and stories he embraced enthusiastically: the Bible. In his early twenties !A/ae learned the rudiments of reading and writing from a kindly German visiting a farm he worked on. Later, using a Bible, he worked the rest out himself.

In his wake !A/ae left a chain of rattled, irritated, and almost always reluctantly impressed farmers, most of whom were happy to see his back. During the 1970s and '80s Namibia's white farmers were steeped in the paranoia bred by the liberation war and the anti-apartheid struggle. They worried that their farms could be subjected to communist infiltration and that snake-tongued activists might persuade their loyal workers to rise up in the night and butcher them in their beds. Many farmers chose to stick almost exclusively with Ju/'hoan labor on their farms, in part because they were considered to be apolitical. "The *kaffirs* and the Bushmen don't like one another," the farmers would say, or "It's only the *fucking* Owambos who play politics." But !A/ae was an anomaly. As much as he had no formal connection to the febrile liberation politics of the time, he was a revolutionary in his own quiet way. He was considered too clever and too difficult to manage. Farmers worried that his articulate questioning of labor practices and fair pay would put incendiary ideas in other Bushmen's heads.

By the time I met him, !A/ae, unlike most other Ju/'hoan men, had foresworn all forms of alcohol.

"When I was young, I would drink," he said. "But the spirits would take me and I would fight. Always fight. Every weekend. I don't know if I ever won a fight, because I would be so drunk that I could never remember. So I stopped one day in 1986. And that was it."

His sobriety and his literacy also meant he could manage a broader range of responsibilities than many of his peers. Added to this, he was seen to be a model father. Early in his working life he had met and married Xoan//a, with whom he produced five children, four of whom survived into adulthood.

!A/ae's repudiation of drink was also a sign that he had abandoned the optimistic fatalism that enabled Ju/'hoansi to succeed as hunter-gatherers and, later, cope with life at the bottom of the social pile in the Omaheke. In contrast to most other Ju/'hoansi, he was determined to become master of his own destiny and became deeply despondent when his efforts to do so were frustrated.

Soon after independence, !A/ae abandoned the farms. He had been foreman on a farm in the northern Omaheke for four years, but he was not happy with the work and saw no difference between his life before and after apartheid.

In 1991, when !A/ae was asked by a group of philanthropically minded farmers' wives to help at a new school being established in the northern Omaheke for Ju/'hoan farmworkers' children, he jumped at the opportunity. But he found school life frustrating and struggled to get along with the white teachers. Even more problematic, the school had neither the space to accommodate his extended family nor was there any grazing for the small herd of livestock he had accumulated. Despite his restlessness and the rags he habitually wore, !A/ae was wealthy by Ju/'hoan standards when I met him. Over the preceding years he had built up a herd of some forty-four goats, twenty-five cattle, and several bedraggled horses. He also owned a rusty blue donkey cart assembled from scrapped cars and a vintage Corona typewriter on which he would later diligently type up notes from our language-learning sessions. So when Skoonheid was designated a resettlement farm with the offer of grazing for settlers, he packed his family into his donkey cart and headed there.

Like with the other Ju/'hoansi at Skoonheid, the fact that !A/ae was considered a "settler" in a land that his ancestors had lived for tens of thousands of years often filled him with despair.

5

Living in the Moment

"Bushmen don't understand time like we do," the farmer explained, puffing up his chest and speaking loud enough for everyone nearby to hear.

We were standing in the forecourt of a gas station on the edge of Gobabis on a hot afternoon in the Kalahari spring of 1994. The gas station attendants watched with interest. A fight between customers might spice up an otherwise dull day. But there was no threat in the farmer's tone, only exasperation.

I had introduced myself to the farmer a few minutes earlier. He had been pointed out to me as one of the local farmers who still paid their Bushmen laborers only in food despite recent changes in the law prohibiting this. I'd also been told that he was, generally speaking, a "good boss," and that he might be prepared to talk to me when other farmers weren't. I explained to him that I was conducting research for a commission of inquiry into farm labor in Namibia on behalf of the president's office and asked if he'd be willing to discuss how he manages labor relations with Bushmen on his farm. I also mentioned that one of his former employees, now living at the Skoonheid Resettlement Camp, had specifically complained to me that this farmer owed him money but had refused to pay.

The farmer was less keen to chat than I had initially hoped. To him my questions invoked the specter of government-sponsored land grabs, witch hunts, and retribution. This was understandable. It was an anxious time for white farmers like him. It was less than five years since Namibia had won its independence from South Africa and many white farmers were yet to make peace with the transition to majority rule—or, as they referred to it, "black rule." Many openly questioned what future they had, if any, in a country now governed by people whom, five short years previously, they had demonized as their enemies, freely exploited as labor, and mocked as racial inferiors. Even though the new government had insisted that it had no plans to seize white-owned farms, many farmers were yet to be persuaded that their landholdings were safe.

The farmer told me that paying "his" Bushmen in food was not only sensible, it was moral. He then explained that doing so helped them to manage their lives better and how, even if they complained, in the end they always appreciated it.

"They know they can't control themselves," he added.

The main problem, as he saw it, was that if he paid his workers in cash, they would squander it immediately on booze and other frivolities rather than budgeting it to last the whole month, with the result that they would run out of food weeks before the next payment was due. He said he had seen it time and time again. As had all his neighbors. The reason, he explained, was that the Bushmen's sense of time was "similar to small children's" because they cared only about immediate gratification, never thought of the future, and had little appreciation of the past.

The idea that Bushmen were "like children" had become so entrenched over the course of Namibia's colonial history that, before independence, it explicitly informed official policy. The most comprehensive government report on the status of South-West Africa's "Bushman tribes," published in 1984, explained that the many development challenges faced by Bushmen were compounded by the fact that "the Bushman lives only for the day and the moment in which he finds himself in" and concluded that "the Bushman is the unlucky child of the moment."

This official view of the Bushmen was a relatively sanitized version of those that preceded it. Only a few decades before, public debate on Bushmen focused myopically on whether they were more animal or human. In 1941, Colonel Denys Reitz, South Africa's minister for native affairs, argued that "it would be a biological crime if we allowed such a peculiar race [the Bushmen] to die out, because it is a race which looks more like a baboon than a baboon itself does . . . We look upon them as part of the fauna of the country."

As much as the belief that the Bushmen were "more animal than human" still loitered in the back of some Omaheke farmers' minds, they were adamant that their understanding of how Bushmen thought and acted was based on hard experience rather than racist dogma. For farmers the Bushmen's "childlikeness" was there for all to see. They complained in particular how the Bushmen's tendency "to live in the moment" was ill-suited to wage labor and farming in particular because almost every job on the farm was future-oriented and the rewards for labor were only ever harvested long after the hard work was done.

Farmers conceded that Bushmen had some desirable qualities that compensated for their shortcomings. They often remarked how Bushmen were "technically gifted" and how many demonstrated "an almost super-natural affinity for mechanics." They also described them as "inventive," "imaginative," and "intelligent." And, despite everything, many farmers also described the Bushmen as "loyal" and "likable." But perhaps the quality that farmers liked the most was that they could get away with paying Bushmen little or nothing for their labor.

It was easy to dismiss the farmers' views of the Bushmen as no more than part of the toxic edifice of racist mythology that underpinned apart-heid. At the time I did. It seemed to me that after half a century of being beaten and punished for tardiness and unreliability, Ju/'hoan laborers were mostly diligent, competent, hardworking, and punctual.

But had someone other than a farmer wriggling out of his legal obliga-tion to pay his impoverished employees their due asserted that some cultures experienced something as apparently fundamental as time differently from others, it may well have come across as both insightful and intellectually provocative.

"You whites don't understand time like we do," explained Old /Engn!au slowly and carefully so that my dust-clogged Dictaphone wouldn't miss a syllable.

I wanted to laugh when he first said this to me. I asked whether he had any idea how many farmers had said exactly the same thing to me in the previous few months, but about Bushmen. He said he didn't but that he wasn't remotely surprised. Farmers may be mean but they are not stupid, he added.

He then set about trying to persuade me that if I and the white farmers considered time to be linear, finite, and evidenced by constant change, then he considered time (at least until recently) to be cyclical, rhythmic, and characterized by the predictability of the seasons and the metronomic periodicity of the movements of the sun, stars, and moon.

/Engn!au seemed impossibly old and frail when I met him. Like many older Ju/'hoansi, he had no idea when he was born and didn't really care. So estimating his age was a question of pegging his memories to documented historical events. But even that was hard. He told me a story of the same event in the mid-1920s—very accurately, given other sources—from the perspective of a boy one time and from the perspective of a young adult the next.

He attributed his long life to good luck, to being a dedicated smoker, and to his knowledge of traditional medicine. His insistence that he was lucky and in good health did not match his appearance. With no teeth left, he could eat only soft food and was nearly blind. He also had lost his right leg just above the knee in an accident that could only be considered extremely unlucky, and in a community plagued by tuberculosis /Engn!au's hacking and wheezing was always the most horrifying.

/Engn!au hobbled around on the same old pair of worn wooden crutches that he'd been given in the hospital after his amputation decades earlier. But crabbing through soft desert sand on pointy old crutches was hard work, so he spent most days sitting in the sand outside of the house he shared with his equally ancient wife, /Ouin/Ouin. The house was an incomplete cement-brick "resettlement" structure with no floor and no door. Except for his bow and arrows, which he had "hidden so the drunks won't find them and kill each other," he and /Ouin/Ouin kept their few worldly possessions inside the house. These consisted of several old blankets, /Engn!au's great coat, his pipe, a collection of homemade musical instruments, and a plastic supermarket bag in which they kept their spare clothes. However, /Engn!au disliked changing his outfit and was almost always dressed in his favorite ensemble, a faux military affair. It comprised a pair of dark trousers, neatly folded and turned at the right leg so it hugged his stump tightly, and a torn and stained khaki military tunic resplendent with frayed epaulettes, pleated pockets, and a double vent at the back. His outfit was completed by a battered khaki military peaked cap of uncertain provenance that was decorated across the band with colorful beads. /Engn!au was immune to heat but disliked the cold. So during winter he either substituted his cap for a torn woolly hat or, if the occasion merited some formality, wore them both, one on top of the other.

Both of /Engn!au's eyes bore the milky-white stains of established cataracts and he struggled to see much farther than the small fire that burned in the sand just beyond the cavity for the front door to his house. But he did not long for clear eyesight again and refused my offers to arrange to get his eyes fixed. As far as he was concerned, it was enough to hear the chaos beyond his fire without having to actually see what was going on. Instead he preferred to sit contentedly and dwell in a magical world that existed behind the fog of his cataracts, a world populated by trickster jackals, naive porcupines, bawdy gods, and pantomimic lions wearing policeman's caps and wielding whips in their paws.

His daily journeys into this private universe were aided by a steady supply of *zwaa*, marijuana, which, like his tobacco, he kept hidden in a small pouch that he buried beneath the sand floor of his house.

"Sharing is important," /Engn!au explained when I asked him why he kept his *zwaa* hidden. "A person who does not share is not a person, but, like the meat of a springhare or tortoise, my 'special tobacco,' that *zwaa*, is not for everyone. A man should have at least four children before he can smoke *zwaa*, and anyway I need it for my health. The young men sometimes try to steal it. That is why I keep it hidden. I won't share it with them."

/Engn!au and /Ouin/Ouin were in no state to care for themselves. /Ouin/Ouin was small and frail and looked permanently on the edge of starvation. Like many older Ju/'hoan women, her skin was a dizzying fractal of wrinkles and folds that clung loosely to her bones. She also had a palsy of some sort that made her hands tremble and her head shake from side to side. Neither /Engn!au nor the angry nurse at the Epukiro clinic could diagnose the cause of her palsy or treat it. /Ouin/Ouin and I never did much more than greet one another. She had forgotten what little Afrikaans she knew, and my Ju/'hoan was never good enough to distill much meaning from what she said, as her palsy played havoc with her diction.

So whenever the emergency food rations that Skoonheid's settlers depended on were issued, /Engn!au and /Ouin/Ouin's would be collected by others on their behalf. And every day, as long as these rations lasted, /Engn!au and /Ouin/Ouin would be presented with a bowl of maize porridge softened with a little oil or powdered soup to share accompanied by mugs of very sweet black tea.

———————

I first met /Engn!au at Skoonheid Resettlement Camp in the winter of 1994, nine months or so into my first period of long-term "fieldwork" there. He introduced himself to me by offering me a medicinal "tea" when I lay whimpering with a fever. It turned out to be an emetic of some sort. I vomited and dry retched for several hours, convinced that I had been poisoned before falling asleep. I awoke eighteen hours or so later feeling much better despite the sense that my internal organs had been boiled. /Engn!au wanted to know how well the medicine had worked and to ask me for some tobacco and a bottle of acetaminophen in case he also got sick. He explained that the medicine he had given me never agreed with him. "It made me shit blood," he said.

For a man who lived to talk, /Engn!au was singularly disinterested in sharing the details of his own life. As far as he was concerned, it was a dull subject that offered none of the enjoyments offered by stories of the "First Times." It took several months to piece together the outlines of his life history from anecdotes that arose tangentially from other stories.

/Engn!au was absent from Skoonheid for much of the first nine months that I lived there. He had been working at a farm some fifty miles or so to the south. That particular farm was a predator sanctuary and also, at the time, the closest thing to a tourist attraction in the Omaheke. Semidomesticated orphaned baboons in disposable diapers roamed the tourist accommodations, but the main attraction was a haggard parade of lions and other large carnivores that moped about in wire enclosures while tourists ogled and gawped. The farm's owner had persuaded /Engn!au to act as a living display for the tourists. He hoped that /Engn!au's presence would add a little authenticity to the place, as the Ju/'hoansi who worked at the farm already were not sufficiently traditional to satisfy the tourists' expectations. /Engn!au, who was promised a monthly salary as well as "meat every day," agreed to go. He remained there for six dull months, spending the days sitting in a small traditional grass hut adjacent to the tourist accommodations wearing his old leather thong, a bow and arrow by his side and a traditional beaded headband on his head. He spent most of his time there twiddling his thumbs, shuffling his arrows about, and cheerfully telling tourists to fuck off in Ju/'hoan through a wide smile when out of earshot of the farmer's adult children, both of whom spoke good Ju/'hoan.

Eventually, dissatisfied with the less-than-generous meat rations and bored with being photographed and being rude to tourists, he asked the farmer to give him the money he was owed and to take him back to Skoonheid. The farmer responded by chastising /Engn!au for his ingratitude and told him that if he wanted to leave he could do so whenever he wanted. But he wouldn't get any money and wouldn't be given a lift. So /Engn!au whipped off his leather thong, put on his old clothes, grabbed his bow, arrows, and battered old crutches, and hobbled off to the main gravel road to Omawewozanyanda. After a series of lifts he was eventually deposited back at Skoonheid's gate.

/Engn!au considered his experience as a one-man tourist attraction to have been little more than an inconvenience. "That is just how *Boers* are," he explained, pulling what I came to think of as his stoic face.

———

/Engn!au believed that the old served a single important purpose: storytelling. He regretted that the young were now no longer as interested in "old" stories as they were when he was small, but he did not let that bother him. And in me he found a willing audience who always had tobacco and food to share. Besides my apparently bottomless supply of tobacco, my relationship with /Engn!au was built on our shared interest in the past, although his sense of precisely what history was proved very different from my own.

Prior to meeting /Engn!au, my efforts to document a Ju/'hoan perspective on the history of the Omaheke yielded nothing of use: just a series of individual life stories from otherwise bored interviewees that would not have stuck around were it not for my cigarettes. They revealed not only no shared sense of collective history but also a distinct lack of interest in the past beyond the obvious fact that "the farmers and Herero stole all the land" and "walked over the Ju/'hoansi as if they were sand." And when it came to questions about the distant past, very few people had anything to say at all.

"Go and speak to the Old Time people," they told me, referring to those that had grown up hunting and gathering. "Maybe they will remember something."

/Engn!au, by contrast, had plenty to say and plenty of time to say it. And when we talked, we would sometimes be joined by some of Skoonheid's other Old Time people. They would sit and listen to /Engn!au, occasionally nodding, often laughing, and interjecting once in a while to offer advice or elaborate on or dispute something /Engn!au said.

/Engn!au took the view that there were three periods in the history of the world. These were "First Times," "Old Times," and "New Times." First Times was the period soon after God created the world. It was a time "when animals were people and people were animals and they married each other." Old Times was the period when people and animals were no longer the same and no longer intermarried but instead shared the land and occasionally ate one another. The third and final phase of history, New Times, began when the *goba*—black people—and the */hunsi*—white people—arrived, claimed the land for themselves, and set in motion an era of continuous and unpredictable change.

I was a creature of New Times, he explained, and so was pretty much everyone else here at Skoonheid besides him and his cohort of geriatrics. New Times, he explained, was a period of constant, dramatic, and unpredictable change. Those Ju/'hoansi whose sense of the world was shaped by life on the farms or in the townships or by working for *goba* were "New Time people." As were those who liked to drink alcohol, attended school, or "prayed to Jesus." /Engn!au did not particularly care for New Times. Nor did he care a great deal about what New Time people thought. This was probably a good thing for /Engn!au, because New Times had chiseled a generation gap into a society where none had existed before. Like their contemporaries in inner cities across the globe who viewed the elderly as ignorant relics of another era, many younger Ju/'hoansi were openly scornful of the Old Time people like /Engn!au. They blamed them for being weaker than the whites, for not having cattle like the Herero, and for not understanding guns, cars, or work. And so instead of referring to them by the respectful term *ju!ae!ae*, meaning "elders," they occasionally addressed them as *ju≠angsi*: "worn-out" or "useless" people.

First Times was the setting for /Engn!au's favorite stories. These had the quality and manic absurdity of dreams. This was an age when the identities of both animals and people were fluid and during which different species intermarried and preyed on one another. G//aua, the trickster deity, also featured frequently in these stories. He embodied and engaged with the full spectrum of human behaviors, emotions, and motivations but had access to powers denied to ordinary men. He exercised these with very little restraint or self-awareness. To Ju/'hoansi, G//aua was capable of being all things. He was a creator and destroyer, a life giver and life taker, the bringer of cool rain and the harbinger of drought. He was jealous and trusting, vindictive and warm, lustful and lewd, perverted and prudish, self-loathing and proud. He was also capable of extreme and self-destructive behavior. He repeatedly and outrageously violated the norms that governed Ju/'hoan social life simply to entertain himself. In one story G//aua cuts off, cooks, and serves his own anus to his family and then laughs hysterically while they compliment the tastiness of the dish. In others, he cooks and eats his wife, rapes his mother, steals beautiful children, and kills haphazardly in a jealous rage.

The end of this period and the beginning of Old Times was marked by a division of the species and the fixing of their identities: humans became humans, zebras became zebras, lions became lions, and so on.

/Engn!au talked at length about Old Times, for he was after all "an Old Time man in a New Time world." He described how he was born in Old Times and how this was a period during which Ju/'hoansi were "alone" and were free to hunt and gather—a period that came to an end only "when the Boers and Herero came with guns and cattle." He told me what animals the Old Time people hunted, how they hunted them, how people got married, what foods they gathered, how and why they danced, how they moved with the seasons, what games children played, and what songs people sang. But what was extraordinary in these narratives was that neither /Engn!au nor any of the others had any stories to tell about specific events or even memorable characters. Regardless of how much I badgered them, I was told no tales of great hunters, notorious seductresses, madmen, or powerful shamans. Nor, for that matter, was I told stories of brutal murders, famous love affairs, wars, feuds, or alliances. Similarly I was told no specific stories of desperate droughts, dismal dry seasons, or exceptional rains. Instead I was told that sometimes there were terrible droughts and great hunger and that sometimes there were tremendous rains when the pans and the *omiramba* filled with water and what people would do in the event of them. I was also told that among Ju/'hoansi there were always good hunters and bad hunters, jealous lovers, loyal husbands, and powerful shamans, and that this "was always how things were during Old Times," when the present was not the sum of all past events but rather a novel and always original re-performance of them.

The only anthropologist to have written about how foraging Bushmen thought about time and history in any detail was George Silberbauer, the Bushman survey officer for the Bechuanaland Protectorate during the 1950s and '60s. Born in Australia and seconded to the Bechuanaland colonial administration, Silberbauer was more comfortable camping under the stars and hunting for the pot than being bolted to a desk. As a result, he spent the better part of a decade living and working among the G/wikhoe, the custodians of one of the Kalahari's toughest neighborhoods, an area now known as the Central Kalahari Game Reserve. Time and history were not Silberbauer's principal interest. His academic work focused mainly on the relationship between the G/wikhoe and their environment. But it was something that in the end he felt could not be ignored. One particular event sparked his interest in it.

When the spectacular comet Ikeya-Seki appeared smeared across the early morning sky in the southern hemisphere in the spring of 1965, Silberbauer reported that the G/wikhoe thought it "would perhaps kill them." He was surprised. What about Halley's Comet, which had been visible both day and night for months only fifty-five years previously? Or any of the other less dramatic comets that were visible in more recent years. The central Kalahari still offers among the clearest views of the heavens of any place on earth, and the G/wikhoe were keen observers of the stars and other celestial bodies. Surely someone must remember hearing about them if not seeing them? Yet nobody remembered Halley's or any other comet. As a result, they took the view that Ikeya-Seki was a harbinger of disaster but reasoned that there was "nothing they could do about it," so they went about "their daily occasions" as normal.

This moment of cosmic amnesia puzzled Silberbauer. His time among the G/wikhoe gave him no reason to doubt their intelligence, memories, or abilities when it came to induction, extrapolation, abstraction, and logic. Indeed, like many other anthropologists to have worked among foragers, he was far more conscious of his own intellectual shortcomings in resolving questions that were considered straightforward by his hosts. As a result, he concluded that these kinds of historical details simply did not matter when people's lives were so firmly focused on meeting present needs.

For the G/wikhoe, as with the Ju/'hoansi, while change was immanent in the world around them, it was constrained by systematic predictability. Every season was different from those that preceded it, yet any differences between seasons, whether marked by drought or rain, would fall within a range of predictable change. In this sense, successive summers were simultaneously different and the same. Unlike in New Times, when making sense of the present required roping a series of disparate and wholly unpredictable events into sequential chains of causality, in Old Times there was no need to do so.

In a world where the past and future have so little importance, the dead were also soon forgotten, their spirits left to loiter while their bodies and others' memories of them dissolved into the sand pits in which they were buried. Nobody sought to define themselves according to who their ancestors were, or reckoned their identity or entitlement in terms of ancient lineages stretching back in time. There was no need to. Like the other animals they shared the world with, their presence was entitlement enough.

———

The idea that Old Time Ju/'hoansi did not care particularly for the past, imagine different futures, or hold themselves hostage to aspirations and ambitions may explain why they did not bother much with history. But it does not explain quite how or why hunter-gatherers thought about time so differently from others. In the end the best explanation came from another anthropologist, James Woodburn, who had worked among the Hadza of Tanzania, another hunting and gathering society with a small but nevertheless distinct linguistic and genetic link to the Khoisan.

A contemporary of Richard B. Lee's, Woodburn was also interested in how hunter-gatherers made a living. Like Lee, he was surprised at quite how good a living the Hadza made. But what interested him most was the fact that Hadza undertook very little economic planning, even in the short term. Like the Ju/'hoansi whom Lee worked with, the Hadza typically went out gathering or hunting only when they needed to. They made no effort to store food and always gathered only enough food to meet their immediate needs. In seasons when wild fruits were at their most abundant, the Hadza didn't change their behavior to exploit this abundance, perhaps by drying fruit to eat when the seasons turned. Similarly, if for some reason hunting was particularly easy at a certain time of year, they didn't exploit the opportunity to kill and store meat for use when times were lean. Instead they were grateful for an easy hunt but would not hunt again until all the meat was consumed. Among foraging Ju/'hoansi, the idea of killing more than could be reasonably eaten before it rotted meant risking social and spiritual sanctions.

To describe the Hadza's economic approach, Woodburn coined the term "immediate-return economy."[1] By this he meant a society in which almost all labor effort is focused on meeting an immediate need, like the next meal or a shelter to sleep in that night. He contrasted this with "delayed-return economies," characteristic of all production-based economies from early agricultural societies through modern industrial societies as well as a handful of arctic and subarctic hunting societies in which they depended on seasonal surpluses.

In delayed-return economies, labor effort is focused on meeting future rewards. To a farmer it means planting a field to harvest when the season turns. To a salaried employee it means working for a paycheck at the end of the month to pay off a mortgage, fund a pension scheme, or provide a future for his or her children. As an investor it might involve buying a stake in a business in the hope of disposing of it at a higher value some-time in the future.

Woodburn intended the distinction between immediate- and delayed-return economies to be explanatory rather than prescriptive. It was meant to evoke a general set of ideas about how people thought about the relationship between work and time rather than offer a hypothesis that had to be tested rigorously to be accepted. This was because the Hadza, like the foraging Ju/'hoansi, obviously undertake some future-oriented actions. Making a bow, arrows, or a digging stick is future-oriented, as is moving to an area where game is more plentiful or praying for rain. A boy practicing with a mini–bow and arrow and imagining his first successful hunt and getting married is aspirational. Similarly, people in industrialized and farming societies also engage in immediate-return activities, usually in pursuit of short-term pleasures with obvious future costs. It's also obvious that even in complex, highly stratified societies, all of our economic choices have both immediate- and delayed-return elements. Does a beggar who lives from hand to mouth live only in an immediate-return economy? Does the bond trader who may throw an occasional penny in a beggar's hat yet spends the day making high-yield short-term trades for instant gain live exclusively in a delayed-return world?

Despite these obvious challenges, the differences between delayed- and immediate-return economic behavior help us to get a sense of how hunter-gatherers' experience of time—like ours—is tied to what they do to make ends meet and how we do it.

And it raises an obvious question: If hunter-gatherers like the Hadza and the Bushmen worked almost exclusively to satisfy only their immediate needs, what enabled them to have the confidence to do this? Surely they would have had to have tremendous faith in both the providence of their environments and their own abilities to get what they wanted from it whenever they needed it.

6

Tsumkwe Road

There is talk that the main road to Tsumkwe, the closest thing to a town in Nyae Nyae, will soon be tarred. But for now, at least, it remains as it has since the South Africans in the 1970s bulldozed their way through the manketti groves, acacia scrub, and fossilized dunes that lie between it and the farming town of Grootfontein two hundred miles to the west. Before then, getting to Tsumkwe was hard work. It required navigating erratic and uncharted sand tracks littered with broken tree roots, stubborn termite mounds that rose like cement stalagmites, and long stretches of deep, soft sand that pushed even the most robust engines to a point of mechanical exhaustion.

Tsumkwe is not far from Namibia's eastern border with Botswana and is home to roughly 3,500 people. It lies at the heart of Nyae Nyae, a place that is a synonym for remoteness in a country where almost everywhere is remote. It is also home to the northern branch of the Ju/'hoansi. They once claimed a much larger territory than the 3,500 square miles that now officially form Nyae Nyae. Much of the land south of the sixty-mile-long game fence that now marks Nyae Nyae's border with Hereroland was once their exclusive domain. As was much of the Khaudum National Park that lies just to the northeast. And until the 1970s Ju/'hoansi moved freely across the border with Botswana, where their kinship and gifting networks extended as far as the Tsodilo Hills.

Established a little over five decades ago, the town extends from a single intersection in the gravel road linking the regional capital of Otjiwarongo to the west and the Botswana border, fifty miles or so to the east.

Tsumkwe has not changed much in the twenty-five years I have known it. Like some of the Ju/'hoansi who dress in second- and thirdhand clothes far too big for their frames, Tsumkwe still struggles to fit into its formal designation as a "town." Two-thirds of the three thousand or so Ju/'hoansi in Nyae Nyae are only occasional visitors to the town. They prefer to spend their time in the network of small villages that are scattered through the bush and are reachable only by dusty tracks that meander off the main gravel road. In the villages they can avoid the siren call of informal traders selling beer and moonshine.

Ju/'hoan is not the only language spoken in Tsumkwe. Now the guttural rumblings of Afrikaans, the rolling alliteration of OshiHerero, and the melodic rhythms of Oshiwambo and Kavango also fill the air. Many of those speaking these other languages are government employees who have been dispatched to Tsumkwe to provide state services or to teach at the school.

Not all of these "strangers," as the Ju/'hoansi often refer to them, are in Tsumkwe on government business. Namibia is larger than France and Germany combined but is home to only around two million people. Nearly half of Namibians depend in part on subsistence agriculture to survive. But with most of the productive agricultural land owned privately by commercial farmers, people are always on the lookout for new places to graze their cattle or plant their crops. And Tsumkwe is one such place. To many of the neighboring Herero pastoralists the vast open spaces now reserved mainly for wildlife in Nyae Nyae are a criminal waste. For where they see a herd of eland or zebra grazing, they imagine instead long-horned cattle, mottled in red or black, grazing in their place. Local Kavango farmers also hold similar ambitions. But where Herero imagine herds of cattle, they conjure images of fields of millet, maize, and sorghum ripening in the sun.

And then there are the small-scale entrepreneurs: men and women with few resources of their own who have come here to carve out a basic living by brewing beer, which they sell from their huts or small improvised bars.

Most of Tsumkwe's homes are scattered haphazardly along a series of sand tracks snaking off the main road. Some live in dilapidated single-room cement-brick houses built by the South African military. Some have built shacks from corrugated iron or simple mud huts. Others still have just claimed space in between houses and sleep in flimsy shelters carelessly fashioned from bits of plastic sheeting, old blankets, and any other items that are ready to hand. Small fires burn outside of each home. These are the Ju/'hoansi's kitchens, living rooms, and entertaining areas.

Tsumkwe now offers a range of modern services to the people of Nyae Nyae. A chorus of apostolic churches lines a section of the main road. These churches exercise a far greater influence over the local population than the ramshackle state of their buildings suggests. Their message of salvation and sobriety in an otherwise uncertain world means that their services are always well attended. There are also several brick ministerial extension offices, a small police station, housing for government officials, a wildlife office, and a small courthouse visited episodically by circuit court judges to remind the locals that the laws of Namibia extend to every corner of the land.

The main road also hosts the newly built Chief Kxau Kxami Community Learning and Development Centre—a small computing center that offers an erratic Internet connection to the few Ju/'hoansi with the skills to follow digital tracks into the cyberworld beyond Nyae Nyae without having to leave the safety of familiar surroundings. For a few young Ju/'hoansi, the Internet is also a means of earning cash. They run a translation service set up by another anthropologist, a member of the original Harvard Kalahari Research Group and a driving force behind efforts to develop mother-tongue learning materials for Ju/'hoan children. There are also two schools in Tsumkwe. A new primary school building was recently gifted Tsumkwe by the Chinese government. Tsumkwe also hosts a secondary school that has seen better days. The classrooms have broken windows, the boarding-house is a mess, and it has the highest dropout rate of any school in Namibia.

If Tsumkwe has a town center, then it is the Tsumkwe General Dealer, a small shop and gas station that stands proudly on the corner of Tsumkwe's only road intersection. For it is here that most Ju/'hoansi from around Nyae Nyae choose to spend whatever money finds its way into their pockets. It is the grander of the two established shops in Tsumkwe. The other, the now venerable Tsumkwe Self-Help, has seen better days. It used to lure in its customers by playing kung fu movies on an old TV. But now the VHS tapes have all stretched to the point of uselessness, and the TV's cathode ray tube only fires blanks.

Occupying center stage in the General Dealer is a recently installed ATM that, as one Ju/'hoan explained to me, "shits money if you know what numbers to tell it." This idol of commerce is the first of its kind here and it is the only means by which those in Tsumkwe with salaried jobs can translate their digital paychecks into hard cash without traveling two hundred miles to Grootfontein. Beyond this piece of electrickery, all the shop's wares are kept safely behind a series of long wooden counters.

Most of the shop's customers are Ju/'hoansi. But they account for a relatively modest proportion of its total revenues. The big spenders here—those able to regularly purchase big-ticket items like cooking pots, glue, fan belts, knives, ice cream, and motor oil—are mainly government extension workers, teachers from the local school, and Herero from G/am, a settlement south of Nyae Nyae.

Usually the Ju/'hoan shoppers have only small amounts of money to spend. They patiently line up for soft drinks, sweets, maize porridge, tea, and tinned meats, offering crumpled banknotes to the shopkeepers and trusting them to dispense the right change. Some buy alcohol when they are feeling particularly flush, but for most Ju/'hoansi hoping to spend the day drunk, the informal traders selling homemade beer offer far more oblivion per dollar than the General Dealer with its fancy bottled booze trucked in from Windhoek, more than six hundred miles away.

Like Diogo Cão's *padrão* at Cape Cross on the Skeleton Coast, this busy little shop presents itself as an omen of things to come: a pioneering outpost of an expanding cash economy that will soon seduce the Ju/'hoansi into an ever more complex web of money, work, and aspiration. To some of the more senior government employees for whom Tsumkwe is the bleakest of all possible postings, this change cannot come soon enough.

"Soon Tsumkwe will be a proper town," a no-nonsense Herero woman explained to me on a recent visit to Tsumkwe. She was employed in one of the government ministries and we were chatting while we waited in line behind a group of laughing Ju/'hoan women unable to make up their minds about which sweets to purchase at the General Dealer.

"I have heard that a branch of Pep Stores will open when the road is tarred," she added, referring to southern Africa's largest low-cost clothing retailer. "And a China Shop too." She closed her eyes briefly as she lost herself in this vision of prosperity.

But I sensed her optimism may be misplaced, even if only for the time being. Over the two decades I have been visiting Tsumkwe, it has always felt as if it were on the cusp of a dramatic transformation, yet every time I return I am surprised by how little has changed. Her vision of Tsumkwe's elevation from a dusty outpost to a pulsing metropolis also ignores much of Nyae Nyae's recent history. For even after several decades of engagement with the outside world and sometimes intense flirtations with the world of labor exchange and commerce, Nyae Nyae has stubbornly refused to surrender itself completely to the cash economy.

In the 1950s, anthropologists were expected to travel alone to their destinations. "Proper" fieldwork was seen as a rite of passage for neophyte ethnographers, and the journey to remote field sites was considered to be a form of pilgrimage. Once at their destinations, they were expected to immerse themselves completely in the lives of their subjects, severing the ties that bound them to their homes for the duration of their research in the field.

But even though they secured some sponsorship from the Smithsonian Institution and Harvard's Peabody Museum, the Marshall family was neither part of the anthropological establishment nor, thanks to Laurence Marshall's personal fortune, constrained by miserly academic budgets. Their expeditions were grand affairs. In addition to the four members of the Marshall family—Laurence the organizer, Lorna the ethnographer, and children John and Elizabeth—their first expedition was joined by ten others. Among them were a government official from the recently established Commission for the Preservation of the Bushmen—who would later play an important part in shaping Tsumkwe's destiny—two mechanics, a cook, a camp steward, an archaeologist, a photographer, and two "tame" Bushman farmworkers picked up from a Gobabis farm en route after their employer agreed to "lend" them to the expedition to act as interpreters and guides. To carry their party into the northern Kalahari, Laurence acquired a small fleet of off-road vehicles, including two four-wheel drives, two six-by-six trucks, and a variety of trailers kitted out with gasoline, water, food, and enough spare parts for their mechanic to build a new vehicle from scratch. Their expedition was so generously resourced that state officials suspected that the Marshalls were secretly prospecting for diamonds on behalf of a shadowy consortium.

The size of their party was justified by caution. The Marshalls had been warned by government officials, Kalahari cattle ranchers, and missionaries alike of the perils of isolation in the northern Kalahari and the dangers posed by Nyae Nyae's "wild Bushmen." Elizabeth Marshall Thomas recalled in one of her memoirs, *The Old Way: A Story of the First People*, how "we were told that [the Bushmen] would kill us from ambush with their poison arrows, and we'd never even see who shot us."

Their concerns were understandable. Beyond the journals of some of the hunters, refugees, and explorers who had passed through Nyae Nyae in the nineteenth century, little was known about a place that was assumed to have existed in almost complete isolation for millennia. So by the time the Marshall expedition set off for South-West Africa, Nyae Nyae had assumed the mythical quality of a "lost world."

On arriving in South-West Africa, the Marshalls soon learned that Nyae Nyae was not entirely isolated. In the 1870s around one hundred Afrikaner pioneers, the Dorstland ("Thirst-land") Trekkers, had passed sluggishly through Nyae Nyae in their ox-drawn wagons as they meandered northward into Africa's interior in the hope of finding their own private Canaan as far from British interference as possible. White hunters also ventured into Nyae Nyae in the mid-nineteenth century intent on gunning down elephants and ostriches to feed Victorian Britain's growing appetite for feather dusters, extravagant hats, ivory-keyed pianos, and snooker balls. But with the end of the ivory boom in the 1880s and the corresponding decline in elephant numbers in the Kalahari, the white hunters soon disappeared. Over the next fifty years the only contact Ju/'hoansi in Nyae Nyae had with white people came in the form of one German military patrol in 1905, two mounted police patrols, and, in the 1930s, a small expedition that was dispatched to map the border with the Bechuanaland Protectorate (Botswana), which up to then had only existed as a neatly ruled line running north to south on maps.

Genetic studies confirm that Ju/'hoansi living in Nyae Nyae had very little contact with the agricultural Bantu-language peoples who had spread across the more fertile parts of the subcontinent over the preceding two millennia. Contacts between Ju/'hoansi and Bantu speakers increased in the nineteenth century during the period of great upheaval. But where Bushmen in many other parts of the Kalahari found themselves suddenly competing for space with pastoralists in search of new lands, in Nyae Nyae contact between Ju/'hoansi and others remained sporadic. The single largest influx of Bantu into Nyae Nyae came about in 1904 when thousands of Herero refugees, battle broken, starving, and escaping the guns and concentration camps of the German *Schutztruppe*, fled eastward through the desert in the hope of reaching British protection in the Bechuanaland Protectorate. Some followed the course of the Eiseb Omuramba, the valley that later guided the Marshall family into Nyae Nyae. The Herero's sojourn in Ju/'hoan territory was brief but long enough to persuade the refugees that, should they ever return to Namibia, Nyae Nyae might be a good place for them to rear their cattle.

As isolated as Nyae Nyae was when the Marshalls set off on their first expedition, the Ju/'hoansi who lived there knew more of the outside world than the outside world knew of them. They had heard stories of life on the Omaheke farms. Unsurprisingly, it took the Marshalls some time to persuade the Ju/'hoansi that their intentions were no more sinister than a desire to learn from and about them.

The Marshalls made eight more trips to Nyae Nyae over the following decade, accompanied by their usual string of camp attendants and cooks as well as an ever-changing cast of photographers, taxidermists, linguists, and socialites. Each expedition was as grand as the first. In the process they documented the Ju/'hoansi's lives with empathy, affection, and an eye for detail. Between them they produced arguably the richest and most compelling account of any documented hunting and gathering people. The Marshall expeditions were instrumental in changing how Bushmen were perceived in the world beyond the Kalahari. Their films, reports, and books showed that, far from being the wild men of popular mythology, the Ju/'hoansi were a people who were both ordinary in their behavior and yet extraordinary in the way they lived.

While the rest of the family moved on to other things after their last shared expedition in 1961, John Marshall rebuilt his relationships with the Nyae Nyae Ju/'hoansi in the 1980s and continued to visit and work with them until his death in 2005. Over this period he would play a pivotal role in helping the Ju/'hoansi to protect their land rights as Namibian independence approached. But as much as his loyalty to the Ju/'hoansi was a sincere expression of their mutual affection and respect, his continued involvement with them over the next few decades was motivated in part by a sense that the Marshall expeditions were instrumental in bringing Nyae Nyae and its people to the attention of the colonial state. For in demystifying the last of the "wild" Ju/'hoansi and carving a route to Nyae Nyae, they unintentionally persuaded the South-West Africa administration that it was time to extend the rule of law into this last "wild" outpost of Namibia.

On Christmas Eve 1959, the people of Nyae Nyae welcomed another white visitor, Claude McIntyre. Having recently served as secretary to the Commission for the Preservation of the Bushmen, he was considered the ideal candidate to serve as South-West Africa's first "Bushman affairs commissioner."

McIntyre was more familiar with the Kalahari and its peoples than any other government official at the time. As well as accompanying the Marshalls on their first expedition to Nyae Nyae in 1951, he had also spent several years as the native commissioner in Hereroland East, the "native reserve" established for Herero on the southern border of Nyae Nyae. Appropriately, one of his responsibilities in Hereroland had been to appease angry Ju/'hoansi there who resented the influx of Herero into their lands.

McIntyre's first job in Nyae Nyae was to establish an administrative "capital." The location he chose for this was a centrally located area adjacent to a deep natural pan with good water. Referred to by the Ju/'hoansi as Tjum!ui, it was subsequently rechristened by McIntyre into the click-less form, Tsumkwe. Had McIntyre bothered to check what "tjum!ui" meant, he may well have thought twice about inscribing this name on the official map. In Ju/'hoan, "tjum!ui" means "woman's pubes."

Remembered as a companion of the Marshalls, McIntyre was welcomed by the Ju/'hoansi. The /Gautcha band, who had adopted the Marshall family, hoped that McIntyre's party might become similarly gracious and generous visitors, and McIntyre had no problem persuading some of them to join him at Tsumkwe.

McIntyre's ambitions were soon made plain to the local Ju/'hoansi by the most senior government official in South-West Africa at the time, the administrator Daniel "Daan" Viljoen. He visited Tsumkwe soon after McIntyre had set up camp there and took the opportunity to address a small assembly of Ju/'hoansi.

"The government takes great interest in you as one of its peoples and wants to give you a chance to become civilized and lead normal and happy lives," Viljoen announced to the Ju/'hoansi before explaining that in order to do this they must become "self-supporting," like "other people."

I've never been able to track down any Ju/'hoansi who remembered Viljoen's address. But it is not hard to imagine the expressions on his audience's faces as the interpreter translated the administrator's words. Few in the audience would have had much sense of what a "government" was and none would ever have had good reason to doubt either the "normality" or "happiness" of their lives. And the idea that they were not self-sufficient would have made even less sense. It was surely obvious to the administrator, they must have reasoned, that everyone there was self-sufficient and no one there was self-sufficient. No one was self-sufficient because the environment provided their needs, even if it was occasionally miserly; and because everyone shared the resources among kin and extended groups, they were interdependent. But they were also self-sufficient because they knew how to make a good enough living out of this apparently hostile environment when others clearly struggled to do so.

As bizarre as they would have found this idea, it was the administrator's other key message that would have caused the greatest alarm.

"Europeans and Natives could soon turn this wild uninhabited land into an area to support many people," the administrator warned. "They would achieve this by their knowledge and hard work. These two factors—knowledge and hard work—are the essentials for any people to survive in the world today. Without them any people must eventually starve and die."

Forgetting for a moment that the land was quite obviously not "uninhabited," Ju/'hoansi in Nyae Nyae were aware of the fate of the Ju/'hoansi in the Omaheke. They may also have understood that as far as "Europeans" and "Natives" were concerned, for land to be "owned" or "inhabited" in a meaningful way meant that it had to be worked, transformed, and rendered productive. But it is unlikely they would have grasped the full sense of what the administrator meant, for the Ju/'hoansi's own relationship with their environment was based on a very different reality.

McIntyre did not share the Ju/'hoansi's confusion about the administrator's words. He had been in influential voice in the recently dissolved Commission for the Preservation of the Bushmen, which was set up to determine how the Bushmen would be dealt with under the apartheid master plan that South Africa had determined to impose on Namibia. As much as the work of the Bushman commission was steeped in the racist doctrine of apartheid, the commissioners' motives for establishing a reserve for the Bushmen in Nyae Nyae were compassionate. They worried that if steps were not taken to protect the Bushmen and their lands, the Bushmen would become "extinct." In private the chairman of the commission, Professor P. J. Schoeman, harbored doubts about whether the "wild" Bushmen of Nyae Nyae could ever be "tamed." He was of the view that they "seem to lack something . . . some inner spiritual quality" that would enable them to adapt to modern life. But the commission had concluded that establishing a reserve was the only way to prevent them from "exterminating all the big game" and becoming a "continual nuisance to Natives and the European Farmers."[1] Based in a large part on the commission's recommendations, the South-West Africa administration set aside an area of 6,770 square miles centered on Nyae Nyae as a native reserve for the Bushmen, which they christened, unimaginatively, "Bushmanland."

The apartheid master plan for Namibia, like that for South Africa, was based on the simple logic that each of South-West Africa's ten officially recognized ethnic groups should be allocated "homelands" where they would be free to practice their cultures and traditions. Doing so served another important purpose for the South Africans: it made it very difficult for black Namibians from different ethnic backgrounds to form a united front against white domination.

As much as the establishment of Bushmanland ensured that the Nyae Nyae Ju/'hoansi retained some control over their traditional lands, they lost access to an area roughly twice the size of that which they were able to hold on to. With the Ju/'hoansi's northern territories incorporated into a national park and their southern territories ceded to Herero, they no longer retained enough land to make a good living as hunter-gatherers. Fortunately, the gears of government turned slowly in this part of the world, and it was not until 1970 that the territorial restrictions on the Ju/'hoansi had a material impact on them.

Nyae Nyae was only home to around 10 percent of Namibia's Bushmen when Bushmanland was established. For people like the Hai//om, the Khwe, the Nharo, the Omaheke Ju/'hoansi, the !Xo, and the !O-!Kung scattered through the rest of Namibia, the creation of Bushmanland put an end to any hopes they had of maintaining autonomous access to land. The administration took the view that Bushmanland was for "all Bushmen." If Bushmen elsewhere in South-West Africa were dissatisfied with their lot as landless indentured farmworkers, the administration reasoned, and if their employers gave them permission to leave, they could just trek to Bushmanland. After all, in the administrators' minds, Bushmen were "nomads" and so should think nothing of the inconvenience.

But Bushmen were not nomadic. As much as they were mobile within their traditional territories and did not build permanent dwellings, they were arguably the least mobile of all Namibia's peoples, with individual groups maintaining historical associations with the same places for potentially tens of thousands of years. They also did not think of land as some form of alienable property. Rather, they conceptualized ownership in terms of specific social rights to use their resources without asking others for permission to do so. Different Bushman peoples expressed their relationships with their territories in slightly different ways. The Ju/'hoansi were fairly relaxed about letting others share resources within their *n!ore*s as long as correct protocol was followed. If hunters pursuing an animal they had shot in their own *n!ore* tracked it into another *n!ore*, they were expected to ask permission of the *n!ore*'s owners to continue the hunt. They were also expected to share a portion of the meat with them. By contrast, !Xo in the dryer southern Kalahari, where resources were scarcer than in Nyae Nyae, were far more intolerant of others using their resources than the relatively well-off Ju/'hoansi.

McIntyre was energized by the administrator's visit. He set about translating his vision for Bushmanland into reality. His approach was relatively simple. First he intended to persuade Ju/'hoansi living nearby to relocate to Tsumkwe with offers of sugar, maize porridge, salt, meat, and tobacco, in return for which they would be required to participate in small-scale agricultural projects. He reasoned that once they abandoned their traditional territories, other Ju/'hoansi would in turn occupy them, thus giving McIntyre a chance to persuade them to also move to Tsumkwe. His plan worked. Like hunter-gatherers elsewhere, Ju/'hoansi never sneered at offers of free food.

Despite his gardening project falling foul of a succession of insect plagues, blights, and drought, McIntyre managed to persuade a hundred or so Ju/'hoansi to settle around Tsumkwe. Although only a few old and infirm Ju/'hoansi settled there permanently, many others became episodic if frequent visitors, in particular during lean seasons. By their reckoning, receiving regular food rations in exchange for a little work was preferable to enduring the hunger associated with the lean months in early summer.

Over time, Tsumkwe became an ever more established part of the Ju/'hoan social universe. During seasons when the veld foods and hunting were good, it resembled an old-age home for retired foragers. But during lean seasons it bustled with life as a significant proportion of the thousand or so Ju/'hoansi in Nyae Nyae added a spell in Tsumkwe to their seasonal cycle.

Soon the Dutch Reformed Church, an organization that never shied away from opportunities to demonstrate to less fortunate souls the path to salvation, also set up a mission station in Tsumkwe. And with religion came commerce. In addition to building a small church, the missionaries also built a small trading store. But this neither drew Ju/'hoansi into the world of labor exchange nor locked them into the cash economy. Unable to force them to work with threats of violence, as white farmers did, McIntyre and his successors despaired at how unreliable the Ju/'hoansi proved as laborers. They came and went as they pleased, were prone to disappearing for long periods of time, and seemed immune to any form of systematic material incentivization. Offers of increased payments, food rations, and tobacco were of course welcomed by Ju/'hoansi. But—contrary to the expectations of the commissioners, who hoped that the additional rewards would inspire the Ju/'hoansi to work longer and harder hours—it had the opposite effect. They worked less because now they could get the same rewards they had previously but in return for less effort.

———

The most substantial and sustained incursion of the cash economy into Tsumkwe would not come about as a result of government development initiatives or the efforts of missionaries. Rather, it came about because of war.

Over the course of the 1960s, black and "mixed-race" Namibians became increasingly vocal in expressing their opposition to apartheid and South Africa's continued rule over Namibia in defiance of United Nations resolutions. South Africa responded to their demands with whips and birdshot. In 1966 a peaceful popular uprising transformed into a small-scale insurgency. Then, when neighboring Angola gained its independence from Portugal in 1974, the liberation movement—the South-West African Peoples Organization (SWAPO)—gained a territory from which to launch more substantial military operations into South-West Africa. The war escalated rapidly and coalesced into a flashpoint of the Cold War, with the Soviets and Cubans supporting Namibia's liberation movement and the United States and other Western powers clandestinely supporting the South Africans.

The militarization of Namibia's Bushmen began soon after this escalation. Portuguese forces in Angola had successfully persuaded some !Kung-speaking Bushmen there to join an irregular unit of trackers and reconnaissance commandos tasked with hunting down enemies of the colonial government. With !Kung in Angola having been brutalized over the previous half century by Bantu-speaking pastoralists, joining the Portuguese military offered them some protection and the opportunity to exact revenge. The sudden collapse of the Portuguese administration in 1974 left these soldiers adrift and vulnerable. So they gathered their families, headed south, and forded the Kavango River into South-West Africa. There they were picked up by the South African military, which soon set about using these new immigrants to form the nucleus of their own Bushman unit.

The Bushman unit expanded rapidly as the liberation war escalated. First the South African military concentrated on recruiting Bushmen groups like the Barakwena who lived in areas adjacent to the Angolan border. Along with the Angolan !Kung, they were consolidated into a single battalion.

By 1978 the Bushman battalion had achieved something of a mythical status. Their tracking skills in particular were in high demand in a guerrilla conflict where conventional military tactics were ineffective. As a result, the decision was made to intensify efforts to recruit Bushmen elsewhere in Namibia, including in Tsumkwe. The administration of Nyae Nyae was ceded to the military authorities in 1978, who immediately began an aggressive recruitment campaign there, building a small base in Tsumkwe itself and two larger bases to the west of Tsumkwe to house the !Kung soldiers from Angola as well as some Bushmen from elsewhere in Namibia. Within a few years almost every able-bodied Ju/'hoan male in Nyae Nyae had signed up.

By 1981 army recruits in Nyae Nyae were paid salaries far higher than the national average in Namibia, and Tsumkwe suddenly became awash with cash. It remained so until the sudden end of the Cold War sucked the energy from this conflict and the South African military machine disengaged from Namibia. The South African army not only dispensed khaki uniforms and military kits to the people of Tsumkwe, they also embraced the "civilizing" mission started by McIntyre. They built schools and public clinics and established several ambitious new development projects ranging from gardening to craftmaking. They also made sure not to neglect the spiritual welfare of the Ju/'hoansi and other Bushman soldiers. Military chaplains counted on the help of a procession of "church missions"— volunteers from South Africa all keen to share a message of salvation with the Bushmen of Nyae Nyae.

But as the military became ever more established in Nyae Nyae, the Ju/'hoansi grew increasingly ambivalent about the changes that had been visited upon them. Easy money, regularly issued government food rations, and shop-bought foods bred indolence among those families supported by military incomes and fueled jealousy among the few that were not. Social institutions designed to manage conflict in small hunter-gatherer bands couldn't cope with the strains of living cheek by jowl in Tsumkwe, the trauma of war, the boredom, or the sense of discontinuity and helplessness many Ju/'hoansi felt. Copious amounts of alcohol added a poisonous new element to the mix. Ju/'hoansi had no history of alcohol consumption, and the sweet liquor sold by traders proved hard to resist. Soon military clinics spent more time stitching up wounds earned in drunken fights than they did treating soldiers injured in battle, and Ju/'hoansi started talking of Tsumkwe as "a place of death."

Many Ju/'hoansi had grown tired of life in Tsumkwe by the mid-1980s. Food may have been plentiful, but the other "benefits" of modernity started to grate, and people began to feel nostalgic about their old lives. Talk about moving "back to the land" soon turned from idle fireside chatter to a tangible yearning.

Soon small groups packed up their few belongings and returned to their traditional territories, where they could be far from the influence of the military, the alcohol traders, the missionaries, and the shops. Supported by a small charity established by John Marshall, they were given assistance in trying to support themselves by farming now that the creation of Bushmanland had much reduced their traditional territories.

By the late 1980s it became clear that the war would soon come to an end and that the South Africans would be departing. Over the course of the military occupation of Nyae Nyae, Ju/'hoansi developed an increasingly more sophisticated understanding of the issues behind the liberation war. And their sympathies for the South Africans declined proportionally to their growing excitement about Namibia's looming independence. In this optimistic atmosphere the smiles of those who had left Tsumkwe to return to their *n!ores* persuaded others to do the same.

While still partially reliant on government rations, those who had returned to their *n!ores* tried to pick up where they had left off. But no Ju/'hoansi were under any illusions that they could return to the life they once had. And then, when Namibia became independent in March 1990, a series of new challenges presented themselves, the most urgent of which was to protect their rights to the land they had retained through the apartheid era. Three thousand Herero had recently been repatriated from neighboring Botswana. They had been resettled just south of Nyae Nyae and were eyeing Tsumkwe's grasslands for their cattle herds.

Even if many Ju/'hoansi wanted to avoid Tsumkwe town life, none wanted to abandon some of the obvious benefits of modernity, like antibiotics or reliable access to water. Many also wanted their children to attend school. But none of this dented the determination of the Ju/'hoansi to reconnect with their traditional territories, which they diligently mapped with the help of John Marshall's charitable foundation. Marshall's foundation also assisted the Ju/'hoansi to develop a community organization, purchase small herds of cattle for several villages, and drill new wells to provide year-round water.

In the end, only a few Ju/'hoansi embraced cattle herding with the enthusiasm needed to make a success of it in an environment as unforgiving as Nyae Nyae. Where their Herero neighbors' hearts beat in time with those of their cattle, Ju/'hoansi struggled to work up any real passion for these docile beasts except when eating them. Herding was sometimes difficult work, and it had few obvious or immediate rewards. On top of this, even the most diligent cattlemen in Nyae Nyae struggled to get their herds to multiply. Lions treated the cattle as convenience food, and thirsty elephants routinely wrecked the borehole pumps the Ju/'hoansi depended on for water. The cattle also succumbed to ticks that infested their dewlaps, routinely consumed poisonous plants, and sometimes simply disappeared in the dead of night.

The failure of the cattle program accentuated many of the already acute tensions brought about by several decades of rapid and confusing change. With some Ju/'hoansi advocating the need to "develop" and others hoping to return to a past that they all knew deep down was gone forever, Nyae Nyae bristled with tension.

After several years of frustration, confusion, and anxiety, the people of Nyae Nyae agreed to take a different approach to securing their land and future livelihoods. New legislation was passed in Namibia in 1994 to incentivize rural communities to protect rather than kill potentially troublesome wildlife. The idea behind the legislation was to transform the elephants and other problematic wildlife into assets capable of generating greater monetary returns to communities than the damage they caused. Income was to be generated from tourism, harvesting wild plant products, and selling animals to trophy hunters. The latter activity was where the real value lay in Nyae Nyae, which was too far off the beaten track and too sparsely populated to attract the numbers of photographic tourists that would have been needed to make a success of it.

Now, nearly a quarter of a century after the military's withdrawal, and a period of sustained economic growth that has seen small district and regional capitals that were not much larger than Tsumkwe before independence expand beyond recognition, Tsumkwe is not much bigger than it was in the 1970s. The main difference is that now Ju/'hoansi complain about how poor they feel compared to the government officials they see gunning up and down the gravel road in their fancy four-wheel drives or the Herero farmers who still sneak their cattle through holes in the southern game fence so they can graze on the rich pastureland of the conservancy. But their complaints are not made with sufficient energy to spur them to systematically explore economic opportunities beyond Tsumkwe, or even to seize opportunities around the town. One Ju/'hoan schoolteacher with a regular salary has set up a small store in his village from which he dispenses sweets, sugar, tea, maize porridge, and other basics, but other than him all the entrepreneurial small traders in Nyae Nyae hail from elsewhere.

As much as Nyae Nyae has experienced changes unimaginable in the 1950s, Ju/'hoansi have maintained both a practical and emotional relationship with their land. More than half a century after McIntyre started his farming project, one-third of Ju/'hoansi still regard veld foods gathered as their single most important source of nutrition, and more than two in three adults still gather and hunt regularly, even if doing so provides only 15 to 30 percent of their caloric intake.

For government officials in Tsumkwe, the Ju/'hoansi's continued dependence on gathering is a concern. "They need proper jobs," I am told again and again. Gathering remains such an important food source for Ju/'hoansi in Nyae Nyae in part because most Ju/'hoansi cannot always afford to purchase food from the General Dealer. But to say this is the main reason would do Ju/'hoansi an injustice. Over the years they have had many opportunities to fully embrace other forms of making a living but have not done so. Despite the huge amount of money, effort, and time poured into farming projects in Nyae Nyae since the early 1960s, fewer than one in ten Nyae Nyae Ju/'hoansi interviewed in 2010—some fifty years after McIntyre's first agricultural projects—considered farming to be an important food source.

In choosing to remain in their traditional territories and participate selectively in the ever-expanding capital economy around them, it may appear that Ju/'hoansi still have "few needs easily met" and that they have reconfigured their "primitive" affluence into a contemporary form. This may be true to the extent that many have chosen the relative serenity of village life over the insecurity of searching for jobs beyond Nyae Nyae's borders. But they are now acutely aware of how they are materially much worse off than most other Namibians. As much as it is possible to feel content with not very much, it is very hard to feel affluent when you are often hungry and others can afford flashy four-wheel drives and meat every night. There is also a pervasive sense of fragility to life in Nyae Nyae and a muted acceptance that change in some form or another is inevitable.

But for the moment, at least, the fact that foraging still plays an important role in Nyae Nyae speaks to the extraordinary resilience of hunting and gathering.

PART TWO

THE PROVIDENT ENVIRONMENT

7

The Hollow Tree

When I first arrived at Skoonheid Resettlement Camp in 1994, Anu was a toddler. She was one of a gaggle of children who would occasionally sit around and listen while Old /Engn!au told me stories and smoked my cigarettes. The children were fond of the old man. He liked them too. They often helped him onto his crutches and led him beyond the settlement area when he needed to relieve himself. They were also his eyes and hands when he wanted to go to the bush to look for medicinal plants. I accompanied /Engn!au on these trips a few times, but when it came to recognizing things worth gathering, it was a case of the blind leading the blind. In the end he declined my offers of help. His view was that my time was far better employed in procuring things for him that others couldn't. Things like tobacco, bread, sweets, meat, and tea.

For Anu and her friends, having a /hun, a "white," living among them was a novelty. They had learned from their parents that most whites, whether they were farmers, policemen, or priests, were potentially dangerous creatures. Everyone agreed that the priests were the most harmless of the lot, but because they carried the judgment of the Lord with them and because some were known to be lustful when in the presence of young women, they too needed to be treated with caution.

Like their parents, the children were keen observers of their white neighbors and bosses. For them, understanding their peculiar ways was as important to survival in this part of the world as knowing the ways of other potentially dangerous creatures like lions, elephants, and black mambas had been for their grandparents. Ju/'hoan children marveled at the farmers' wealth but wondered why the farmers were seldom cheerful when they always had more food than they could possibly eat.

Skoonheid was bleak when Anu was small. People had little to live for, so violence came easily and death, whether by disease or by someone else's hand, was never far away.

But, like children everywhere, who have no reason to doubt the love of their parents or the affection of other adults around them, Anu and her friends found joy amid the mayhem.

When I visited Skoonheid in the late summer of 2014, Anu had become both a mother and my sister-in-law as a result of her marriage to !A/ae Langman's youngest son, Frans. Because I had been absent from Skoonheid for nearly a decade, she asked if I remembered her and I admitted that it was hard to translate the memories of the myriad small faces that buzzed around two decades ago into their now adult forms. She was indignant when I told her this. Why did I not remember her specifically? she asked. It was a good question. Because as an adult she shimmers with an energy that only ever seems to sag when Frans goes away to work on distant farms.

/Engn!au died in 2008. But he was admired in death in a way that he never was when he was alive. Anu told me how she and others wished they had learned more from "the old man" and how much they missed his tales of irritable spirits, trickster jackals, and randy lionesses.

———

The 2014 rainy season was particularly welcome, coming as it did after a dreadful drought. That autumn Anu insisted that we go to gather veld foods—"Just like the old people did."

"/Engn!au taught me how to find plants in the bush," she added. "He knew so many things."

"Where will we go gathering?" I asked. "Not here, surely? Haven't the cattle eaten everything?"

"Yes, /Kunta. Here!" she said. "We will go into the bush just behind !A/ae Langman's home. The rains have been good. !A/ae and Xoan//a came back with a bag full of marama beans just the other day. But Xoan//a ate all of them while everyone still slept."

When Anu was very small, it was nearly impossible to find veld food in any useful quantities at Skoonheid. But back then we were in the teeth of a drought so intense that even the local Herero prophets began to wonder nervously whether the parables of eternal fire that they peddled might actually come to pass.

Anu's husband, Frans, and her uncle Kaace both armed themselves with digging sticks. They joined us as Anu led the way across the fence line, her baby strapped to her back and two skinny dogs lurching behind. We walked a respectful distance beyond the "shitting zone" just behind the house and turned our attention to the world around us.

That morning we were looking for marama beans. These plants grow from large tubers that establish themselves a foot or so under the desert soil. The tubers are edible and moisture filled. In times of drought they provide an emergency source of drinking water. But it was the series of long, soft, spindly stems, five to ten feet in length, that grow from the tuber and radiate across the sand that were the focus of our efforts that morning. After good rains they are surprisingly easy to find. Decorated by neat yellow flowers, they have distinctive elephant-ear-shaped leaves that ladder their way up the stems. Hidden in among the leaves are green pods with burgundy streaks, each about the size of an infant's hand. Each pod hosts what look like two big, creamy broad beans. They are tasteless and slimy when raw. But they are packed with complex proteins and other nutritional wonders, and once they have been roasted gently on a fire they transform into a moreish, rich, oily, nutty treat.

Anu mentioned that Old /Engn!au always insisted that marama beans were not only a strong food but a good medicine. "For stomach pains and diarrhea," she added thoughtfully, aware that over the years I have been known to turn down offers of tripe, brains, and other offal on the grounds of a "weak stomach."

The maramas were prolific that year, and our bag soon filled with oval pods. But we were not only looking for maramas. Anu pointed to a seemingly innocuous stem, no larger than a couple of inches tall, marked by a few slim leaves, and Frans began to dig. His efforts revealed a small potato-like tuber with distinctive hairs at the base. This wild potato is known locally as "hairs resembling a sand grouse." It is delicious when pulped and cooked, especially with animal fat. Over the next two hours we found several of its cousins, each slightly different and some harder to find than others. To me the telltale stems were impossible to differentiate from any number of the other small plants poking out of the sand. But to Anu, Frans, and Kaace, they were obvious.

We also found fat green mopane worms—a local delicacy sometimes fried and served as a pub snack in Botswana hotels—as well as half a dozen zebra beetles, whose wings were quickly snapped so they could not escape. Kaace insisted they were delicious. But the next day I noticed that when everything else was eaten, the hapless beetles still lay broken-winged and twitching in the otherwise empty gathering bag.

We returned home with a full bag after only a couple of hours and having walked no more than two or three miles. Our haul was so generous because few others at Skoonheid had been gathering with serious intent that year. With the good rains, they were content to live off the produce from their vegetable gardens and the maize porridge still provided from time to time by the government. If they had been gathering, I suspected our bag would have been a lot emptier than it was. Later we podded the marama beans and placed them in an old tin can to roast on the coals overnight so that they would be ready for breakfast.

Anu was determined that we should go gathering again soon. But she insisted that when we did, she would wear a traditional leather apron and that I must photograph her, as if to project her into a past that she had never fully experienced.

There was something distinctly different about this gathering trip compared to many others I had been on. There was an almost overwhelming sense of nostalgia to what we were doing. It felt almost like an afternoon hike in a European woodland hunting for fresh mushrooms to add to our pasta or a fishing trip on a beach holiday with the aim of throwing our catch onto a barbecue.

Like gathering, hunting too is now largely a thing of the past at Skoonheid. The last really good hunter at Skoonheid committed suicide in 2011 soon after his release from prison for murder. By then only a handful of other people retained the skills necessary to sneak onto the farms and successfully track and kill an oryx, kudu, or warthog, but they were old, and the risk of a stiff prison sentence if caught was sufficient to persuade them to stay home. A few months before our gathering trip, a bewildered kudu doe stumbled into the main compound at Skoonheid. Harassed by the Skoonheid dogs, it found itself cornered between two fences, where it was brought down in an orgy of clumsy stabbing by a group of young Ju/'hoan men unskilled in the use of spears. The older men and women who witnessed this episode mocked the young men mercilessly but then grew angry when they would not share the meat according to the old customs.

A nostalgia-packed gathering trip at Skoonheid and the chaotic killing of a kudu offers only a distorted view on how hunting and gathering shaped the Ju/'hoansi's sense of the world and how, as foragers, they came to view their environments as provident. To get a better feel of this requires traveling 150 miles north of Skoonheid to Nyae Nyae, where people still gather regularly and where they are free to hunt.

———

Overlooking a shallow pan in the heart of Nyae Nyae that transforms into a serene, shallow lake when the rains are good stands a magnificent baobab tree that is now approaching the end of its life. With a trunk circumference of around 125 feet, no one doubts that this particular tree is at least a thousand years old. Exactly how old, though, is a matter of debate. Silver-tongued tour guides claim it is four thousand years old, making it one of the oldest trees standing on earth. Others put its age more reasonably at somewhere between a thousand and fifteen hundred years old. Unlike most other tree species, baobabs don't generate concentric rings to mark seasonal growth cycles, and on particularly old trees like this one the central trunk often partially hollows out. So the only option is radiocarbon dating, but that also presents its own challenge, because it requires finding the oldest growth on the tree.

Even in the protracted moment of its death this baobab still dominates the horizon on which it squats like the twisted corpse of a giant spider. Over the centuries its contorted, flabby, gray, gout-ridden limbs have been pulled downward and outward by gravity. Now, apart from a single central branch that stretches skyward, all the others radiate almost horizontally from the central trunk. With nothing nearby serving as a reliable yardstick, it is hard to get a sense of quite how big this tree is until you stand in its shadow. Then you realize why it dwarfs the elephants that sometimes congregate at its base to gouge moisture-filled chunks of bark and wood from its mottled silver trunk.

This particular baobab's bark bears the scars of centuries of periodic harassment by thirsty elephants. But over the last two decades it has lost its aura of invincibility. First the largest of its limbs—which stretched almost horizontally out from its trunk to form a natural arch under which elephants shaded themselves—collapsed under its own weight. Then, nearly two decades later, in 2013, following one of the countless lightning strikes that this tree has endured over its lifetime—another of its huge limbs collapsed, shearing away a portion of the trunk and exposing the fibrous guts of the tree to the elements.

As resilient as ancient baobabs are when alive, their moist wood dries out quickly and deflates into a soft fibrous mess when they die. The softness of its wood is one of the baobab's cleverest environmental adaptations. It allows the trees to suck up and store moisture like giant sponges, transforming them into massive arboreal reservoirs. Typically around four-fifths of a healthy baobab's bulk is made up of water, and trees as big as this one might store up to fifty-five tons of water at any given time. This not only enables them to survive the longest of droughts but also shrug off the wildfires that blaze through large stretches of Nyae Nyae every dry season. Water also gets caught in the flabby creases that form on their branches, creating a series of tiny elevated ponds that in turn attract insects, birds, lizards, and small mammals, and the snakes and raptors that prey on them.

The desert elephants appreciate the baobab's water when the nearby pan is dry, but its fruit pleases them even more. Once the fruits within easy reach of their trunks have been plucked, elephants have been known to stare wistfully into the tree's boughs in the hope that a gust of wind might dislodge a few more. This is an exercise in unfamiliar patience for elephants. A few nudges from a big bull would be enough to get any more modestly sized tree in the Kalahari to drop its fruit.

For Ju/'hoansi harvesting out of reach, baobab fruit requires less patience than it does for elephants. They can be easily dislodged with a well-aimed stick thrown into the baobab's branches or by climbing into the tree and plucking them. The smooth skinlike bark of the baobab is deceptively slippery, but scars and irregular growths on the trunk provide easy footholds for agile climbers.

The fruits are packed into hard, olive-green, oval seedpods that can grow to about eight inches in length when mature. The pods are easy enough to crack open with a rock. Doing so reveals a lattice of neatly packed fruits. Vivid white and each roughly the size of a small hard candy, they are packed with vitamin C, iron, and antioxidants. The fruits are sometimes crushed and mixed with water to make a refreshing if wincingly tart drink. Other times they are ground into a porridge. But as often as not, people just pop the fruits in their mouths and suck them as if they were acerbic sweets.

This particular baobab tree is called the Holboom, meaning the "hollow tree" in Afrikaans. It is the most impressive of a triumvirate of giant baobabs that mark the territorial boundaries of the small Ju/'hoan community from the village of Djokxoe in central Nyae Nyae.

I was first shown the Holboom by yet another of my many name fathers, /Kunta N!a'a, who lived in Djokxoe. This was when I first stayed in Djokxoe in the late 1990s, a short while after the first of the Holboom's great limbs had collapsed. By then an old man with stiff knees, a small white beard, and tired eyes, /Kunta N!a'a was one of the *n!orekxausi* (custodians) of Djokxoe and so was one of the "owners" of this tree. He liked to remind me of his venerable age and of the fact that when he died I would then be left with only one other namesake in Djokxoe, then a snotty toddler who peed on my shirt when I held him.

With his stiff knees, /Kunta was not keen on walking long distances. But we had a four-wheel-drive vehicle, unlimited tobacco, and sweet biscuits, which meant that, for now at least, he was happy to accompany me on a visit to see this legendary tree. He also insisted that one of the children from the village who spoke reasonable English join us to help translate, because my Ju/'hoan was "so bad" that he had trouble understanding me.

The Holboom and one of its sister trees, another majestic if slightly smaller baobab, loomed into view a short way past the village at Djokxoe as we looped around the dry pan before coming to a halt at the the Holboom's base. The boy immediately scrambled out of the vehicle and shimmied up the trunk into the lower limbs of the tree. Apparently he wasn't there to translate after all. His job was to check on whether a beehive in the hollow of one of the Holboom's branches had been recolonized. /Kunta for his part wandered around the base of the tree clasping a pack of biscuits in one hand and a lit cigarette from my pack in the other. He kicked the broken shells of seedpods as he walked past and nodded his head when the boy reported that the bees had not come back that year. /Kunta pointed to a small broken branch protruding from one of the baobab's limbs and explained how in the days before the South African army came to Nyae Nyae he'd often come here with other young men to gather the fibers from broken branches and use these to make strings for their bows. They don't bother doing it anymore, he explained. It's far easier to unpick the hessian or plastic fibers on the large bags of maize porridge left by the government if they want to make string or rope. Furthermore, since the tree had been struck by lightning recently, using its fibers might bring bad luck and throw the coming rainy season into chaos.

I asked /Kunta whether the fact that this tree had lost one of its great limbs saddened him. He shrugged. So I asked whether there were any famous stories or myths about the tree. Again he shrugged. He explained that it was a good tree for honey and it produced lots of pods. Its proximity to the pan was also a good thing, for when the pan filled with water, many animals would come to drink, and the tree provided easy concealment for hunters. He also mentioned that the few tourists who came that way liked the tree. But, beyond these incidental benefits, there was nothing special about this baobab, just as there was nothing particularly special about any individual plant.

———

Farming communities across Africa think about their environments very differently from hunter-gatherers. Among these communities, baobabs approaching the size and age of the Holboom are often the subjects of stories and myths that bind people to place, to each other, and sometimes to the heavens.

A farmer's job is to persuade his land to conjure up reliable harvests of yams, wheat, or any of the thousand plant species that have been carefully selected by his ancestors over generations. But to do so requires that the farmer engage with and think about a landscape in a way that a hunter-gatherer doesn't. Whereas a hunter-gatherer finds something, a farmer must produce it. To the hunter-gatherer, an environment is autonomously productive. It will produce whether the hunter-gatherer is there or not. For a farmer, however, a landscape left to its own devices is only potentially productive. To become fully productive, it requires the farmer's agency. Where the hunter-gatherer engages skillfully if opportunistically with his environment, the farmer repurposes his environment according to his intentions.

But there is a catch. All farmers, from the smallest subsistence farmers on the edge of the Kalahari to technology-intensive, industrial-scale wheat farmers on the prairies, must strike bargains with their environments if they are to be coaxed into yielding harvests. The terms of this bargain differ from environment to environment and from people to people. But in every instance the principal currency of the transaction is work. And when a farmer ceases to work the land, the bargain inevitably collapses: weeds grow and harvests fail. Similarly, if a farmer works hard but a landscape fails to produce a harvest, the bargain will fail and the farmer will feel let down. Farming also involves some luck. And when their luck fails, farmers often attribute the failure of the bargain to other agencies—gods, witchcraft, inaccurate weather forecasts, and regulatory red tape—and will make sacrifices variously to gods, ancestors, scientific institutions, government ministers, and any number of experts to help them maximize their productivity and minimize their risks.

When an environment offers something for free—for example, in the form of vitamin-rich seedpods from a giant baobab—the farmer cannot help but view its gift as a transaction that needs to be reciprocated. In some instances the farmer responds by nurturing the tree in much the same way that wild truffle hunters on Mont Ventoux in the South of France or wild berry pickers in a Surrey woodland might look after their preferred foraging patches and hedgerows. But as often as not the transaction is fulfilled in symbolic form simply through the expression of gratitude to the gods.

Some hunter-gatherer societies like the Mbuti in Congo or the Nayaka in Tamil Nadu describe their environment's providence as "generosity." But they do not do it in the same way farming peoples do. Instead they typically describe their environment as a "parent" that expresses affection by sharing its abundance with the many creatures that consider it their home.

Foraging Ju/'hoansi don't animate their environment like the Mbuti. They also don't talk about animal spirits or speak of conscious, living landscapes. Rather, they describe their environment's providence in more matter-of-fact terms: it is there and it provides them with food and other useful things, just as it does for other species. And just as importantly, even if they consider their environment to be provident, they don't think of it as "generous"—firstly because it can sometimes be austere, and secondly because Ju/'hoansi do not think of their environment as a "thing" capable of agency. Rather, they describe it as a set of relationships between lots of different things capable of agency—plants, insects, animals, people, spirits, gods, and weather—that interact with one another continuously on what Ju/'hoansi called the "earth's face."

———

Over the last 30 years the earth's face, at least around Tsumkwe itself, has become increasingly cluttered. This is because while most households in Tsumkwe diligently keep their small yards and homes clear of trash, many public parts of Tsumkwe are now buried under a sea of litter. Plastic bags made brittle by the sun cling to thornbushes, and in some parts of town the desert sand is barely visible beneath a chaos of rusting tins, weathered plastic, broken glass, and sun-bleached animal bones.

For tourists who stop at the General Dealer en route to Khaudum National Park, the litter is a disappointing eyesore, a nail in the coffin of their expectations. Why, they wonder, if Bushmen are supposed to be so "at one with nature," are they so obviously indifferent to living knee-deep in trash? Visiting development workers and government officials feel the same way. But where the tourists mutter under their breath about the mess, government officials occasionally take it upon themselves to lecture the locals regarding the dangers of their "unhygienic habits."

Ju/'hoansi in Tsumkwe aren't exactly happy about the amount of rubbish lying around. They just aren't unhappy enough about it to deal with it. It annoys some, frustrates others, but, crucially, it doesn't offend. Many of those more accustomed to town life joke how it's only when the state president visits, as he does every five years or so, that any concerted efforts are made to tidy up. Things could be a lot worse, though. There is now a municipal rubbish dump in the bush just south of Tsumkwe and a rubbish collection service, in the form of a tractor and trailer, that occasionally collects trash from the government buildings, the churches, the lodge, and the shops.

The villages are not nearly as litter-ridden as Tsumkwe. But this is not because people consider litter to be any more offensive in the villages than they do in Tsumkwe. Instead it is because in the villages there are fewer purchased goods around in the first place and anything that can be reused or repurposed—which is pretty much everything—sooner or later is. It is also because in the villages all space forms part of someone or other's household. But even in the villages people pay no more heed to the occasional torn plastic bags or sweet wrappers that dance across the sand when caught by a gust of wind than they do to a pile of manketti shells. And the reason for this is because for many thousands of years there was no litter in Nyae Nyae.

The absence of litter in the past was not because there was no waste but because, to Ju/'hoansi, there simply was no such thing as litter.

All societies and all peoples have strong albeit often very different ideas about what anthropologists generally refer to as pollution. What constitutes pollution is determined by the way people divide up the world around them and organize it into categories. Something that is where it shouldn't be according to these divisions is pollution. Food on a plate is dinner; food on the floor is pollution. A rose in a rose bed is a flower; a rose among runner beans is a weed. Ju/'hoansi, like all people, have strongly held views about pollution. Defecating too close to the village is viewed as repulsive.

For most of the tourists who come through Nyae Nyae, litter is a form of pollution. It is something that is where it shouldn't be. This is a learned behavior, one that grew out of necessity as people lived in larger cities and the connection between public health and effective waste disposal became increasingly obvious. However, the tourists' concern about litter in Tsumkwe is not based solely on their outraged sense of hygiene. It is also because many of them associate Nyae Nyae strongly with an idealized vision of nature and imagine the Bushmen to embody a particular vision of natural living.

The idea that nature should be "pristine" and unpolluted by the detritus of human life is, of course, a relatively new one. In most complex societies, after all, "natural" or "wild" places are still considered to be dangerous or at the very least inhospitable. And while it is true that most societies conceptualize humans as something distinct from the natural world, foraging societies like the Ju/'hoansi simply do not. To them everything in the world is natural and everything cultural in the human world is also cultural in the animal world, and "wild" space is also domestic space. So while Ju/'hoansi consider the litter to be an irritation, few see it as pollution—at least in the way the tourists do. To most of them, the litter is no more offensive than the leaves that fall from the trees in the Kalahari autumn or the broken baobab seedpods that litter the soil near the Holboom.

8

Strong Food

Gathering trips in Nyae Nyae are cheerful affairs. Even though people now only go gathering when there is no store-bought food available or when something particularly tasty happens to be in season, many in Nyae Nyae still consider it to be their most important food source. But when Ju/'hoansi still depended exclusively on hunting and gathering, they would usually go out gathering on most days.

Men often tag along on gathering trips now as they did in the past, but the trips are almost always initiated and led by women. Foraging parties typically set off early in the morning to avoid the worst of the day's heat. Mothers carry infants, while children old enough to walk follow along in a chaotic, playful gaggle. For the kids these trips are as much a pleasurable excursion as an informal school outing in which they learn to recognize what is edible, what is not, what is in season, and what will soon come into season.

Foragers depart their villages armed with little more than a bag or leather pouch in which to store what they find and a digging stick made from fire-hardened Grewia wood. No more than a couple of feet in length and with a tip that tapers into a point, this is the perfect tool for digging roots and tubers from the soft Kalahari sand. No store-bought spade is more practical or effective in this environment. It is also light to carry but hard enough to club a snake should the need arise.

In the late dry seasons, a few months after the last of the summer rains have fallen and veld foods are at their most prolific, even a brief forage in the bush can yield a surprising array of foods. Ju/'hoansi in Nyae Nyae classify around a hundred different plant species as edible. They also consume a variety of plant parts: fruits, stems, gum, seeds, flowers, stalks, roots, tubers, and bulbs. But not all of them are equally desirable. Some are only suitable as emergency rations—something to be eaten through gritted teeth when the specter of famine looms. Ju/'hoansi classify veld foods on a spectrum ranging from "strong" to "weak" according to their nutritional qualities, how easy they are to find and prepare, and whether or not they are especially tasty. All other hunting and gathering Bushman peoples across the Kalahari classify their foods in a similar way. But what fruits and vegetables fall into these categories varies from place to place. For example, the G/wikhoe, who live in a part of the Kalahari with no permanent water sources, consider plants with the highest moisture content to be the "strongest."

In Nyae Nyae the Ju/'hoansi have privileged access to one particularly bountiful source of "strong" food that is rare in many other parts of the Kalahari: the manketti nut.[1]

Like baobabs, mankettis are impressive trees. But where baobabs are stout and flabby, mankettis are lean and tightly muscled. Adult trees grow to around sixty-five feet tall. Their limbs spread out in an orderly chaos from a straight and well-proportioned trunk to form neat rounded crowns about half as wide as the tree is tall. Manketti trees are gendered, and solitary trees cannot procreate. As a result, mankettis typically gather in groves of more than five trees. But, like many Ju/'hoansi, they are uncomfortable in large crowds, and any single grove rarely exceeds twenty trees.

Manketti trees are particularly well adapted to Nyae Nyae. They have deep roots that help them cope well with drought and, like many other species adapted to this climate, when the rains come mankettis waste no time in responding. Their branches quickly become heavy with dark green leaves punctuated by small off-white flowers. Within a few weeks these fall away to reveal green oval fruits that grow to the size of a ripe plum. As they grow, the fruits change color from green to pale brown, at which point they fall to the ground, where they continue to ripen. The reproductive success of mankettis depends on their producing large quantities of fruit. In a good season these can lie knee-deep at the base of a big tree.

Manketti fruits contain a thin layer of sweet, sticky flesh just beneath their skins. The flesh is packed with both sugar and vitamin C and tastes a bit like a pungent, ripe date. But the fruit portions are meager when compared to the size of the manketti's stone. The Ju/'hoansi sometimes chew the flesh off the stone but just as often cook it to make a sweet jam-like paste that goes well with meat. Even though it can be dried for later use, much of the fruit is left to rot. This is in part because the fruit is at its best at the same time of year that the Kalahari is most generous in providing the Ju/'hoansi with other food, and they are spoiled by the number of choices. But it is also because it is the stone inside the fruit rather than its flesh that makes the manketti so important for the Ju/'hoansi.

Resembling rounded walnut shells in appearance, manketti stones are very hard—so hard that even elephants, who love the fruit, struggle to crush them with their brick-size molars. This is another successful adaptation by the manketti, because it ensures that elephants spread the seeds widely, depositing them in a rich bed of manure to aid their germination. However, the hard shells are no match for a sophisticated tool user. They can be easily split or crushed when hammered between two hard stones. And when shelled they reveal two small nuts, each about the circumference of a penny. The nuts are tasty raw and even tastier once roasted. Over half a nut's mass is made up of a rich, fatty oil packed with antioxidants. A quarter is made up of protein and the remainder comprises various minerals and vitamins.

In the past, Ju/'hoansi set up temporary camps near the best manketti groves every year. But now that they live in established villages, visits to manketti groves are less of an occasion than they used to be. When they do go, they often camp out there for a day or two before returning home with bags filled with nuts. And as if to remind harvesters of how quickly the world around them is changing, a new market for manketti has sprung up that sometimes sees whole groves cleared of all their fruit in a single sweep. Kavango and Herero brewers in Tsumkwe town have discovered that mashed manketti fruit makes powerful *kashipembe*, a squint-inducing clear liquor capable of knocking out even the most accomplished alcoholics.

The manketti nut also seeded the idea of "primitive affluence."

When Richard B. Lee analyzed the nutritional health of hunting and gathering Ju/'hoansi in 1964 after having been "struck by the apparent lack of effort that went into the food quest," it was the manketti that made all the difference. Lee patiently weighed and measured everything the Ju/'hoansi ate over twenty-eight consecutive days. He concluded that manketti nuts constituted around a quarter of the volume of food eaten by Ju/'hoansi yet accounted for well over half their total caloric intake. Meat accounted for a third of their diet by weight but provided only half the caloric value of manketti nuts. Other foraged fruits and vegetables made up the remainder of their diet by volume yet accounted for only an eighth of their total caloric intake.

Lee also wanted to get a better sense of how hard the Ju/'hoansi worked to get their food as part of a simple energy input and output equation. He established that on average during this survey period healthy adult Ju/'hoansi worked 17.1 hours per week on food collecting, with that number skewed upward by hunting trips, which almost always took up much more time than gathering excursions. For women, the workweek rarely exceeded twelve hours.

Lee's survey also revealed that the Ju/'hoansi ate well. Adults consumed on average over 2,300 calories of food each day. This is more or less the recommended caloric intake for adults according to the World Health Organization and was considered more than adequate by the Ju/'hoansi.

Many of the foods Ju/'hoansi gather come into season in a neatly staggered sequence, meaning that at almost any particular time of year something is in season. Paradoxically, the period just after the first rains fall and when the Kalahari becomes a sea of green is considered the leanest time of the year. This is the period when hunting is hardest, as animals are able to move farther away from waterholes, sustaining themselves from puddles, seasonal waters, and in many cases the moisture content of newly germinated grasses. It is also the time of year when most of the food plants the Ju/'hoansi rely on begin a new seasonal cycle of growth, with the result that their tubers or fruits are too small or immature to make good eating.

Ju/'hoansi complained a great deal about hunger at these times. They also grumbled about the additional effort involved in gathering enough to get by. Lee didn't extend his detailed nutritional survey to these months, but over successive years he and other researchers measured people's weight variations at different times of the year. This revealed a mixed picture.

Some researchers suggested that Lee's data was unrepresentative and that Ju/'hoansi typically experienced noticeable nutritional stress during lean seasons. Others suggested that Lee was right and that Ju/'hoansi suffered only minimal seasonal weight variations.

When evidence like this points in two different directions, then the simplest solution is to assume that they are both right. Rain is so variable in the Kalahari that the difference between a good year and a bad year can be extreme. Some years are much leaner than others. In lean years Ju/'hoansi inevitably had to work much harder to get enough food, and when the energy they expended hunting and gathering exceeded the nutritional value of the foods they procured, they lost weight and condition and women's reproductive cycles were interrupted.

But focusing on this short-term variability obscures the most important point raised by Lee's work. This is simply that Ju/'hoansi were not captive to an interminable food quest and were content to expend no more effort than was strictly necessary to meet their basic short-term needs even in the toughest months. In other words, even when the food quest was difficult, Ju/'hoansi never lost faith in the abundance of their environment. And just as importantly, when foods were superabundant, as was often the case, Ju/'hoansi did not wallow in their plenty or try to maximize short-term benefits by gorging themselves. Instead, they ate to the point of satisfaction and appreciated the fact that the daily food quest hardly took any effort at all.

———

Ju/'hoansi in the Omaheke often commented on the size of local Afrikaner farmers. They liked to remind me that at a mere six feet and weighing only 165 pounds, I was but a child when compared to most of them. They also liked to remind me that "when white men get married they get very fat, very quickly" and that I should expect the same to happen to me.

The physical size of most white farmers invited lots of speculation among Ju/'hoansi about the farmers' attitudes toward food. They reasoned that farmers lived in constant temptation because they always had pantries packed with good things to eat. But even so, Ju/'hoansi were puzzled as to why farmers didn't eat more moderately.

Some Ju/'hoansi took the view that the farmers struggled to control their appetites because of all the alcohol they consumed. After all, Ju/'hoansi also had a hard time keeping a lid on their basic desires after a few drinks, and the farmers did drink an awful lot of beer and brandy. Others took the view that it was because most white people were simply incapable of controlling their appetites, their tempers, and their sexual desires. A few Ju/'hoansi reached the conclusion that it was a cultural matter and that greed was something that was taught in "cities." They noted that the few Ju/'hoansi who had been given fancy jobs in the capital after independence fattened up so fast that they may as well have been bitten by puff adders.

Most Ju/'hoansi in the Omaheke complained that they rarely had enough to eat and would gladly be much fatter. But after years of watching obese farmers wheeze and puff as they went about their business, they had no doubt that obesity was unhealthy. Ju/'hoansi noted how the farmers' knees grew fragile from bearing so much excess weight, and how the fatter they got, the quicker their legs became tree trunk–like, gout ridden, and irritated by sores that never seemed to heal. These would almost certainly be the same observations made by any epidemiologist passing through the Omaheke, except that the epidemiologist would be quick to point out that obesity was now a global epidemic.

The obesity epidemic first raised its flabby hand in the industrialized West during the economic boom that followed the relative austerity of the Second World War. And then once the Cold War ended, the epidemic gobbled its way into the former Soviet republics and eastern Asia. Now it also afflicts the upper- and middle-economic echelons of developing countries like Namibia, and Ju/'hoansi have been quick to note that most senior government officials are no slimmer than the white farmers.[2] Unsurprisingly, the costs associated with managing health problems related to obesity globally now exceed those associated with problem drinking and smoking.

Of the many factors that are said to have contributed to the obesity epidemic, the sedentary nature of modern life has probably received the most attention. With the majority of people in developed economies employed in the amorphous services sector, our lives have become a narrative of moving from one chair to another. Children, who once played outside or worked in the fields, now spend much of their time slumped behind desks or melting into sofas while their thumbs dance over the screens of their smartphones. It was not always like this, so the story goes. When we were hunters and gatherers, we led active lives that ensured that we burned off excess blubber merely by doing what was needed to stay alive. Thus surgeon generals and health organizations encourage us to get off our behinds and exercise, even if only for twenty minutes a day.

But this advice may not be all that it seems.

A recent research project undertaken with the Ju/'hoansi's distant genetic cousins, the hunting and gathering Hadza in Tanzania, provides a novel perspective on the relationship between obesity and activity.[3] This research aims to establish how much more energy hunter-gatherers like the Hadza expend compared to sedentary Westerners. To do this well, the researchers had to do more than simply measure caloric yields and make rough estimates of energy expenditure based on activity levels as Richard B. Lee had done with the Ju/'hoansi in the 1960s. This time they went to the trouble of analyzing urine and measuring carbon dioxide levels to get an accurate idea of exactly how much energy the Hadza burned.

The study showed that although modern Hadza walk on average around eight miles a day, they nevertheless burn up no more energy than comparatively sedentary Westerners. This led the researchers to two conclusions. The first was that our level of activity does not play a massive role in regulating our weight. They noted that most of our energy is burned by the background tasks our body does to stay alive, like digesting food and powering our brains. The second, as the lead author of the study, Herman Pontzer, put it, was simply that obesity is on the rise not because people are expending too little energy but rather "because people are eating too much."

———

Cheap refined carbohydrates in the form of white-maize porridge and refined white sugar now account for the lion's share of the trade by volume at the Tsumkwe General Dealer. With little money to spend, Ju/'hoan shoppers almost invariably leave the General Dealer burdened with bags of sugar because, as they point out, it is by far the most cost-effective way to get energy. Over the course of a day, and in the absence of other food, Ju/'hoansi will often drink several mugs of strong black tea containing as many as seven or eight tablespoons of sugar in each.[4] A survey conducted by an anthropologist during the late 1990s in a Nyae Nyac village revealed that sugar accounted for roughly half of most Ju/'hoansi's total caloric intake. It also revealed that average Ju/'hoan body weights in Nyae Nyae had dropped by some 10 percent over the period their diet transitioned from being based largely on hunting and gathering to being based largely on refined carbohydrates. Nurses at the small Tsumkwe clinic are of the view that tea and sugar is still the single largest source of calories in the Ju/'hoan diet. As a result, type 2 diabetes is now a minor epidemic in a community where almost everybody is thin and many are malnourished.

As much as soaring global obesity rates have focused the attention of public health officials, it is worth remembering that, despite the tremendous abundance of food available, many people remain a healthy weight. For some it is a matter of luck. Genetic mutation is an ongoing process and some people are simply better at metabolizing fats and sugars. But for most others the answer lies in another of our genetic adaptations: our ability to shortcut the slow process of evolutionary adaptation by superimposing cultural rules to restrain our seemingly unconscious instincts, from fighting to sex, and now, ever more so, what we eat.

The sum of our attempts to curb our instincts to gorge on sugar are expressed, among other ways, by the emergence of a dieting industry estimated to now be worth over half a trillion dollars annually. But fancy first world diets are an expensive luxury. And when the nurses at the clinics in Tsumkwe or the Omaheke lecture those diagnosed with diabetes about the perils of carbohydrates and sugars when they cannot afford to purchase anything else, they simply nod and ignore them.

9

An Elephant Hunt

In the Kalahari, rain is the great creator and drought the great destroyer.

Rains typically arrive with the heat of summer. In most years the first clouds begin to gather in November once the dry winter cold has given way to a searing heat and troops of dust devils dance across the land before disappearing into clouds of dust and debris. In good years phalanxes of small clouds merge together, forming huge thunderheads that deliver intense and cooling storms. In bad years they squat in the sky, obstinately refusing to do anything. Oftentimes in spring and early summer a few small clouds will coalesce into a halfhearted thunderhead, growl, and discharge some rain only for hot winds to dissipate it into silken gray strands before a single drop reaches the ground. This time of year is called the little rainy season. No one ever expects it to bring much rain, so the rare occasions that it does are a cause for celebration.

The summer solstice signals the beginning of the big rainy season. During the big rainy season equatorial cyclonic fronts suck up millions of tons of water from the Indian Ocean before converging on southern Africa, bringing torrential showers. When this happens the desert bursts into life. Trees that have endured the dry season explode into an efflorescence of color, and fresh grass shoots pierce sand that only days before looked incapable of supporting life. Rain is a cause for celebration in the Kalahari, and even in those rare years where a rain front might blot out the summer sun for several days and make everyone shiver with cold, it is rare to ever hear anyone complain about the rain. The big rainy season rarely lasts longer than a few short, intense months. And within days of the last rainfall the grasslands, now thick and tall, begin to transform from green to gold.

Fluctuations in climate and the absence of topographic features like hills that function as convective funnels in the Kalahari make it nearly impossible to establish where, when, and how much rain will fall. A good year might have ten times the amount of rain as a bad year. And one Kalahari farm may end up having ten times the rainfall of a neighboring farm a few miles away. The rain is also subject to other longer-term climatic fluctuations. Often a long sequence of good rain years is followed by a similarly drawn-out sequence of droughts.

Before the Nyae Nyae Development Foundation of Namibia raised money to drill boreholes that tap ancient subterranean wells across Nyae Nyae, Ju/'hoansi there depended on a network of natural waterholes and springs supplemented by moisture-rich plants to slake their thirst. Only one of the natural waterholes in contemporary Nyae Nyae is permanent. Before the apartheid administration ceded two-thirds of Nyae Nyae to the Herero, Ju/'hoansi controlled three other permanent waterholes. Back then the Ju/'hoansi dispersed across Nyae Nyae during the late wet seasons when the seasonal waterholes sprang into life. Each waterhole was owned by a small Ju/'hoan family group of between five and fifteen people who retained exclusive rights to it and the plant and animal resources around it. These waterholes formed the hearts of loosely defined territories of about twenty or thirty square miles, which Ju/'hoansi from other bands had to ask permission to use. When these waterholes dried up, individual bands clustered together around the permanent waterholes until the rains came again.

This system worked well. During dry seasons, the lands around the permanent waterholes could sustain more people than they could during the wet season, when most of the plants that nourished the Ju/'hoansi were still early in their growth cycles. And gathering together in larger groups gave people the opportunity to catch up with old friends and family and for younger men and women to flirt with new people and perhaps fall in love.

Ju/'hoansi considered rain to be more than the convergence of a set of meteorological phenomena. It was, they believed, the only elemental force tinkered with by the Ju/'hoansi's aloof Creator God, who was otherwise content to let the places, people, and animals He created muddle on without his interference. He left the job of meddling in terrestrial affairs to the other deity figure in the Ju/'hoan cosmos, G//aua, an insecure and jealous trickster with a vicious streak capable of occasional, often surprising acts of kindness.

The Creator God was not the sole agency that governed the rain. In the recent past, Ju/'hoansi lit fires during the late dry seasons "because smoke generates clouds." The rain was also linked to a fundamental property all people and the most important meat animals possessed. Ju/'hoansi referred to this property as *n!ow* and explained how it revealed itself in changes in the weather whenever an important meat animal, like an elephant or eland or giraffe, was killed or whenever a human was born or died.

N!ow featured prominently in the work of the Marshalls, whose books I had diligently combed through before my first period of proper ethnographic fieldwork in 1994. That year the little rainy season began on cue with a terrific thunderstorm in mid-November that soaked the northern Omaheke for an hour or more. But that storm turned out to be the only proper rain of the whole wet season. The sky remained clear of clouds through Christmas and then into January. By February, clouds appeared again, but they never gathered the strength to form the towering cumulonimbi that bring rain. Occasionally a few drops would fall, but not enough to soak the sand before evaporating. By late March it was clear that there would be no big rainy season that year. With no new growth save the few grass shoots that had sprung up after the November shower, the grasslands in the northern Omaheke were transformed into a sea of sand in alternating ripples of red and white.

I asked my neighbors frequently about what they thought had caused the drought and whether it was something to do with *n!ow*. Most shrugged and suggested that there was no place for the magical ideas of the Old Time people now that Christians had come.

Only Skoonheid's small cohort of Old Time people had much to say about *n!ow*. And in time *n!ow* would also become a headache for this small geriatric band because of my nagging questions and inability to get my head around something that was apparently so obvious. As a result, whenever

I brought up *n!ow* in conversation, as I often did during this drought, most would suddenly remember some urgent task that needed doing and quietly shuffle off. /Engn!au, having only one leg, did not have this option.

"If you light a cigarette with a match and the cigarette makes smoke, but then dies as it burns itself out, that is how it is with *n!ow*," he explained to me once, among much head nodding and grunted agreement from his friends, a statement that left me even more confused than I had been before.

N!ow came in two forms, good *n!ow* and bad *n!ow*. Good *n!ow* was associated with rain and wetness, bad *n!ow* with drought. All humans are endowed with *n!ow* when they are fetuses in the womb, and according to /Engn!au it is what gave them life. No one was sure when animals gained their *n!ow* but they were certain that some species, in particular those they liked to hunt the most, like kudu and wildebeest, clearly had *n!ow* because their *n!ow* would interact with the weather after a kill in just the same way as a human's *n!ow* would interact with the weather when he or she was born or died. As importantly, a hunter's *n!ow* would interact with that of an animal he had killed when its blood first hit the soil. How the interaction would manifest was impossible to predict in advance but easy to establish after the fact, because the weather would show you. People's *n!ow* could also affect the weather if they urinated on a fire or burned some of their hair, nails, or dead skin. If the person had good *n!ow* when they did this, it might bring rain. And if the person had bad *n!ow*, doing so might bring coolness and drought.

"What if you slaughter a cow or a goat?" I asked /Engn!au. "Do these animals have *n!ow*?"

"No," he said. "If this was true, the weather near the big abattoir at Gobabis would never settle."

"What about me and the white farmers or the Herero?" I asked. "Do we also have *n!ow* or is it just Ju/'hoansi? What about other Bushmen, like Nharo and !Xu?"

"Of course," said /Engn!au. "Everyone has *n!ow*. But maybe you call it something else. I don't know what other Bushmen call it. These young people here at Skoonheid have *n!ow* even if they don't care about it. It comes to them when they are born and it leaves them when they die."

In the end *n!ow* was something that I only ever made sense of when I ceased trying to understand what it was rather than accepting it as something that existed. *N!ow* was not so much an idea as something empirical, something as real to the likes of /Engn!au as wood or sand or rain. Other anthropologists have had a go at explaining it, but their explanations, like mine, are shortchanged by the words at their disposal. As counterintuitive as it seems to those of us who interpret the world around us primarily through the prism of grammar and words, language is neither the primary medium of culture nor is it a universal tool capable of translating everything from one culture into another. It also reminds us of the limits to understanding that come from only asking questions. Although anthropologists are meant to participate as much as possible in the daily lives of the people we work with, in practice we mainly watch and ask questions. Doing so enables us to describe aspects of things like *n!ow*, but it does not give us the ability to make sense of them. To know *n!ow* and understand it, you have to have been a product of this land, to have been shaped by its seasonal rhythms, and to have experienced the bonds that formed between hunters and their prey.

––––––––––

The elephant's *n!ow* came in the form of clouds at a time of year when the skies should be cobalt blue. These were not rain-bearing clouds but a series of small, almost translucent icy cells that blanketed the eastern sky across Nyae Nyae. And as the sun set, these cells transformed into a mottled purple-gray lattice that resembled the slabs of gray skin that were sliced and tugged from the elephant's carcass earlier that morning.

The elephant had died in a thicket of dense bush five miles or so off from the sand track that led to the small Ju/'hoan village G/aqo!oma in the southeast of Nyae Nyae. The sun was already high when we reached the carcass. By then half a dozen Ju/'hoansi were busy sharpening knives in preparation for a long day of butchery while the hunting party stood in the shade and watched. The elephant was lying on its side, eyes closed as if asleep. Its one complete tusk was half buried in the sand. The other, a broken stump, pointed skyward.

The hunting party comprised a professional hunter (who had won the contract to organize trophy hunts in the Nyae Nyae Conservancy), his dog, a team of Ju/'hoan trackers, and the clients, a middle-aged married couple from Vienna. The husband was a tall, clean-shaven, and soft-spoken dentist. His wife was a no-nonsense, tournament-winning clay-pigeon shooter. Back home they spent their weekends hunting boar on an estate outside Vienna.

The dentist had chalked up plenty of big-game trophies across Africa already. This hunt was a gift for his beloved. His partner's stamina, calmness, and obvious prowess with a rifle transformed her into a goddess in his eyes. For her, killing an elephant was the apotheosis of her art. She said that no other form of hunting was more demanding or more satisfying.

I had visited the hunters at their camp a few days before they bagged their trophy. After dinner that evening they showed me the tip of a broken elephant tusk they had found when trekking through the bush earlier that day. It was just under a foot in length, heavy as leadwood, streaked with thousands of fine black cracks, and stained a buttery yellow by tree sap. Elephants tend to favor one tusk over the other when using them to gouge bark, dig, or shove things about. Here in the Kalahari, where naturally occurring phosphates are scarce, elephant tusks are comparatively brittle and their favored tusks are prone to snap after thirty or forty years of work. The hunters had found this particular broken tusk several days before and decided that its owner was exactly the elephant they wanted.

On the day the carcass was butchered, they brought the broken tusk along with them to see if this was indeed the same elephant. When the dentist held the tusk to the stump with practiced hands it fitted perfectly, and for a brief moment this elephant was whole again in death.

Despite the trauma of the animal's death, there was something serene about this carcass even as one of the Ju/'hoansi plunged a knife through the thick skin at the base of its head before putting his weight behind it and drawing the blade along the elephant's spine to its tail. For after the adrenaline, pain, and panic that coursed through its system after the first volley of shots crashed into its skull, neck, and lungs, the bull had lain down on its side and closed its eyes in contemplation of its death. By then its companions—four younger bulls—had fled trumpeting in panic into the bush, where they would ride out the adrenaline screaming through their bodies, relive the day's trauma, memorize the smells and sounds of the killers, mourn their loss, and contemplate a future without the guidance of this old bull.

———

Of all the tracks that decorate the sand in Nyae Nyae, those left by elephants are the most obvious. In rural Nyae Nyae and the adjoining Khaudum National Park, elephants outnumber people by a ratio of two to one. But it wasn't always like this. When the Marshalls arrived in Nyae Nyae half a century ago, elephants were only occasional visitors: then the most prolific dangerous animals were lions. But over the last three decades lions have become ever more scarce and the elephant population has grown from fewer than a dozen to around four thousand.

No one is certain whether there were large numbers of elephants in this part of the Kalahari in the distant past or not. Scars high up on the trunks of the older baobabs suggest that there almost certainly were, but whether the numbers were comparable to current populations is anybody's guess.

When I ask Ju/'hoansi about it, they explain their grandparents hadn't thought to tell them and they had no good reason to ask, so why should they know? What they do know is that there are many more elephants now than there were fifty or a hundred years ago. They also know that no matter how careful you are, elephants are difficult and sometimes very dangerous neighbors.

There are stories of nursing elephant cows that have charged and killed Ju/'hoansi who have unwittingly disturbed them and their young calves. There are also stories of moody bulls in musth that have turned on Ju/'hoansi in acts of spontaneous biochemical aggression. With testosterone levels sixty times higher than normal, even the most placid bulls become unpredictable and truculent when in musth. When this happens, urine drips from their penises, the temporal glands behind their eyes swell painfully, and a sticky dark soup of proteins and lipids trickles from them to their mouths. Periods of musth are hard to predict and can last from a week to longer than a month. And for the duration of this period, bulls think of little else but mating and fighting. Attractive to female elephants, the smell of these secretions is unmistakable even from far away. This makes elephants in musth easy enough to avoid if you are on foot and downwind from them. But occasionally, when the wind is unfavorable and the bush is thick, it is easy to get too close.

However, it is not the episodic tantrums of testosterone-crazed bulls or the fierce determination of cows to protect their calves that causes Ju/'hoansi to lose sleep at night. Rather, it is the calm intelligence the elephants display when they dismember the windmills and solar water pumps that now provide year-round water to the remote Nyae Nyae villages. As the villagers, aided by government and local development organizations, have devised ever more elaborate ways to protect their wells, pumps, and pipes from thirsty elephants, so the elephants have developed ever more ingenious ways of breaking them.

As troublesome as the elephants can be as neighbors, Ju/'hoansi are content to put up with them. Not just because the trickle of paying tourists who come to camp near the pans like to see elephants, but also because the annual elephant trophy hunting allocation in Nyae Nyae yields around forty tons of meat for the community every year. Each elephant killed also realizes close to $30,000 USD in cash, with the result that trophy hunting generates up to $600,000 USD for the Nyae Nyae Conservancy every year. This money is used to maintain village water points, manage the conservancy, and provide some basic services in the villages. Any money that is left over at the year-end is distributed to all the adults in the conservancy in the form of a cash dividend.

Ju/'hoansi have spent many days over the last two decades debating the costs and benefits of letting trophy hunters loose in Nyae Nyae. For the moment, like the government, they take the view that it is beneficial. But they struggle to make sense of the hunters' motivations. Why would anyone spend such an unimaginably large sum of money just to kill something they wouldn't even eat? And why would anyone hunt something simply for the ivory? But then, Ju/'hoansi have always been confused by the motivations of the big-game hunters who plundered the Kalahari in the second half of the nineteenth century. And these early big-game hunters were almost certainly responsible for the elephants' nearly century-long absence from Nyae Nyae.

———

For the Victorian polymath Sir Francis Galton—discoverer of anti-cyclones, inventor of psychometrics, genitor of eugenics, and father of differential psychology—and his friend Charles Andersson, the western

Kalahari was a trophy hunter's paradise when they visited a century and half ago.[1]

Accompanied by a group of musket-wielding Amraal Hottentots, Galton and Andersson embarked into the uncharted "wilds" northeast of Gobabis in 1851 looking for a route to the legendary Lake Ngami that David Livingstone had chanced upon a few years before. But the promise of discovering a route to Lake Ngami proved to be of less immediate interest to them than the prospect of shooting a rhinoceros, an obstinate omission from the trophy bag they had assembled thus far on their safari, a trip spanning nearly a thousand miles as they trekked from Walvis Bay on the coast and then up and down Namibia's mountainous central spine. So when they eventually reached a waterhole in the southeastern borderlands of "Bushman territory" now known as Rietfontein and found it teeming with game of "every sort," including rhinos, they were easily persuaded to abandon any plans of heading farther east in pursuit of Livingstone's fabled lake. Instead they stayed on at Rietfontein to engage in some "sport" before heading back to the coast and, in Galton's case, a glorious return to London and a shiny medal from the Royal Geographical Society.

The numbers of wildlife that flocked to the spring at Rietfontein astounded them. Andersson described how in one evening he shot "no less than eight" rhinoceroses in the space of five hours before turning in to bed. He probably slept poorly that night, for he follows his description of the evening's carnage with the observation, "But I never took delight in useless slaughter."

Galton also described the good sport he had taking potshots at any animal unfortunate enough to wander into his sights. But he tired of the butchery far sooner than Andersson. Instead he turned his attention to observing the behavior of animals, quizzing the local Bushmen about whether or not unicorns and griffins might be found in the Kalahari (the Bushmen assured him there were), and experimenting with recipes for cooking the growing mountain of meat being produced by the hunters. "A young [rhino] calf, rolled up in a piece of spare hide, and baked in the earth is excellent," he wrote. "I hardly know which part of the little animal is the best, the skin or the flesh."

There was probably more skill involved in Galton's cooking of the rhino than in Andersson's gunning them down. The rhinos in Rietfontein had no reason to fear humans yet and so were more curious than skittish. This was fortunate for the hunters, because Galton's and Andersson's muskets were only reliable at around twenty-five or thirty yards. Galton recalled his "delight" at seeing "two huge white rhinoceroses" and how subsequently "some twenty of us . . . ran helter-skelter . . . till we were pretty near them, and then, as one trotted up to see what was the matter, a volley was blazed into him, that bowled him over like a hare."

There were also plenty of elephants there at the time, but, unlike the rhinos, they were nervous of humans and knew to steer clear of the sounds of musket fire. Europe's appetite for African ivory had begun to affect life even in this "unexplored" part of the Kalahari well over a decade before Galton and Andersson took their first potshots at passing rhinos.

Ivory was the plastic of the eighteenth century, and a staple raw ingredient for many of Europe's emerging industries. Strong, enduring, beautiful, and easy to carve, it was used in everything from combs and cutlery to billiard balls and Christmas baubles. With much of South Africa's wild elephant population having been destroyed within two hundred years of the first permanent European settlements in the Cape, by the early nineteenth century, ivory hunters and traders began to cast their gaze farther north toward the Kalahari. At first the traders stayed on the southern fringes of the desert and exchanged guns for ivory with the Tswana-speaking tribes that were prepared to venture deeper into the desert. But this only realized a trickle of ivory. The Tswana hunters were inexperienced riflemen and hunted on foot. This meant that not only were they relatively unproductive but also, because they had to carry the heavy tusks as well as their muskets, they rarely shot more than one or two elephants at a time. The elephants, for their part, also quickly learned to avoid people or, if they were so minded, run down and crush careless hunters unable to reload their muskets fast enough. But when the European ivory traders began to push into the Kalahari themselves and brought with them wagons and horses, things changed. With horses, hunters' ranges could be extended much farther. Horses could also outrun charging elephants when hunters needed to reload their weapons. And with wagons, hunters could cart ivory back by the ton.

Where Galton hunted for the cookpot, recreation, adventure, and the opportunity to impress those back home with tales of derring-do, hunting professionals was a much less glamorous affair for the professionals. It required manpower, supply routes, start-up capital, and plenty of equipment. One of the first Europeans to realize the potential wealth to be gained from the industrial-scale killing of elephants in the Kalahari was Roualeyn Gordon-Cumming. For a single hunting trip in the southern Kalahari in 1841 he took with him fifty thousand percussion caps, sixteen thousand bullets, four hundred pounds of lead, and five hundred pounds of gunpowder.[2]

Over the next thirty years many more traders and hunters established themselves on the fringes of the Kalahari. Portuguese hunters and traders converged on the Kalahari from the north, German hunters from the west, and American, British, and Afrikaner hunters from the east and south. By 1865, elephants were being harvested at a rate of six thousand per year in the Kalahari, and the path carved by Galton from Gobabis to Rietfontein became an established trade route, with as many as a dozen wagon trains passing through in a single year. In the western Kalahari, one particular hunter, Hendrik van Zyl of Ghanzi (in what is now Botswana), shot four hundred elephants in 1877 and claimed in the following year to have dispatched more than a hundred in a single afternoon's shooting with the aid of six companions.

Van Zyl, who was formerly a member of parliament in the Transvaal Republic, would eventually become the first European to settle permanently in the central Kalahari. A champion of frontier justice, van Zyl came to dominate the local ivory trade. In doing so he made a fortune and developed a reputation of being fearless. On hearing that Bushmen had murdered the child of an Afrikaner trekker passing through, van Zyl invited the accused Bushmen band to share in a feast. Once the Bushmen were well fed and drunk on brandy, he ordered them to be tied up and then invited the family of the murdered child to shoot them. When the bewildered family declined, he instructed his own servants to do so. Thirty-three Bushmen—men, women, and children—were executed that day.

No Ju/'hoansi know with any certainty whether their ancestors hunted elephant or not. In Nyae Nyae and the Omaheke, Ju/'hoansi neither talk of elephant hunting nor have any established techniques for doing so. Perhaps with the disappearance of elephants in the 1870s, this particular skill set was simply forgotten.

Hunter /Ui thought that if Ju/'hoansi hunted elephants in the past, they would probably have ambushed them after having made them chase "a

very fast runner." But even he could not help but laugh at the idea
because it sounded so insane. Elephants were not only dangerous but, like
hippos and rhinos, far too big for even a large gathering of Ju/'hoansi to
eat before much of the meat would spoil. A big eland or giraffe could just
as easily satisfy everyone, and the risk of being killed while hunting them
was much lower. Added to this, the small spears and lightweight bows that
Ju/'hoansi still hunt with are not remotely suited to bringing down something as large as an elephant.

But there are records of Bushmen elsewhere hunting elephants. In 1668
a Cape settler, John Shredder, described how hunters surrounded an
elephant "on flat and sandy ground" before stabbing it from every direction, forcing the animal to turn back and forth while the hunters dodged
its swinging trunk "until at last blood flows from the many spear wounds
and he is worn out and falls down."[3]

But even if Ju/'hoansi were not involved in the ivory trade, some other
Bushmen were. David Livingstone described how the "River Bushmen" of
the Boteti River near Lake Ngami—"at least six feet high, and of a darker
colour than the Bushmen of . . . the thirsty plains of the Kalahari"—killed
many elephants using "long-bladed spears."[4] James Chapman, another
hunter and trader, many of whose descendants still farm in the Omaheke,
gave a detailed description of how the Boteti River Bushmen were forced
by their Tswana "masters" to drive elephants into sticky bogs where they
could be speared at leisure. Chapman expressed particular admiration
for one particularly "dexterous" Bushman with "arms as delicate as a
lady's" but who nevertheless could "kill three elephants of a troop in a short
time."

By the mid-1880s the Kalahari ivory trade fell into terminal decline.
The hunters had been killing elephants at a rate much faster than they
could ever reproduce. All the big tuskers had been wiped out, and elephants
became so rare and nervous that hunters' ivory hauls were no longer large
enough to justify the costs of mounting commercial hunting expeditions.

———

The Nyae Nyae Conservancy would never have survived were it not for
modern ivory hunters.

In the early 1990s conservationists feared that elephants, rhinos, and other important species in Africa would soon be hunted to extinction and the ecosystems in which they lived destroyed. Alarming numbers were being killed every year in central, southern, and eastern Africa. The process was being driven by a straightforward supply-and-demand equation. In Asia there was demand for ivory and rhino-horn and in Africa there were people willing to supply them for relatively modest fees. With no means to counter demand in Asian markets for these products, conservationists in Africa focused their efforts on the supply side of the equation. Criminalizing poaching was not enough. Governments had neither the resources nor the manpower to police the remote areas where game was most abundant.

The problem, as the conservationists saw it, was that African subsistence farmers saw no obvious benefits in protecting wildlife. Wildlife, after all, was sometimes a catastrophic nuisance. Having an elephant herd destroy a year's harvest in a matter of minutes, or being stalked by hungry lions when you go to urinate at night, doesn't compare to the inconvenience of a rat in the larder or a fox worrying the chickens. For many rural subsistence farmers, gunning down elephants for their ivory got rid of hazardous wildlife and at the same time yielded impossibly large sums of cash. The conservationists wondered whether they find a way to compensate local communities for the inconveniences they endured as a result of having problematic animal neighbors and at the same time persuade them to protect rather than poach them?

The solution they proposed was to partially privatize wildlife and other natural resources by vesting limited rights over them to the local communities. They reasoned that if local people were empowered to claim ownership of their wildlife and could directly benefit from their exploitation, then a sustainable balance might be struck. This meant that communities in rural areas could form organizations that would in turn be given rights to develop tourism enterprises and, where appropriate, host trophy hunters for a fee. This model was tried out first in Zimbabwe before it was adopted in Botswana and Namibia, the two states with by far the best records in wildlife conservation in Africa. Nyae Nyae was one of the first Namibian communities to form a "conservancy." It is now one of over fifty conservancies scattered through Namibia.

Established in 1998, the Nyae Nyae Conservancy is now nearly two decades old. And while Ju/'hoansi grumble about it, its longevity is testament enough to its success. While it has made no one rich, it generates sufficient wealth for Ju/'hoansi to maintain a degree of autonomy that would otherwise be impossible. It also enables Ju/'hoansi to choose to stay in their villages and has been instrumental in preventing Herero and others from moving into Nyae Nyae en masse with their cattle. It's impossible to say whether future generations of Ju/'hoansi in Nyae Nyae will feel that the conservancy is right for them. But for the time being, at least, the benefits more than justify the costs.

———

Butchering an elephant is heavy work. Six tons of skin, muscle, assorted organs, teeth, tusks, and bone do not surrender themselves easily to knives and axes wielded by mere men. By midday a dozen or so Ju/'hoan men from the two local villages had shown up and were methodically shearing the skin from the hunted elephant's flesh and the flesh from its bones. Soon its trunk was sliced off and its face was skinned to reveal a fatty white lattice and a single accusing eyeball. The carcass had also swelled to bursting and, with only a thin layer of dermis and fat holding the intestines in place, there was a real risk that it might explode. I was careful to stand on the other side.

To release the pressure, the butchers sliced through the last remaining layer of fat holding everything in place and the swollen intestines leapt wetly from the chest cavity. Every once in a while someone punctured a portion of the exposed intestines to let expanding gases whistle out, filling the air with the smell of dung and death.

More men were expected to arrive to help with the butchery later that afternoon when the conservancy trucks that would later distribute meat to the villages arrived. In the meantime everyone worked contentedly. Meat is a serious business. Some of the butchers were new to elephants, but none were new to butchery: regardless of size, the inside of one mammal is not very different from any other, and so they set about their work with an air of confidence. The younger, more agile men were given the job of clambering into, on, and over the carcass. Their clothes, hands, and feet were soon washed in blood so dark it sometimes appeared black.

The only woman there was the Austrian hunter. I asked Hunter /Ui whether it was bad luck for a woman to be involved in a hunt like this. Among Ju/'hoansi, merely sitting where a woman had recently sat was considered enough to ruin a hunt. "Not this one," he laughed, pointing at the dead elephant as evidence that I was wrong.

"But you whites are different people," he added while gesturing to me to place a lit cigarette in his mouth, as his hands were wet with blood.

When the top flank of the elephant had been skinned, the Austrian hunter squeezed between the Ju/'hoan butchers and cut a fist-size chunk of meat from the carcass, which she threw on a small fire her husband had prepared. Their fire was downwind of the carcass and the smell of putre-fying guts washed over the brazier in nauseating waves. But it would have been rude to the elephant—and to the hundreds of Ju/'hoansi who would feast on it later that night—to decline the offer of a taste of its meat, and to my surprise it was good.

———

Shooting an elephant is not particularly difficult. Modern high-powered rifles can deliver death from afar, and elephants are not much more difficult to hit than the average barn door. But these particular hunters were not after any old elephant: they needed to find a suitably old and large bull that had already reproduced. Before this bull was shot down, the hunters and trackers worked hard. For fifteen consecutive days they had left their camp before sunup and returned after dark without having discharged a round. They tracked and saw many elephants. Each mature bull elephant they encoun-tered was laboriously stalked until they could take a view on its suitability. Was it big enough? Might it still be sexually active? Was it old enough?

The most effective way to age an elephant is by its teeth. The numbers of new molars it has—which arrive at different ages, like sequences of wisdom teeth—and how worn they are is the most accurate measure. But elephants are not keen on having their teeth examined, and so the hunters have to make judgments based on the shape of a particular animal's head, its bearing, the posture of its spine, the size of its ivory, and its footprints.

In this desert where mammalian and reptilian life inscribes every twist, turn, and movement it makes into the sand, it is an elephant's footprints that finally determine whether or not a suitable-looking bull ends up with a bullet in its head.

If an elephant skeleton were reanimated, it would look as if it were walking on tiptoe or as if its ankles were carried by an imaginary set of spongy high heels. The bony mass of the foot is suspended on a soft cushion of fat and connective tissue, and this is what allows it to walk so quietly. The soles of its feet wear into a bloom of cracked and burnished calluses separated by fine cauliflower-like ridges. It is these ridges and calluses that help reveal its age. The smoother, shinier, and larger they are, the older the animal is.

During the first two weeks of this hunt, the party tracked down several large bulls, but in each instance the trackers concluded that they were too young to kill.

This bull was shot on the penultimate day of the clients' three-week trip to Nyae Nyae. Come what may, the following day they would be blasting down the Hereroland road to make their flight home. I had asked them a few nights earlier how they would feel if they went home empty-handed. "We would feel like we had been on a wonderful hiking safari" was their reply.

And the hunters got their money's worth. Having made their kill, there was an easiness in their movement, a sense of belonging, and an almost postcoital calmness to their demeanor that day. In many hunting societies there is something in the act of taking of a life that invokes some of the same emotional and physical depths that we usually associate with the act of creating life. These hunters have no words for this, but for the Ju/'hoansi it takes the form of *n!ow*.

Trophy hunters find it hard to express how their "sport" binds them or to describe to nonhunters how it feels to kill an animal. They get especially tongue-tied in the presence of effete urbanites for whom animals are pets and meat is something served in restaurants or sold in cellophane. For most hunters, hunting is experiential. It finds its expression in the electrified senses, amplified emotions, surging adrenaline, and exhaustion of a hunt and, finally, in the visceral proximity of death. And for these elephant hunters it was no different. They struggled to find words when I asked them how they felt. But then, even Ernest Hemingway, trophy hunting's most articulate champion, struggled to convey anything more to nonhunters than what to them appeared to be an irrational passion for mindlessly butchering wildlife. "Some are hunters and some are not" was Hemingway's view. And so, when he wrote of hunting and fishing, he spoke neither for hunters nor about them. Rather, he spoke to them in passages replete with clubby winks and knowing nudges that would only make sense to others who had experienced what he had.

———

Around five thousand trophy hunters visit Namibia every year. Two-thirds hail from Germany, Austria, and the United States. And when the season starts, they clog up the international airport as they queue for customs clearance for their custom-made Mauser, Remington, and Savage Arms rifles. Hunting is an expensive hobby. And for those who can afford to shoot elephant, lion, or rhino, their trophy cabinets speak as much to their triumph over the human world of commerce as they do to their conquest of nature. Killing one of these animals costs more than the average annual take-home pay of an adult in the world's richest countries. As a result, most other hunters come to Namibia with the more modest ambition of taking down a more reasonably priced animal—like a kudu, oryx, springbok, or warthog—on one of the many privately owned game farms.

It is now standard practice for budget-conscious trophy hunters to preorder their targets from a fixed-price menu, pay in advance for the animals they wish to shoot, and to be more or less guaranteed their kills as long as they show up, are prepared to walk and stalk a little, and can shoot reasonably straight. The farmer will know they have sufficient stock of the animals ordered and likewise will have a good idea where to find them on their farms: water points and salt licks are irresistible to even the most gun-shy of animals. For some hunters the pleasure is all in the pursuit. The best hunting guides ensure their clients get this, often taking them on unnecessary detours to make certain they have a decent story to tell when they get home. For others, how the trophies slot into their collections matters more than anything else. And as soon as they have bagged them, they are happy to sit back, drink beer by the pool, and exchange pleasant-ries with other hunters about calibers, local taxidermists, and whatever creatures are next on their lists. The farmers and their staffs flatter their clients. The sometimes solemn, sometimes jovial camaraderie of blood and death is their livelihood and they work hard to put on a good show. The trackers and laborers who guide the hunters and then process the carcasses do likewise. They and their families usually end up with most of the meat to eat. And some clients, in particular Americans, give generous cash tips that dwarf their salaries.

Pinnacle Point

Pinnacle Point golf estate lies a few miles to the southeast of the natural harbor at Mossel Bay where Bartolomeu Dias's party landed in 1488. High greens fees and the paint-by-numbers luxury of the clubhouse means the golf estate is a hit with both the well-heeled and the aspirant. It perches above a series of sheer cliff walls that descend into a wave-pummeled bay, and its visitors come as much for the mountain and sea views as they do for the golf.

Pinnacle Point is a testing course. Errant golf balls often clatter off the fairway and into the sea far below. Luckily, the golfers are equipped with clubs that give them every advantage when making their shots. Each is precisely weighted and engineered to make them as powerful, accurate, and ergonomic as possible. While it may not occur to the golfers as they are ferried between tees, some seventy-one thousand years ago Pinnacle Point was home to another group of people also preoccupied with trying to get small projectiles to fly accurately over large distances.[1] It might also surprise the golfers to learn that while their golfing gear may be a powerful contemporary symbol of affluence, the projectiles manufactured by the people at Pinnacle Point all those millennia ago played a crucial role in unlocking the equation between effort and nutrition that enabled the original "affluent society" to have more free time for leisure pursuits than most of the golfers at the Pinnacle Point course could ever dream of.

Two hundred feet below the golf course, but safely above the high-water mark, are a series of caves that disappear into the cliff walls. Archaeologists have found evidence of human occupation in the caves stretching back nearly 150,000 years. Archaeologists have also found evidence to suggest that 70,000 years ago these caves were home to skilled craftsmen capable of making sophisticated, multipiece arrows.

Up until recently, most paleoanthropologists agreed that although early Homo sapiens were biologically modern, they were cognitively "primitive." They took this view because, before the discoveries at Pinnacle Point and a few other sites, there was little evidence to suggest that early humans were capable of the kind of complex symbolic thought and problem solving that define who we are now. The paleoanthropologists pointed to the absence of works of art older than 20,000 years as well as the scant evidence for any "complex technologies" requiring complementary but different materials and skill sets to design, construct, or use—things like barbed fishhooks, shafted axes, and spears.

Among the most illuminating finds at Pinnacle Point were hundreds of pieces of ochre that have been provisionally dated to 162,000 years ago. These were excavated at the deepest levels where archaeologists found evidence of human activity. The ochre is of an unusually brilliant red, and the archaeologists have established that it came from a quarry several miles north of the cave. The largest pieces of ochre also show marks suggesting they were ground and scraped to make ochre powder. Based on evidence elsewhere it is almost certain that the powder would have been mixed with animal fat to make a vibrant paste that would have been used as an all-in-one makeup, sunscreen, and insect repellent.

Assuming that the pieces of ochre didn't find their way to this cave by accident, this pushes back the date of the cognitive revolution to soon after the evolution of biologically modern humans. And the practice is likely to have been widespread in southern Africa. Recent excavations at another site—the now equally famous Blombos Cave, which lies around forty miles west of Pinnacle Point—have revealed a 100,000-year-old pigment "workshop" where ochre-based pastes were manufactured and stored in mother-of-pearl-rich abalone shells. Other coastal caves nearby revealed evidence of the manufacture of ostrich eggshell beads identical to those still made by many Bushmen today.

From a technological perspective, the most intriguing finds at Pinnacle Point are a series of small, finely crafted microliths—stone blades of between one and three centimeters in length. The oldest microliths in the cave have been dated to around 71,000 years ago and the most recent to around 60,000 years ago. Slight differences in the size and shape of microliths of different ages found in the cave also show that this technology evolved over this period.[2]

Microliths like these are of little use to anyone unless they are attached to shafts. This would have been done either by using a tree resin–based glue or by binding them onto the shafts using animal sinew or plant fiber strings. It's impossible to tell now whether these projectiles were then used as darts or arrows, because bows and dart throwers—sometimes called atlatls—are perishable and would have disappeared into the dust many thousands of years ago. Given that there was no tradition of using atlatls by Bushmen during the colonial era, there is a very good chance that these particular microliths were used for arrowheads. If so, this would mean that the basic principles behind the hunting technology used by twentieth-century Bushmen and other Paleolithic peoples far predates previously held estimates for the invention of the bow and arrow. It also suggests that early Homo sapiens were a lot brighter than we have previously assumed.

What is most interesting about these particular microliths is that they were not bashed out of any old stone. They were made from silcrete, a hard quartz-like rock particularly well suited to being flaked into blades. Silcrete is neither easy to find nor is it straightforward to work with. It also needs to be heated carefully before it can be flaked precisely. The complex, multistage process of their manufacture—involving quarrying, controlled use of fire, and skilled stone knapping—meant that the ability to manufacture these microliths was the product of years of experience and experimentation with other minerals and processes.

The history of archaeology is littered with broken fragments of grand hypotheses that have imputed extraordinary significance to unremarkable discoveries. Archaeologists make a living from reimagining entire worlds from the accidentally preserved fragments of ancient life. The more groundbreaking their finds, the more cautious most are in saying what they think. In the case of southern Africa's Paleolithic history, their job is further complicated by the fact that sea levels have yo-yoed up and down as successive ice ages have come and gone. At the time the microliths were abandoned in this cave, the sea level would have been only twenty or thirty meters lower than it is today. But around 180,000 years ago the sea level was around 460 feet lower than it is today, meaning that Pinnacle Point would have been situated sixty miles or so inland. This means that any evidence of technical sophistication among coastal dwellers more than a hundred millennia ago will have been buried beneath the waves.

There are other finds that support the evidence of archery in southern Africa long before most archaeologists previously imagined was possible. The most interesting is in an inland rock shelter called Sibudu Cave, seven hundred miles northeast of Pinnacle Point, in what is now sugarcane country in South Africa's KwaZulu-Natal Province. There archaeologists found evidence of 61,000-year-old bone toolmaking technologies of a kind that until recently was thought to have only been mastered 20,000 years later. These included a finely manufactured bone sewing needle as well as microliths with traces of blood and bone on them that had only one obvious function: as arrowheads.[3]

As compelling as these finds are, another rock shelter in modern KwaZulu-Natal, Border Cave, provides the clearest evidence that 50,000 years ago people in southern Africa—and arguably far beyond—had a material culture similar to that of hunting and gathering Bushmen in the twentieth century.[4] The finds in this cave were particularly special because a series of geological accidents left it extraordinarily dry—so dry that that organic material that would have dissolved into dust almost anywhere else was preserved through dehydration. At this cave, archaeologists found 45,000-year-old bone arrowheads, a digging stick, a resin-based glue, and ostrich eggshell beads. The beads were almost certainly made in the same way that San throughout the Kalahari did until they were introduced to the stainless-steel nail clipper, the modern ostrich eggshell bead maker's tool of choice.

Also found in this cave—but dropped by a much more recent visitor from around only 24,000 years ago—is a thin wooden stick with a number of carved notches in it. It closely resembles the poison applicators used by some twentieth-century Bushmen groups to daub poison onto their arrows. When these notches were analyzed, they were found to contain traces of ricin-based poisons. Even though it lacks the antiquity of the other finds in this cave, it still is the oldest strong evidence of the use of poisons in hunting. And it raises the very real possibility that poisons were used by Khoisan hunters many years before. Possibly even by the microlith makers of Pinnacle Point. The proteins in organic poisons have a short shelf life

//Eng doing battle with cabbages and onions at Skoonheid in 1995. JAMES SUZMAN

!A/ae "Frederik" Langman (my adoptive father) in 1995 with Jacobus, his grandson. !A/ae has now been recognized by the Namibian government as chief of the ‡Kxao//eisi (southern Ju/'hoansi).
JAMES SUZMAN

Skoonheid resettlement camp, 1995. JAMES SUZMAN

The male hill at Tsodilo after a summer storm. JAMES SUZMAN

The "python" in the Rhino Cave at Tsodilo Hills. USED BY PERMISSION OF SHEILA COULSON

Old /Engn!au at Skoonheid, 1994. JAMES SUZMAN

A Ju/'hoan farmworker in Gobabis works while his boss looks on. PAUL WEINBERG

After independence, many Ju/'hoan farmworkers in the Omaheke were chased off the farms and squatted in the margins of Herero settlements, such as Omawewozanyanda. ADRIAN ARBIB

John Marshall filming in the 1950s. USED BY PERMISSION OF THE PEABODY MUSEUM, GIFT OF LAURENCE K. MARSHALL AND LORNA J. MARSHALL © PRESIDENT AND FELLOWS OF HARVARD COLLEGE, PEABODY MUSEUM OF ARCHAEOLOGY AND ETHNOLOGY, PM# 2001.29.254 (DIGITAL FILE #97010003)

John Marshall at a Nyae Nyae community meeting in 1989. ADRIAN ARBIB

The South African Army comes to Tsumkwe. PAUL WEINBERG

Ju/'hoan soldiers on parade in Nyae Nyae, 1989. PAUL WEINBERG

Anu demonstrates an "old bushman pipe" while out gathering. JAMES SUZMAN

When the rains are good in Nyae Nyae, the pans fill with water, transforming them into shallow lakes. JAMES SUZMAN

/Kunta N!a'a leads a procession past the Holboom. JAMES SUZMAN

/Kunta N!a'a. JAMES SUZMAN

After a good day's gathering, a bag is filled with marama beans, brachystegia, and other delicacies. JAMES SUZMAN

Manketti nuts in abundance. USED BY PERMISSION OF MEGAN LAWS

Butchering an elephant is heavy work. JAMES SUZMAN

Making arrows in Nyae Nyae. PAUL WEINBERG

Hunters rarely set off on their own. JAMES SUZMAN

/I!ae, Skoonheid's best hunter in his prime, was very particular about being photographed.
JAMES SUZMAN

Without fire, meat is difficult to eat. JAMES SUZMAN

One benefit of the drought in 2013 was plenty of meat from the cattle that died. JAMES SUZMAN

With many lions on the prowl in Nyae Nyae during the late 1980s, people built ever more robust kraals for their cattle. ADRIAN ARBIB

Kids dancing outside of "Tsumkwe Rock Star," Tsumkwe's finest—and only—brick and mortar bar.
JAMES SUZMAN

//Eng showing off her garden in 2014. JAMES SUZMAN

and when exposed to the elements it doesn't take long before they disappear without a trace. So it is no surprise that evidence of ancient poison use is hard to come by. It is, however, almost certain that early hunter-gatherers experimented with local toxins. Far less sophisticated primates like chimpanzees and capuchin monkeys demonstrate an often surprisingly subtle knowledge of medical plants, so it's reasonable to assume that some of the smarter hominids may well have used poisons in unsophisticated ways.

All documented hunting and gathering Khoisan peoples used similar tools and technologies. The hunting equipment traditionally used by !Kung far to the north of Nyae Nyae is similar in both design and function to that used by /Xam in the Cape over two thousand miles to the south.

If, as the genetic record suggests, Khoisan in the northern Kalahari and those in the south separated as long as 35,000 years ago, then these basic technologies were almost certainly in widespread use well before then. And the fact that these technologies have not been superseded in any substantial way since is a testament to their technical refinement and effectiveness.

Except for iron arrowheads and spearheads, the hunting equipment used by hunters in Nyae Nyae today closely resembles that used by Bushman hunters across southern Africa. Ju/'hoan hunting kits comprise a short-shafted spear with a metal spearhead that extends eight inches from the shaft; a hardwood digging stick sharpened to a flat point on one end that doubles as a club; and a bow and a set of arrows stored in a neat, almost perfectly cylindrical quiver made of hard bark that is bound by three or four neat twists of heavy sinew and topped with a perfectly fitted cap of rawhide. Also bundled within the kit are other essentials for a night in the bush: sticks for making fire, a leather blanket for warmth, spare bowstrings, and perhaps an axe. Some Ju/'hoansi like to attach shoulder straps to their quivers, to which they latch their spears and digging sticks. Others prefer to carry their equipment in neat bags made from the entire skin of a small antelope, into which the quiver is bound. The entire hunting kit weighs no more than five pounds, and when hung from a hunter's shoulder it finds an easy balance, making it light enough not to be a burden but weighty enough to stay in place when the hunter runs.

The bow is the most important part of any hunter's equipment. The strings are traditionally made from the hind leg or back sinews of a giraffe, eland, or oryx although many hunters now prefer nylon because it doesn't soften in the rain or fray so quickly. The shaft is made from a single supple and springy piece of a debarked hardwood, like that of the Grewia, with tapered tips. Neat bands of sinews are dried onto the shaft to provide a hand grip at the center and to fasten to the bow's tips to hold the bowstrings in place. But a bow is of little use without an arrow, and it is the arrow that most clearly reveals the subtle sophistication of this technology. It is also the arrow that helps us to understand why Bushmen did not bother making the larger, more powerful bows used by other bow-hunting cultures.

The arrows look anything but formidable. Individually, they weigh no more than an ounce and rarely exceed twenty-five inches in length. The shaft of an arrow is made from a single stiff, hollow reed reinforced with fine sinew threads. A small solid piece of bone and wood, usually three or four inches long and tapered at both ends, is slotted securely into the shaft. Finally an arrowhead is attached to the tapered link by means of a collar made from dried sinews and often reinforced with tree resin. The arrowheads used to be made from bone, but now they are almost always made from fencing wire that is beaten flat and then sharpened into barbed heads no more than half an inch wide and three-quarters of an inch long.

Using his small bow, a hunter would struggle to kill anything larger than a squirrel with these arrows alone. The key to their effectiveness is poison.

Ju/'hoansi and other Bushmen could easily have built much larger bows capable of delivering larger arrows with much greater force. But these would not have been as effective. It is only recently that easily portable bows have been manufactured that are powerful enough to kill an animal the size of a giraffe or eland with any reliability. For modern bow hunters armed with precisely engineered and geared compound bows, the recommended minimum draw weight for hunting a giraffe is 95 pounds—some 10 percent greater than that of the immense longbows used by English archers at the Battle of Agincourt and nine times greater than that of the Ju/'hoan bow. And even then a shot needs to be perfectly placed if it is to cut into either a lung or the heart.

But for a Ju/'hoan hunter to be guaranteed a kill with this diminutive bow, all he has to do is make sure that his arrow is delivered with enough force to break the skin anywhere on an animal's body. Where the arrow finds its mark only makes a difference in terms of how quickly the animal succumbs to the poison. A shot in the neck or near the lungs and heart will make the process go much quicker than a shot in the meaty flanks or legs. As soon as an arrow hits its mark, the reed shaft separates from the barbed head embedded in the prey's skin. This not only makes it harder for it to become dislodged, but it also means that the animal is less likely to be spooked by an arrow protruding from its body. This is important: depending on the size of the animal, a poison can take anywhere from a few hours to a few days before it disables the animal enough to let the hunter approach and kill it quickly with a spear.

The poisons used by Bushmen differ from place to place.[5] The poison compounds found in Border Cave were made from acids extracted from indigenous castor beans. The Hai//om of Etosha gently cooked sap bled from the roots of the impala lily (*Adenium multiflorum*, a plant that now graces many first world greenhouses) for their poison.

Developing poisons that can kill by entering the bloodstream of an animal in small quantities and not make the meat toxic must have involved a lot of potentially fatal trial and error. Bearing this in mind, the poison used by the Ju/'hoansi and other northern and central Kalahari groups is especially remarkable—not only because it is so effective but also because it comes from a source that is far from obvious.

———

Scattered across the Kalahari are small groves of *Commiphora africana*, commonly referred to as African myrrh. These small, scruffy trees rarely grow taller than the height of a man and flower early in the spring, producing small inedible red berries. Their leaves are the favorite food of an innocuous-looking beetle called *Diamphidia* that resembles a ladybug in shape and size but is the color of burnished copper. *Diamphidia* lay their eggs on the stems of *Commiphora* leaves before covering them with a protective coating of feces. In time an egg falls to the ground, stimulating a small deep-orange larva to hatch from it. This digs a yard or more into the sand, where it waits, sometimes for a year or more, before it pupates.

The larvae aren't easy to find. Ju/'hoansi usually have to dig around the base of several *Commiphora* bushes before they find some to harvest. To make the poison, hunters first soften the larvae up by rolling them gently between their fingers. Afterward they pop the heads off and squeeze the pulped innards directly onto the bases of their arrowheads. Sometimes the larvae are dried and then crushed into a powder that can be rehydrated into a paste sometime later by mixing it with spit or tree sap. Only a few drops are ever applied to an arrowhead. Anything more would be wasteful. Hunters approach the job of applying poison to their arrows with the care of a watchmaker and the caution of a neurosurgeon. They always check their hands and fingers for small cracks or cuts before applying the poison and make sure that nothing is around that might distract them. Once poisoned, arrows are always carefully stored in the boughs of a tree or on the roof of a hut—anywhere far out of the reach of curious children.

The only time I ever saw an adult Ju/'hoan raise his hand to a child was when his infant son startled him while he was giving me a demonstration on how to apply poison to an arrow. No one chided this man for hitting that child, even though Ju/'hoan toddlers were generally free to play with all sorts of dangerous things—like axes, knives, and machetes—that would send most parents in other countries into a state of panic. But there is no antidote for *Diamphidia* poison. Once in the bloodstream, it starts rupturing red blood cells, reducing the oxygen-carrying capacity of blood. But in starving their prey's organs of oxygen, this poison brought life to the Ju/'hoansi. It made hunting in an environment where animals are elusive and attuned to avoiding danger far easier. It also enabled a hunter's success to be determined by his stealth, stalking ability, skill, and knowledge rather than his strength.

Ultimately, this elegant piece of technology enabled hunters to acquire between a third and half of their total caloric intake and most of their protein from meat with relatively little risk in environments where hunting was often difficult. Those like the Ju/'hoansi in Nyae Nyae, with their productive mankelti groves, got a little less. Those like the Hai//om, who lived in areas where the game congregated in vast herds, acquired a little more. In this respect, Khoisan hunter-gatherers were typical of most hunting and gathering societies that weren't confined to arctic and subarctic climates, for whom animal products constituted most of their diets.

———

Europeans who encountered Bushmen during the colonial period seldom saw any artistry in their apparently archaic technologies. But then, only a few of them saw much to admire in the lives of Bushmen at all. As far as they were concerned, the Bushmen's technology, like their art, was "child-like" and "primitive"—a product of their isolation, poverty, and racial inferiority. Yet, despite appearances, hunter-gatherer societies like the Ju/'hoansi were happy to embrace innovation. Unlike agricultural societies, hunter-gatherers were neither slaves to tradition nor, if the behavior of contemporary hunter-gatherers is anything to go by, dogmatic adherents to practices that didn't serve an immediate and obvious purpose. They were just particular about which innovations were worth embracing. But if something helped them to hunt or gather more effectively—and it was ready to hand—it was adopted enthusiastically. And the history of contact between hunting and gathering Bushmen and others shows how quickly San embraced new materials and pressed them into service to their own way of doing things. San groups across the vast expanses of the Kalahari all embraced the use of iron for their arrowheads almost as soon as they were introduced to it. And they did so entirely independently of one another.

Similarly, over the course of the last two centuries, hunting and gathering Bushmen across the subcontinent have enthusiastically embraced wire, plastics, rubber, twine, various fabrics, glass beads, files, mugs, knives, axes, pots, pans, rifle cartridges, cigarette lighters, matches, shoes, and water bottles, to name a few items. And as often as not these objects were repurposed into something entirely new. Cartridge cases were usually transformed into pipes for tobacco, oil tins were fashioned into musical instruments, and plastic bags were melted and remolded into heavy club heads for their digging sticks. San were also quick to make use of dogs as hunting partners when they were introduced to one another even if they did not demonstrate great affection for them. In the Omaheke and beyond, some Ju/'hoansi acquired firearms in the late nineteenth and early twentieth centuries. They were impressed by their accuracy and power. But neither ammunition nor gunpowder grew on trees, and Ju/'hoansi were not particularly interested in regular trade. And firearms also proved dangerous. Possessing one made it far more likely that someone else would shoot you or try to rob you. Old Dam at Skoonheid told a story of how his grandfather had stolen a rifle from some Germans in Steinhausen in the western Omaheke at the turn of the century. He also told me how his grandfather never shot anything with it and in the end broke it up to use the barrel as a digging stick and the stock as a club.

———

Hunting in as sparse an environment as the Kalahari is challenging. Good hunters need skill, perseverance, courage, and plenty of patience. They also need luck. The margins between success and failure on a hunt can be tiny. Releasing an arrow a split second too early or a gentle shift in the wind's direction can ruin a careful stalk and waste several days' effort. As a result, hunters did whatever they could to tip the spiritual odds in their favor. Among a host of individual rites to bring them luck, they avoided eating certain foods and abstained from physical contact with their wives when preparing for a hunt. They also occasionally asked the trickster god, G//aua, to send a large meat animal into their paths, but they were aware that G//aua was just as likely to ignore their request or even send them bad luck as he was to do as they asked.

Foraging Ju/'hoansi rarely hunted when there was still meat in the village. Doing so was considered excessive and inappropriate. It also might lead to some kind of spiritual sanction from God or more likely the spirits of recently dead ancestors. But if people were hungry for meat, Ju/'hoan hunters never passed up the opportunity to kill a meat animal that crossed their path. Porcupines, springhares, birds, and even jackals were always taken if meat was needed. Two-thirds of all the animals that hunters regularly killed were small. Even if they killed more small animals than large ones, it was the large meat animals that populated hunters' dreams.

A Gift from God

"It is a gift from God!" //Uce explained through a mouth full of half-chewed heaven. Rich fat dripped down her chin and onto her dress. Everyone else who squatted in the yard of the abandoned farmhouse at Rosenhof—the farm immediately adjacent to Skoonheid—was in a similarly cheery mood as they ladled the fatty, meaty, bony stew from the large black cauldron into an assortment of battered enamel plates and mugs. Hundreds of thin strips of red meat decorated the branches of a big camelthorn tree while flies buzzed around them in small excitable clouds. A small pack of dogs had gathered too. They sat motionless, mouths agape and eyes fixed on the branches, hoping that some of this odd fruit might fall to the ground.

The feasting had begun early that afternoon following a morning of cooperative slaughter. It started with the liver, which had been thrown directly onto the coals of the fire. It was followed by a pot of boiled tripe garnished with kidneys and the rubbery heart. The remains of the greasy stew of knuckles and marrowbones that now bubbled in the nearly empty cauldron was the final act of the day's meat orgy. And now that the sun was setting, everyone was beginning to look waxy. Their bodies, unfamiliar with so much protein and fat in such short order, were struggling to process this nutritional overload. Unlike the Ju/'hoansi at Skoonheid, a few short miles away, the people here were squatters and so weren't entitled to food aid. This farm had been purchased by the government at the same time as Skoonheid, but no one as yet had decided what to do with it, so it was gradually colonized by a random group of squatters, including, for several months, myself in 1994 and 1995 when the violence at Skoonheid got too much.

The "gift from God" had announced its presence just before dawn that morning when everyone was awoken by a frenzied clanging, shaking, and rattling from the southern side of the perimeter fence by the old farmhouse. This was followed by a chorus of excitable yapping as the dogs became apoplectic. //Uce's children trotted off to investigate, having lain awake and bored while their parents snored beside them. They sprinted back wide-eyed, yelling, "Meat! Meat!"

The remainder of our small compound's residents emerged bleary-eyed from their slumbers and stumbled behind the children to find an oryx bull, its eyes wide with fear and its head twisted awkwardly below its shoulders as if kowtowing to an unseen god. Somehow its meter-long rapier horns had become trapped in the chain links of the perimeter fence erected around the farmhouse during the liberation war.

As the small crowd approached, the oryx pushed off its front legs and jerked its head frantically upward in a bid to escape. Its predicament ran counter to every instinct it had evolved to maximize the defensive value of its horns. When fleeing is not an option, the oryx is a fighter. It protects its rear by backing into thornbushes and forcing its adversaries to confront it head-on. With much of an oryx's quarter ton of mass concentrated in its neck and shoulder muscles, anything that takes one on runs the risk of being skewered. There are few things more intimidating than watching two oryx bulls charging, thrusting, and stabbing one another in the blind fury of a rut.

But the fight had already fled from this oryx. With the crowd standing there, its horns held captive by the fence, and its body fully exposed, its sense of vulnerability must have been absolute and it slouched as if in surrender. Four hundred pounds of desperate muscle, bone, and sinew gaped at us, overwhelmed by its implacable stainless-steel captor.

It was hard to tell how long the oryx had been there or how it had gotten itself into this fix. Why hadn't the dogs barked earlier? Had it taken fright at something and run blindly into the fence? Had it charged a shadow or been spooked by a leopard? Inspection of its spoor showed that it had approached the fence at a walk, a fact that only added to the mystery of its capture. It appeared to have carefully pushed its horns through the links of the fence to a point that it could no longer escape.

The small crowd that gathered did not speculate for too long on precisely why the oryx had found itself in this predicament. The only urgent question on anyone's mind for the moment was how to kill it. With the sharp points of the animal's horns safely on the other side of the fence and no energy left in its legs, would it be simpler to club it to death or cut its throat?

The debate did not last long. Long Oubob, a middle-aged man who lived a solitary, no-nonsense existence in a small shack just beyond the water reservoir, ambled up with a long spear in hand. Barefoot, he made his way through the small crowd and, without saying a word, thrust his spear into the oryx's flank, just behind its shoulder. Once the spear was buried up to the wooden shaft, he then pulled it back without withdrawing it completely and, putting all his weight behind it, shoved it in again, this time giving it a twist. The oryx shuddered as the first spear thrust penetrated its ribs and cut into its lungs. By the time the second thrust was pushed home, pink blood frothed from its mouth as its front legs trembled, sagged, and gave in. The gift from God now awaited the butchery of men.

When //Uce exclaimed that the oryx was a gift from God, I asked her which god she had in mind. Was it G//aua, the Ju/'hoan trickster god, who would occasionally persuade meat animals to blunder into the path of hungry hunters? Or was it the Christian god, who, despite being all-powerful, seemed so unduly demanding of gratitude even when he was being manifestly ungenerous?

But //Uce and I had lived in the same compound for several months already, and in that time she had made it clear that I should save my questions about gods, nature, history, and other topics of interest to anthropologists for those who gave a damn. She certainly wasn't going to be drawn into conversation now. Her silence notwithstanding, like most Ju/'hoansi here, she was open-minded when it came to questions of the cosmos. Farmers had shoved the Gospel down Ju/'hoan throats for generations.

Recently, groups of enthusiastic late-teen Pentecostalists from Pretoria or Bloemfontein or somewhere else in South Africa had begun to descend on Skoonheid every few months. They would hold impromptu church services under a tree before clambering back into their minivans and heading off to whatever farm they were staying on. These evangelists avoided bashing their audience with doctrine and instead focused on persuading Ju/'hoansi that they needed a "personal relationship with Jesus." They also stressed how important it was for Ju/'hoansi to show proper gratitude to the Lord for their many blessings. This always amused /Engn!au. He joked that the government must be God, because they provided everyone's food here at Skoonheid and the government-appointed camp administrator always demanded the settlers' gratitude. But many others found comfort in the evangelists' promises of salvation and so embraced their message.

To everyone who shared its meat, this self-sacrificing oryx was evidence of some kind of divinity. Meat was the most valued of all foods among Ju/'hoansi, and since the arrival of the white farmers, game meat had become a rare treat. On some farms, farmers would shoot a kudu or oryx for the workers to share among themselves every month or two. On others a goat or a bullock might be slaughtered once in a while.

It was not only the white farmers' bullets that scythed their way through the Omaheke's once abundant wildlife. The barbed-wire fences the farmers built to manage the movements of their livestock immobilized the herds of migratory game like wildebeest, hartebeest, and zebra while ever more abundant cattle herds bullied them off the seasonal grasses.

Some species of indigenous game adapted well to this new reality. To the elegant kudu, which carry their helix-shaped horns like giant crowns, the cattle fences were minor obstacles that could be gracefully hurdled. Smaller antelope like red-hided steenbok and duiker also found niches for themselves on the cattle ranches. They did not need to hurdle the fences. Instead they crawled under them and took comfort from the fact that the farmers had wiped out most of the carnivores that preyed on them. Other animals, like jackals and honey badgers, survived by forging new careers as bin raiders and casual thieves. Farmers had little patience with big predators. Lions, wild dogs, and hyenas had long since been hunted out by the time I arrived in the Omaheke. Only leopards and cheetahs remained. Leopards survived because they are the ghosts of the cat world and can disappear from the realm of men with a sudden flick of their tails and cheetahs because they are paranoid and cautious and will flee from a fight if given half a chance.

Old Time people like /Engn!au lamented the disappearance of the great herds of game that now grazed only in the old people's memories or on the private reserves that hosted hunters willing to pay big dollars for easy trophies. He would often solemnly recite the names of the species that he once hunted, counting off each one on his hands as he did so.

"Eland! Kudu! Gemsbok! Wildebeest! Red hartebeest! Duiker! Steenbok! Giraffe! Zebra!" he would sing. "We hunted often. And when we married, we consummated our love with this meat and gave it to our wives and their parents to eat."

By his own admission, /Engn!au was never a particularly gifted or enthusiastic hunter even when he still had two legs and good eyesight. But nevertheless he lamented the fact that so many of the young Ju/'hoansi no longer knew the ways of the animals that their ancestors had depended on, couldn't make a decent bow, and had no idea where to find *Diamphidia* larvae to make arrow poison. As far as he was concerned, it was the absence of hunting that accounted for most of the social ills at Skoonheid. At the same time, though, he was grateful that the young men didn't know how to find the arrow poison or make decent bows. If they did, he reasoned, they would probably all kill each other.

———

But at Skoonheid in 1994 there were no paranoid white farmers watching the Ju/'hoansi's movements, time was abundant, and food was often in short supply. Some men keen on procuring fresh meat concentrated their energies on what they knew best: stock theft. A few others who still retained the skills to hunt big game ranged silently over the white farms in pursuit of kudu, oryx, and warthog. Most, however, were fearful of being arrested for poaching and so were content to pursue small game within Skoonheid's boundaries.

Skoonheid's legion of children preferred catapults to any other hunting weaponry. They fashioned them from stiff wooden forks that they tempered in hot sand and rubber from the inner tubes of abandoned tires. Young boys practiced with their catapults all the time. Most could send a stone flying unerringly at the heads of unsuspecting guinea fowl, ground squirrels, and jackals from farther away than seemed possible. Mainly, though, they shot lizards, snakes, and small birds. The snakes and lizards were left where they fell, but the birds were roasted whole on the embers of a fire, the feathers melting into a crispy shell that, once cooked, could be peeled from the little carcass like the silver foil on a chocolate egg.

There were also plenty of springhares at Skoonheid. Springhares look like they have been improvised from spare parts left over at the moment of creation. Their kangaroo-shaped torsos and bizarrely muscular hind legs sit above long rabbit-like feet and in front of a long, bushy, cat-like tail. Their permanent look of mousey surprise is emphasized by their hairy pink ears that look too big for a squirrel but too small for a rabbit. At Skoonheid they were hunted in the traditional way—the only way that worked if you didn't have a rifle and a spotlight. This involved waiting for the springhares to retreat into the underground dens they rested in during the day. To catch them, Ju/'hoansi made a special kind of spear from a series of thin yard-long sticks that were attached end to end with articulating joints made from sinew or rubber. Instead of a normal spearhead, Ju/'hoansi attached a sharpened hook made from fence wire. This assembly of sticks would be eased into a springhare hole and snaked along its passages until it reached the lair where the springhare hid. With a swift push and pull a springhare could be hooked and held fast, giving the hunters time to dig it out from above before dispatching it with a club or a twist of its neck. I was often graciously offered the head—which, once boiled, stared at me, its teeth exposed in a rictus grin. Being a good guest, I always gave most of my portion to others.

If springhare hunting involved a lot of digging, hunting fowl required lots of planning. Among the many birds they hunted, the largest—like guinea fowl, francolin, and bustard—were the most prized. These were usually caught with spring-loaded snares improvised out of slim Grewia-wood saplings, a small circle of twigs embedded in the sand, and a stretch of twine with a slipknot at one end.

Hunting springhare, porcupine, guinea fowl, and other small game offered tasty distractions. But even the meat of a large springhare or porcupine wouldn't go far. Most who shared in it would only get a mouthful or two and perhaps some fatty broth to wet their maize porridge.

The inability of most Ju/'hoansi on the farms to freely hunt larger game left a chasm in their lives, one for which there was no obvious substitute if they didn't have a job. Many filled the vacuum with alcohol, which at least provided them an opportunity to vent their frustrations. Hunting was much more than a means of providing nutrition among foraging Ju/'hoansi. It animated men's relationships with the world around them, gave them purpose, and imbued the cosmos with a sensate touch of the real. The meat that it provided not only filled the Ju/'hoansi's bellies and gave them strength, it created a visceral sense of pleasure so profound that they insisted it was the glue that bound men and women together in love. For where the farmers sanctified their marriages with rings and promises of fidelity, Ju/'hoansi sanctified their unions with meat.

The experiences of Ju/'hoansi in the Omaheke echoed those of most of the Kalahari's other Bushman populations who still hunted autonomously in the first half of the twentieth century. The lands of the Hai//om—the most energetic hunters of all San peoples—around the great Etosha salt pan was proclaimed a national park. And in 1948 the Hai//om's presence in the park was declared incompatible with nature conservation and so they were loaded into trucks and then dumped on neighboring white farms to serve as laborers. By 1961, !Xo and Nharo-speaking San in the southern Omaheke were forced to surrender the last of their lands to white farmers and Herero. The !Kung in the far north of Namibia had their lands ceded to the Ovambo kingdoms, the Nganjera, Kwanyama, and Ndonga. Across the border in newly independent Botswana, new laws enacted in the 1970s didn't recognize hunting and gathering as a legitimate form of land use, and so cattle farmers quickly moved into areas where they could access groundwater. At the same time a government program there to move Bushmen into permanent settlements helped foster a culture of dependency.

By the 1980s, even though many of the remaining seventy thousand or so Bushmen in Botswana and Namibia still hunted and gathered occasionally, none lived by hunting and gathering alone. But in a few places, like the Central Kalahari Game Reserve and the Khutse region in Botswana, as well as Nyae Nyae and the Caprivi Strip in Namibia, communities at least retained the ability to hunt as their fathers and grandfathers had.

Hunting and gathering Ju/'hoansi were not fussy eaters. Almost all of nature's abundance was consumed without complaint and, more often than not, visceral pleasure. But there was no elaboration or refinement in their food. To a large extent the joy of eating came from the extraordinary internal celebrations their bodies made when supplied with nutrients they craved—which as anyone who has been truly hungry will tell you is a joy far more profound than the rarefied epicurean pleasures offered by a Michelin-starred plate to an already overnourished customer. There was very little that was edible that wasn't eaten, especially meat. Leopard, caracal, cheetah, and a handful of other predators were eaten only rarely but were said by the few people I have met who had tried them to be surprisingly tasty. Lion, I was told, was an acquired taste and its meat was only really suitable for consumption by the elderly.

Hyenas and vultures were avoided except in desperate circumstances because they tasted "like shit" and could make you ill. Baboons, which were confined to the ridges of the southern *omiramba* in the Omaheke and a few rocky areas like the Tsodilo Hills, were also avoided. Unlike other species, all of which were considered by the Ju/'hoansi to be animal-people, baboons were far too much like people-people. Only domestic and wild dogs were considered completely inedible.

Hunter-gatherers in the arctic and subarctic regions speak of how animals like moose and reindeer can fall in love with people. They explain that these animals demonstrate their love through "offering" themselves to hunters by standing still, gazing at them, and providing them an easy shot.

Ju/'hoansi found the idea of animals willingly surrendering themselves to hunters hysterically funny when I told them what I had learned about the arctic hunters. They reminded me that even an old injured wildebeest with worn-out teeth, sunken eyes, and barely a breath left in its lungs would lurch away clumsily, panic in its eyes, if confronted by predators. This was because, like humans, animals "love life" and are understandably paranoid about losing theirs in a neighborhood where all manner of predators wish to eat them.

Among the large herbivores that roamed southern Africa over the last hundred millennia, only adult elephant and rhino felt free to spend their energy contemplating matters other than whether something nearby intended to eat them or not. Among the rest, natural selection favored those that were best at detecting and avoiding danger. Some species focused their energies on defense. These creatures, like the porcupine with its phalanxes of sharp quills or the honey badger with its folds of thick, loose skin that enabled it to squirm out of even a leopard's bite, were in the minority. Others mastered the art of concealment through camouflage or by secreting themselves in underground burrows with enough emergency exits to allow them to surreptitiously escape should their den be visited by a python or a jackal. But for most of the larger ungulates here, natural selection favored those with a nervous disposition, sharp eyesight, excellent hearing, a sophisticated sense of smell, lightning-fast reactions, and, when they needed to flee, amazing acceleration.

There were times when the Kalahari hosted much higher densities of animal life than it does now. The sheer number of animals still supported by the wetlands in the Okavango Delta provides a sense of how prolific animal life must have been in the northern Kalahari when it was a complex of shallow mega-lakes eleven millennia ago. But even fifty years ago the vast dry plains of the Kalahari supported almost unimaginably large herds of wildebeest, springbok, and hartebeest that migrated along well-established routes to seasonal water sources. !Xo Bushmen in the southern Kalahari and G/wikhoe on the eastern edge of the Central Kalahari Game Reserve in Botswana still remember watching herds that would stretch far beyond the horizon and take as long as three or four days to pass. These herds were wiped out in the end by Botswana's love affair with beef, as a result of which a series of veterinary cordon fences were erected after 1954 to prevent the spread of diseases among their cattle. With their traditional migratory paths to seasonal watering points blocked, migratory wildebeest perished of thirst in the tens of thousands, their carcasses littering the fence line. In 1983 alone it was estimated that up to seventy-two thousand wildebeest died attempting to navigate a fence that blocked their access to Lake Xau just north of the Central Kalahari Game Reserve.

But even when the Kalahari still hosted huge migratory populations of wildebeest and hartebeest, hunting was not simply a question of marching off into the savanna and clubbing the preferred dish of the day on the head. As often as not, hunters returned to their camps empty-handed.

Two generations ago, all Ju/'hoan boys in Nyae Nyae were expected to learn to hunt and all adult men were expected to hunt regularly. But like any rule there were always some notable exceptions. Men with particularly poor eyesight or a physical disability were exempted from hunting duties, as were the few men not interested in marriage who simply felt more comfortable hanging out with the ladies back at the encampment. Now that Ju/'hoan children in Nyae Nyae are encouraged to attend school (even though few bother for more than a year or two) and people can no longer hunt as freely as they once did, there are far fewer young men in Nyae Nyae who are skilled or even competent hunters. But men who can't hunt, or don't have access to cash to buy meat, have a hard time persuading their lovers to become brides. And this is because, among Ju/'hoansi, women both *like* meat and *are like* meat.

Women *are like* meat because young men with love in their eyes "hunt" them and because the process of courtship mirrors the flirtatious dance of the stalk, when hunters aim to get closer and closer to their prey so that they can eventually penetrate them with their arrows.

Women *like* meat because "all Ju/'hoansi like to eat meat." For meat is the "strongest" and tastiest of all foods, and a man who can provide his spouse with plenty of meat is a man worth keeping. The raw grunt of sexuality implied in the phrase "Women like meat" is much the same in Ju/'hoan as it is in English.

———

When Ju/'hoan women demanded meat from their spouses, they were expressing a sentiment that was instrumental in shaping the direction of Homo sapiens' evolutionary development.

Around five million years ago our genetic ancestors ate very little meat. Their bodies and their digestive systems were similar to those of modern gorillas. They may well have eaten termites or nibbled at bits of carrion just as many herbivorous primates do when their bodies crave specific minerals, but otherwise they secured almost all of their energy and nutrients from eating plants.

Being an herbivore is hard work, at least in nutritional terms. It also leaves little time for doing anything other than eating, and leaves very little energy for doing anything other than digesting. Most of the grasses, leaves, and fruits eaten by gorillas are not particularly nutritious. They also require a lot of processing to digest. As a result, gorillas spend half the day eating and most of the remainder of their time resting and digesting. At some point, probably around two and a half million years ago, our ancestors developed a taste for meat that set them on a very different evolutionary path from their cousins, whose descendants, the other primates, remained content to chew through piles of fibrous leaves and vegetables all day long.

We know that early hominids ate meat because of telltale butchery marks found on fossilized animal bones. These take the form of scratches, pitting, and percussion breakages made by rudimentary stone tools. While the practice may well have started much earlier, the oldest solid evidence of this sort dates to around two million years ago in eastern Africa. The makers of these tools and the breakers of these bones were most likely Australopithecus, important members of the rapidly expanding hominid family tree. Smaller than modern Homo sapiens, Australopithecus were morphologically similar to modern bonobos and chimpanzees though with marginally larger brain cavities. The most obvious difference between their meat-eating habits and those of modern chimpanzees—who like to catch, tear apart, and eat colobus monkeys every once in a while—was that the Australopithecus were almost certainly much more versatile meat eaters and developed the ability to hunt some species physically larger than themselves. They were also probably accomplished scavengers, capable of chasing other predators from the carcasses of their prey just as Ju/'hoansi and other peoples like the Masai in Kenya still occasionally do with lions. For Australopithecus, as with modern hunter-gatherers, there was a clear advantage to eating flesh from larger animals, because bigger animals typically had much more fat and provided far greater energy relative to the effort involved in acquiring it.

Evidence of Australopithecus's taste for meat coincides with a period in hominid evolution that was marked by rapid brain growth and an increasing tendency to bipedalism that left their arms free to do other tasks and enabled the evolutionary refinement of dexterous hands able to do very clever things.

The evolutionary transition from Australopithecus's immediate successor, Homo habilis, to Homo erectus and ultimately on to modern Homo sapiens occurred over a period of around two million years. Over this period their brain sizes more than doubled. The stimulus for this rapid growth came from a number of selective pressures, but it would have been unlikely to happen at all if hominids had not become increasingly fond of eating animal parts. Growing and maintaining big brains requires much more energy than could be acquired through a strictly vegetarian diet. Despite constituting no more than 2 percent of our total body weights, our brains consume roughly 20 percent of our energy resources when we are at rest. For chimpanzees this number is closer to 12 percent and for most other mammals it is usually well below 10 percent. Building and maintaining such big brains requires consuming nutritious food as well as finding a means to divert energy from other organs, most notably hardworking digestive systems, to our heads. Eating nutrient- and protein-dense meat helped enable both.

Meat eating on its own, though, was unlikely to be enough to enable the continued advances in hominid intelligence. Even though meat is rich in calories, amino acids, and other nutrients, it is also slimy, tough, and hard to chew unless thoroughly minced into something resembling steak tartar. It's no surprise then that the other key variable that helped transform early hominids from occasional meat eaters to dedicated omnivores was cooking. Cooked meat is easier to consume and simpler to digest, and cooking generally makes meat taste better.

Cooking also vastly extended the range of other foods that the hominids could eat.[1] Many tubers, stalks, leaves, and fruits that are indigestible—or even poisonous—raw are both nutritious and tasty when cooked. Cooking made hominids much more versatile eaters than most other creatures. Their dietary adaptability combined with their ability to concentrate nutrition through cooking also meant that hominids were no longer hostage to specific ecological niches and could improvise a living in a far broader range of habitats than most other creatures. Fire also must have helped hominids navigate the perils of life on the savanna, while other higher primates remained confined to the relative safety of forests. Fire sticks—and more recently disposable lighters and matches—are as vital a part of a Ju/'hoan hunter's kit as his bow. A good campfire is still the most effective means of deterring unwelcome visits by lions, hyenas, and elephants at night in Nyae Nyae.

Evidence of systematic fire use by early hominids is patchy. Until recently there was very little that anyone could point at to show with any certainty that systematic fire use predated the evolution of modern Homo sapiens. But the recent discovery of the million-year-old remains of camp-fires in a cave in South Africa's northern Cape suggests that cooking may well have played an instrumental role in determining our evolutionary path from at least a million years ago if not a great deal longer. While there is no strong archaeological evidence for it, it is not implausible that Homo habilis—the first tool users and so the first "real" hominids—cooked some of their food and that Homo erectus—who appeared on the scene around 1.8 million years ago—were the beneficiaries of this legacy in terms of brain growth.[2] Homo habilis made routine use of basic stone tools, and if you crack enough stones together, sparks will occasionally fly and possibly ignite dry grass nearby. It is not too much of a leap of faith to imagine that a creature with twice the brain size of a chimpanzee would grasp that by cracking the right stones together he could reliably harness such an obviously elemental force as fire.

If fire helped mostly vegetarian hominids access the nutritional treasures of meat, then it also probably contributed to shaping our modern physiology. Primates like chimpanzees and gorillas have much larger long intestines than humans. They need this additional colonic real estate to give their gut bacteria sufficient time and space to prize nutrition from their fibrous, leafy diets. By "predigesting" foods through the process of cooking, fire enabled hominids to get by without a significant proportion of the digestive plumbing their leaf-munching ancestors depended on. Cooking also played a role in redesigning our faces. Eating softer, cooked foods meant that big-muscled jaws ceased to be a selective advantage. So, as hominid heads grew, their jaws shrank, a process that aided the development of our unique vocal capabilities and—because the morphology of our teeth did not evolve as rapidly as our jaws shrank—ensures that orthodontists are never short of work.[3]

Another possible legacy of our ancestors' passion for meat is the clogged cardiovascular wards in our hospitals and the healthy dividends enjoyed by investors in the ever-widening array of drug therapies for heart disease. Despite the advice of medical authorities, first world diets are still very meat rich. The global average for meat consumption is currently around 50 kilograms per year, roughly double the recommended "safe" level of 70 grams per day. Across most of Europe, North America, and Australia, where household incomes are highest, average meat consumption is four times the recommended amount. In the United States it's five times. And in the rapidly developing economies, those that have enough cash to afford it now eat as much meat as those in the West. Meat, it seems—even the tasteless, miserable, factory-farmed, steroid-ridden meat that fills the shelves of many supermarkets—still exerts a very powerful hold on our species.[4]

By Richard B. Lee's calculations, Ju/'hoansi still dependent exclusively on hunting and gathering ate first world quantities of meat. But where meat currently provided around 15 percent of most people's caloric intake in the United States, meat provided roughly double that proportion among foraging Ju/'hoansi. This was because Ju/'hoansi didn't have loads of carbohydrates to eat and because they preferred cuts of meat with lots of fat, offal, and gristle, with their higher energy, vitamin, and mineral content. Ju/'hoansi also preferred to boil meat rather than grill it on an open fire so that rendered fat was not lost to the flames.

When compared to other well-researched hunting and gathering societies, foraging Ju/'hoansi were among the most moderate meat eaters. Excluding the almost entirely carnivorous arctic peoples, most other hunting and gathering societies acquired around two-thirds of their caloric intake from animal and fish products. Australian Aboriginals in Arnhem Land, for example, acquired 77 percent of their nutrition from animal products; the Aché in Paraguay, 70 percent; and the Khoisan's closest genetic and linguistic relatives outside of southern Africa, the Hadza of Tanzania, 48 percent.[5] Isotopic analysis of Paleolithic hominid collagen tissues suggests that these higher proportions were the norm throughout the history of modern Homo sapiens. Contemporary wisdom regarding the perils of meat eating suggests that eating as much meat as hunter-gatherers would be an evolutionary cul-de-sac. But it clearly wasn't, a fact now latched onto eagerly by contemporary advocates of "Paleo" diets.

The science of understanding the relationship between what we eat and who we are has a long way to go. And it would not surprise anyone if the official advice on eating meat and animal products were to be reversed yet again in the near future on the basis of new evidence. There is also no real clarity on why hunter-gatherers have had such low incidences of cardio-vascular disease despite their meat-heavy diets. It certainly isn't genetic. Among the handful of urban Ju/'hoansi and other San who have had enough money to eat what they want, when they want, bulging waistlines are the norm and heart disease has cut many of these lives tragically short. The most persuasive suggestion is that meat eating at the levels hunter-gatherers do in the context of their broader diets that include high fiber and antioxidant intakes combined with hardly any carbohydrate-rich foods, has probably made the difference. Exactly why it has made a difference, though, is uncertain. Perhaps it has something to do with the fact that they had to spend so little time working.

It was not only the particular nutritional qualities of meat that helped hominids develop their intelligence. Hunting itself changed the dynamic between hominids and other species. Where Australopithecus's ancestors focused almost exclusively on gathering static foods, successive generations of hominid hunters applied their intelligence to outwitting creatures that did not wish to be eaten and, just as importantly, were also much more agile and intelligent than a head of lettuce. And the success of hominid hunters would have benefited from their ability to mimic and adapt the hunting techniques of other predators—a factor that may well have favored the process of natural selection that led to the development of Homo's very pronounced Broca's area, the segment of our brains associated with our ability to communicate complex ideas.

In the absence of effective weaponry, it's likely that early hominid hunters devoted their energy to catching smaller game. If Homo erectus hunted rather than scavenged some of the larger animals that we know he liked to eat, he most likely employed a strategy still used by a handful of Bushman hunters, the aptly named persistence hunt, a technique that probably helped to develop our species' uncanny endurance-running abilities. This form of hunting, which is still practiced by a handful of !Xo in

Botswana, involves pursuing animals like kudu over very long distances until they are immobilized by exhaustion and can easily be approached and killed.

But in all the learned discussions among anthropologists and archaeologists about the relationship between hunting, meat eating, and human evolution, one of the most distinctive of all human traits has been largely ignored: our ability to empathize with others, people and animals alike—to project ourselves into their worlds and experience them from their perspectives.

12

Hunting and Empathy

Dog adopted me early in the New Year of 1995, six months or so into my first spell of fieldwork. He was the bravest of all the dogs at Skoonheid in seeking affection. The others moped around, their tails between their legs, trying to be invisible. They shied away from physical contact with people but would respond with surprised and simpering gratitude if it was offered. Most of their interactions with people came in the form of kicks or flying stones.

The dogs' only real joy came when they joined a foraging party, went looking for lost goats, or assembled in a pack to tear around the village and the surrounding bush. Only then would they wag their tails.

Each dog was attached to a household in the village but was not considered an object of affection or "part of the family." There was rarely enough food to go around, and dogs were expected to take care of themselves. So they scavenged for scraps around fires at night and, if these were inadequate, hunted lizards, mice, insects, and all manner of other desert creatures. One man claimed his dogs had learned to hunt and eat snakes, although they did so less often after one was killed by a cobra.

Dog adopted me because I had food to share and was happy to give him affection. In return Dog offered me companionship in a place that was—back then, at least—alien and unsettling. Out of sight of others, I slipped Dog leftovers from my plate and, later, gave him his own bowl. I scratched his ears and chest and he'd sit curled at my feet by the fire. Dog would have accompanied me everywhere if I had let him. But the one time I took him in my truck, he panicked. So I left him to fend for himself whenever I had to travel elsewhere.

Dog was a typical Africanis, the distinctive landrace of dogs pictured in Egyptian hieroglyphs. It slowly insinuated itself into human settlements across Africa around two millennia ago. And wherever it became established, it evolved over successive generations into sub-breeds better adapted to their particular environments. Fossil remains suggest that these dogs first arrived in southern Africa around 1,200 years ago and were adopted by some Kalahari populations around 700 years ago. Here the environment selected the fast and the stealthy—those that could hunt independently, scavenge from predators and humans, and get away quickly when they needed to. Standing only a foot and a half at the shoulder, Dog was more a whippet than a muscled lion hunter like his distant hybridized cousin, the Rhodesian ridgeback, a descendant of a sub-breed of Africanis once used by Khoi herders in the Cape. He was also brindled rather than the breed's characteristic beige. But then few Africanis in the Omaheke did not bear some obvious genetic traces of recent forebears' indiscretions with imported farmers' dogs.

My relationship with Dog was short-lived. Several months after adopting him, I returned from a trip to find him cowering deep in a thicket of blackthorn acacia—a place where no one could reach him without getting shredded by thorns. His tail thumped the ground when I called, but some primal fear would not let him draw close enough for me to grab him. Through the lattice of thorns I could see the problem. There were several patches on his back where his hair, skin, and flesh had dissolved. The white of his ribs was visible as if they had been bleached and the flesh around them was black and scalded. A little investigation revealed the cause of his suffering. Some of the children had found a bottle of industrial acid that I had purchased to clean a pipe and carelessly left out. Having seen me play with it, they had experimented with its corrosive powers, first on various objects, then on another dog, and finally on Dog. Dog cowered under that bush for another day or so as his organs shut down. I pushed some food and water into the thicket but he did not respond. In the end we hacked into the bush to retrieve him. By then he was barely alive and in great pain. Once we had brought him out, my friend Kaice quickly clubbed Dog on the head with a spade, which I then used to dig him a small grave that I marked solemnly with his bowl and an unspecific prayer.

My demands that the children should be punished and made aware of the pain they had inflicted confused my Ju/'hoan neighbors. They said that "Dog was a dog" and that the children should not be punished for demonstrating curiosity.

They had found my habits of feeding and petting Dog odd enough. The idea of giving him a human burial just seemed absurd. But it was not completely without reference. The Ju/'hoansi often commented on what they considered to be white ranchers' peculiar relationships with their pet dogs. Dogs usually were offered the passenger seats in ranchers' trucks while Bushman workers were confined to the truck beds. Dogs were fed meat and lavished with affection when Bushman farmworkers were given maize porridge and complained of being regularly beaten. Ju/'hoansi were rarely if ever allowed into a farmer's house, whereas dogs were known to sleep in farmers' beds—a cause of general hilarity among the Ju/'hoansi and the source of oft-repeated jokes that never seemed to get old.

Eventually Kaice broached the uneasy topic with me.

"/Kunta," he said, "the problem with you whites is that you think dogs behave like humans or even that your dogs think that they are humans. They are not humans. They are dogs. Their ways are different."

Even if dogs were "different," this didn't help me make sense of the Ju/'hoansi's apparent indifference to their and other animals' suffering. It seemed at odds with the idea that Ju/'hoansi and other hunter-gatherers had developed profoundly empathetic relationships with the animals they lived among. But in time I learned this is precisely what justified their indifference.

Ju/'hoansi insisted that animals were people of a sort—not humans but people, because they too lived and thought. They asserted that each species of animal had its own distinctive physical forms, customs, habits, and ways of experiencing and interacting with the world.

Most pet owners claim that the love they "share" with their pets is based on an empathetic relationship with them built on traits our two species have in common: in the case of dogs, their sociability, their loyalty, their affection, and their gratitude. But this is a different understanding of empathy from that which hunter-gatherers like the Ju/'hoansi had for their animal neighbors. For them, empathy with animals was not a question of focusing on an animal's humanlike characteristics but on assuming the whole perspective of the animal. To empathize with an animal, you couldn't think like a human and project your thoughts and emotions onto it; rather, you had to adopt the animal's perspective.

To Ju/'hoansi, adopting the perspective of animals did not mean feeling compassion or sympathy for them so much as understanding that—in the broader scheme of existence—happiness, death, and suffering were simply part of how the cosmos was ordered. And in this cosmic order all animals accepted their roles. Many were meat. Others were hunters. And a few, like humans and dogs (which leopards find particularly tasty), were both meat and hunters, depending on circumstances.

Ju/'hoan hunters' empathy with their prey was not unique. Many other hunting populations across the globe have described feeling similar forms of empathy for their prey. This kind of empathy arises out of the performance of the hunt and, for the Ju/'hoansi, found its most graceful expression through the art of tracking, arguably one of the earliest and most enigmatic forms of reading.

———

Among Skoonheid's residents only one man, /I!ae, held his dogs in particularly high esteem.

"These dogs are brave hunters," he explained when he first showed me his scrappy terrier-size mongrel and another, larger dog that offered no obvious clues to its pedigree other than that it was strong and brindled and had good teeth. Both were gnawing cooperatively on the femur of something big. When not hunting with /I!ae, his dogs ran free across Skoonheid. Unafraid of anything and under the protective halo of their master, they stole scraps from other peoples' fires, rummaged in refuse pits, and occasionally chewed on children.

Ten or fifteen years my senior, /I!ae was Skoonheid's most prolific hunter. Tall by Ju/'hoan standards and stocky, /I!ae exuded menace. Local farmers were wary of him and the local constables made sure to inquire after him whenever they popped into the resettlement area. Others at Skoonheid treated him with caution and were grateful that his capacity for explosive violence was defused by hunting.

/I!ae was not much of a talker and never shared much about his past. But he liked being photographed. He dressed with piratical flamboyance and would always pose carefully for photos, usually with a prop of some kind: the jaws of a warthog he had recently killed, a homemade guitar, or a newly decorated item of clothing. He always made sure that his large hoop earring was in the shot and that his elaborately beaded hat was given the prominence it merited. He also liked to pose with an open shirt, displaying the prison tattoos that decorated his chest: a stylized Soviet military star on his left breast and a cross mounted on a stone plinth on his right. Both had been made by cutting into his skin with broken glass and then staining the incisions greenish-black with ash. When I asked what they meant, he shrugged: "Other prisoners had these tattoos. They looked good. So I made them like this." These were complemented by a series of smaller tattoos on his face: three small circles, each no bigger than a large freckle. These were cut into the skin below each eye and in the center of his chin.

/I!ae was unusual in that he preferred to hunt with only his dogs for companionship. He would often disappear surreptitiously before dawn and return in the darkness some days later, usually with meat in hand. As a result, /I!ae did not bother to contribute his labor to any of the community projects at Skoonheid. He received his food aid regardless and, because of his ability to provide meat, was locked into a network of sharing relationships that meant his household very rarely went hungry.

Farm life did not agree with /I!ae and he certainly did not agree with it. So he made himself the master of his own universe and, in doing so, enjoyed more freedom than most other Ju/'hoansi in the Omaheke. Farm fences enabled rather than restrained his movements. To him they were portals into places where he felt alive and at ease, where he could dissolve into the world around him and, if he was lucky, merge his being with that of the quarry he stalked.

/I!ae hunted anything and everything. He kept his bows and arrows secreted somewhere in the bush, far out of reach of any drunks in a fighting mood. But his specialty was the warthog, a species now more prolific than most of the game species that traditionally sustained Ju/'hoansi in the Omaheke in the past. Every few weeks he would offer me warthog teeth as souvenirs, pointing out that local white farmers found enterprising uses for them as key-rings or bottle-opener handles.

For /I!ae, his downtime at Skoonheid could never live up to the sense of freedom he felt poaching on the farms with his dogs. And as he became more frustrated with resettlement life, he began to drink more. Gradually liquid spirits drowned out the call of the animal spirits and sapped his spear arm of its energy.

I saw him last in the spring of 2001. By then he had abandoned his flamboyant outfit in favor of a torn military greatcoat that he wore even in the searing heat of summer. His skin had darkened and blotched, his muscles had wasted, and his body had shrunk into itself. We did not talk beyond greeting one another, and, surprisingly in hindsight, he did not ask me to photograph him. I guessed afterward that he had contracted AIDS, which by then had begun to steamroll its way through many communities across the Kalahari, leaving those infected looking like walking ghosts as they waited for death.

When I returned to Skoonheid a few months later, /I!ae was gone—not, as I had anticipated, to his grave, but to prison. I was informed that he had strangled his wife in a drunken rage one night and carefully arranged her corpse against a tree as if she was napping before making his escape. But he was soon picked up by the police, sent before the court, and sentenced to ten years in jail. His decade behind bars and the absence of corrosive homebrew apparently restored his health. But when he was released he did not return to Skoonheid. He was fearful of being hounded by his wife's family. So instead he trekked to the relative anonymity of Omawewozanyanda, where he celebrated his freedom with a drink and welcomed the g//ausi—the spirits of the dead—back into his soul. Under their spell he was accused of raping and beating a young woman. Sobering up he learned that she'd gone to the police and that it was only a matter of time before he'd be forced to endure another spell in prison. The police found him later that day. He was swaying gently from a bough of a large camel-thorn tree on the ridge of the omuramba on the outskirts of the village, an improvised rope around his neck.

But long before this happened, during my first year at Skoonheid, /I!ae agreed to try to teach me to track. He had thought it an odd request, because, as he explained, tracking was something that you could show people but you couldn't teach it to them. Tracks were there for everybody to see, he insisted, but to read them you had had to understand why they were made.

Ju/'hoan hunters' tracking skills are as important as their poison arrows. For without them hunting is near impossible in the vast, flat Kalahari. Here there are no hills to afford hunters a view of their prey grazing on plains below. Dense scrub often limits a hunter's view to just a few meters. And while climbing a tree or scrambling up a termite mound offers a little additional perspective, the only reliable way of finding animals in most of the Kalahari is to be able to read fluently their tracks in the sand.

/I!ae was right about tracking not being something that could be taught. My efforts to become a competent tracker under his and, later, several others' guidance over the next two decades never came to much. To be a good tracker requires engaging in a constant physical dialogue with the environment and ultimately an ability to project oneself into the animals that left the tracks. Like poetry, tracks have a grammar, a meter, and a vocabulary. But also like poetry, interpreting them is far more complex than simply reading sequences of letters and following them where they go, a task that was hard enough for me because tracks that were obvious to /I!ae, like the slight bend in a blade of grass or an apparently meaningless scuff on a rock, were invisible to my eyes. Tracking required an ability to read between the marks and infer their maker's mood, circumstances, and intentions. To do this required a lifetime of practical experience and an intimate knowledge of the animals that made the tracks. But if I gained no particular skills from /I!ae's lessons, they revealed that as much as hunting in the Kalahari is all about tracking, tracking is not all about hunting.

Tracks were a source of constant entertainment for /I!ae. In the grassless central compound at Skoonheid, he cheerfully recounted the comings and goings of others as revealed through their footprints. To those who could read tracks well, nothing at Skoonheid was secret. Every movement a person made left a legible trace in the sand. Even though many of the resettled Ju/'hoan families at Skoonheid had not known one another previously when I arrived there, it wasn't long before almost everyone there recognized everyone else's footprints so well that unfamiliar ones would be immediately remarked on and inquired about. Illicit liaisons between lovers had to be carefully planned and stock thieves on goat-raiding missions were known to steal others' shoes to try to disguise their identities.

But unlike the gossips who liked to keep tabs on their human neighbors, /I!ae far preferred the stories he read in the sand some distance away from Skoonheid's busy center.

/I!ae experienced the desert as a vast interactive canvas animated by the stories its many creatures inscribed into the sand. He insisted that if you walk through this part of the Kalahari looking only ahead of you "like people in the town do," it is a dead place, a home only to birds, flies, livestock, and the dung beetles that followed them. As he walked, his eyes would dart back and forth across the ground, picking out interesting stories from the cacophony of narratives etched into the sand. And as he did so, his right hand and fingers would dance as if painting the animal that made the tracks back into the empty landscape in front of us.

He once showed me the small crescent arcs that marked the path taken by a large black mamba and the scuff marks left by an elephant shrew that fled after it sensed the snake's approach—and then, a few meters away, where the shrew had been struck, died, and consumed by the mamba, which he warned was concealed somewhere nearby. He also showed me where a honey badger and jackal played a game of wits with one another as they clashed over the rotting bones of a goat and where a cheetah had hidden its young when some people were nearby.

But as a hunter it was the tracks of warthogs, kudu, oryx, and steenbok that excited /I!ae the most. Out of a seemingly insignificant set of indistinct prints, scuffs, and twisted grass stems he would conjure detailed descriptions of their movements and motivations. He'd explain where they were going and why, what they were doing, and where they had been. He'd also tell me their gender, their size, and whether they were healthy, hungry, nervous, or agitated. And if the tracks were fresh enough, he'd wonder aloud whether he should take me back to Skoonheid, retrieve his hunting kit, and summon his dogs.

/I!ae considered the animals he hunted to be both companions and adversaries. They knew he was a hunter and were right to fear him, just as he was right to try to outwit and kill them.

/I!ae described the different species he hunted according to characteristics like how they behaved, what they ate, and how they socialized. He
told me how kudu males care little for the females, how they are bullies
and not very bright, and how females by contrast care a great deal for each
other and hate being alone; how oryx are brave and solitary; and how
warthogs are clever, sociable, and vengeful.

/I!ae would talk at length about the idiosyncrasies of individual species
and would group species together according to habit, diet, color, gender
behavior, teeth, treatment of young, fat content—anything that was meaningful. But he found it far harder to make a broad categorical distinction
between humans and other species—not least because humans, being so
adaptable, had so many things in common with so many other species.
Humans could climb trees like baboons, stalk like big cats, run like wild
dogs, dig like porcupines, and fight with the ferocity of bull elephants. To
his mind there was just a single world in which different species interacted
with one another. And in this world the only thing that most of the
nonhuman species had in common was that it was permissible for people
to eat them. The Ju/'hoan term that most closely approximates the word
"animal" is *!ha*, a generic term for meat. According to this reasoning, if
leopards ever discussed their animal neighbors among themselves, they
probably referred to Ju/'hoansi—along with other creatures they considered edible—to be different kinds of meat as well.

I never hunted with /I!ae. I was too clumsy, loud, and slow. Also, he did
not care for company when hunting, and I was too terrified of the consequences of being caught poaching. On one of our walks he killed a female
porcupine that his dogs were worrying at a safe distance. Without a moment's
thought he stunned it with a well-aimed rock before bashing it on the
skull with a stick. On the way back to the compound, he talked anima-
tedly about how its fatty skin was the sweetest of all meats. And after he
plucked it, he gave me a handful of quills as a souvenir.

/I!ae's difficulties in describing how other animals saw the world were
not only because he was a man of action but also because his sense of an
animal's view of the world was experiential. It was something that was felt
and so could not be easily translated into words. When he discovered fresh
tracks of something he wished to hunt, he shivered briefly, as if tickled by

this trace of the animal's presence. It was a sensation, he explained, that he felt in the back of his neck and sometimes his armpits. Dogs also feel something similar when they pick up a scent, he said, and added that this is one of the reasons that people do not eat dogs, no matter how hungry they are.

/I!ae was one of the few Ju/'hoansi at Skoonheid who toyed with the idea of heading to Nyae Nyae after independence. Others, no longer used to sharing water with hyenas and elephants, expressed reservations about returning to such a life and worried about the savagery of the Ju/'hoansi there. "They might shoot me with their poison arrows!" some exclaimed. But /I!ae thrilled at the thought of being able to hunt all the time. Two other Ju/'hoansi he knew from the Omaheke had trekked to Nyae Nyae back then. And, having been deprived of the ability to hunt freely on the farms, both soon joined the ranks of Nyae Nyae's most prolific and dedicated hunters, their thrill of reengaging with the animal world in this way intensified by their years of alienation from it. Yet, like most others, /I!ae remained in the Omaheke, his spirit captive to the sense of belonging to the place he knew best.

———

Few hunters in Nyae Nyae are in the habit of heading off on their own like /I!ae. But then, unlike hunters in the Omaheke who had to worry about white farmers on the lookout for poachers and trespassers, Nyae Nyae Ju/'hoansi only had to conceal themselves from their prey. Traditional hunts can last several days, and most people prefer some companionship if they are to sleep out in the bush. Also, two or three hunters working together almost always stand a better chance of success than a hunter working alone.

Nyae Nyae is also by far the largest of the last few places anywhere in southern Africa that San can hunt without fear of being prosecuted for poaching. But even so, far fewer men hunt regularly than did in the past. The most prolific hunters in Nyae Nyae are middle-aged and they complain about how only a few young men are interested in hunting and fewer still are skilled hunters.

While Ju/'hoansi in Nyae Nyae are free to hunt whenever and wherever they wish within the Nyae Nyae Conservancy boundaries, they are forbidden to hunt using anything but "traditional methods." The only people allowed to hunt in Nyae Nyae with rifles are the trophy hunters, who pay big money for the privilege. There are also a number of species that Ju/'hoansi are forbidden to hunt by law and others they are forbidden to hunt by conservancy rules. These include giraffe, once a favorite meat for the Ju/'hoansi, and pangolin, much loved by the Ju/'hoansi but now endangered because of poaching to feed the Chinese medicine market.

No one resents the requirement that they must only use bows and arrows, spears, or traditional traps, and hunt only on foot—especially the few men who still hunt regularly and experience their environments in a similar way to their fathers and their grandfathers before them. For them the practice of hunting is a process in which their bodies and senses progressively merge with those of their prey up to and beyond the moment that the fatal spear thrust is delivered.

Unlike gently paced gathering trips, hunters usually set out with light-footed urgency, often chatting among themselves as they scan the ground for tracks. Sometimes they spread out to cover more ground, but just as often they march together in single file, their fingers pointing out tracks in a twinkle of practiced gestures while their mouths talk about other matters. If the hunters are lucky they may find suitable fresh spoor early in the hunt. But it is not uncommon to walk for days, find nothing, and return home empty-handed.

Most of the larger meat animals Ju/'hoansi hunt, like kudu or wildebeest, aren't particularly fond of the heat. It saps their energy and makes moving around a chore. So when the sun climbs above the tallest trees, they seek out patches of shade in which to disappear and will usually remain there until late in the afternoon. This is the best time to hunt. It gives hunters a chance to gain ground on prey that may have left a set of tracks five or six hours previously. It also allows the hunters to capitalize on one of their most obvious advantages over many prey species: their physical endurance and ability to cover large distances relatively fast.

Hunters will often choose their individual prey on the basis of its tracks alone. From among the tracks left by a herd of kudu or hartebeest, for example, it is easy enough for the hunters to establish which individual in the herd best suits their needs, which is likely to be easiest to kill, and which will have the most fat. Once the hunters decide to follow a promising set of tracks, the tenor of the hunt changes. Their pace increases and, if they talk, they do so in hushed, urgent tones, communicating only by means of hand signals. If the wind is favorable or there is no wind at all, the hunters will follow the track as it is written. But if the tracks lead downwind and the animal may be nearby, they will tack back and forth, intersecting the animal's tracks now and again, so that they can approach it with the wind in their faces. And as the spatial distance between them and their prey closes, the hunters' senses begin to merge ever more completely with those of their quarry.

Once they locate their prey, each movement they make is dictated by an amplified awareness of their prey's immediate sensory universe: what it sees, what it smells, and what it hears. Moving silently, knees bent and shoulders stooped, bows in hand, they experience the world around them from the perspectives of both the hunter and the hunted. As the hunted they are alert to every sound and movement the hunters make. As the hunters they are singularly focused on dissolving into the landscape and emerging undetected close enough to get off a good shot. A glassy shard of cloud passing overhead can reveal their presence as the passing cool of its shade induces a momentary breeze, as can a bird taking flight or a ground squirrel or lizard scurrying for cover. It is only once the hunters have stalked within forty yards or so of their target and an arrow has been released and found its mark that this hypersensory bubble dissolves.

If the shot finds its mark, the light reed shaft of the arrow falls to the ground often before it has been noticed by the prey, which feels no more pain in that moment than it would if it had been bitten by a particularly vicious horsefly or stung by one of the angry wasps that terrorize casual visitors to waterholes. Even then the hunters will be careful not to reveal themselves to their prey. Doing so would almost certainly spook the animal, causing it to flee. If it is not spooked, it is usually sufficiently disoriented by the pain that begins to seize it to remain close to where it was shot. At best death comes in a couple of hours, but if it is a particularly big animal, like a giraffe or eland, it can take more than a day before it weakens enough for hunters to approach and kill it with their spears.

There is little point in following a particularly large animal once it has been shot. The stress of pursuit can affect the meat. It also saps the hunters' energy. In these circumstances hunters will memorize the individual animal's spoor and camp for the night where they are or, if they are not too far away, return home. But returning home brings with it an additional set of risks. During the period a hunter and his prey are linked by the poison; hunters describe feeling shadow pains, often in the corresponding part of their bodies where the arrow struck their prey, or they feel unsteady as the poison gradually starves the animal's organs of oxygen. But these sensations are neither overwhelming nor particularly distracting. They have form and presence yet no substance.

Returning into the human world of the village while waiting for the poison to do its work also risks severing the empathetic thread that binds the hunters to their prey. Back in the village the sense of shared anticipation, even if not vocalized often, amplifies the hunters' anxiety that something may go wrong. Was the poison on the arrowhead sufficiently fresh? Was there enough? Did the arrow penetrate deep enough for the poison to enter the bloodstream? Might a rainstorm wash away the spoor and the animal die needlessly?

On these occasions they also avoid eating the meat of any other animals in case doing so breaks the empathetic bond with their prey. They also avoid contact with women, who, after all, are "like meat" and so can also break the empathetic bond. But doing so can be hard for a hungry hunter who has walked and run ten or twenty miles over the course of the day. In the late 1990s at N≠amtjoha, a village in southern Nyae Nyae, one hunter who shot a bull roan antelope that he intended to follow and kill the next morning shared the meat of a tortoise with his mother and wife. Later he woke up with a pain in the night that stopped suddenly again just before dawn. Convinced that the sudden disappearance of the pain meant his bond with the roan had been severed, he started to follow the spoor from first light. He soon discovered the carcass being shredded by hyenas.

In the same village a few years previously, a Ju/'hoan man who had recently moved with his family from the Omaheke to Nyae Nyae and who only paid lip service to what he thought of as archaic customs was said to have slept with his wife after shooting a giraffe, the largest and most desired of all the meat animals. The giraffe fell to the poison the next day. But before they even built a fire to cook the fresh liver, Nyae Nyae's sole game warden found them, placed the entire village under arrest, and confiscated as much meat as he could fit into the back of his tiny Land Rover. No one let this hunter forget the incident up until the day he died a few years later under mysterious circumstances after "falling" from the back of a truck.

But if all goes well, the final stage of the hunt is usually a formality. If the animal has not been spooked, then there is a good chance that it will still be somewhere near where it was first shot. But if has run or the poison works too slowly, the hunters will have a long walk before they claim their prize. Once they find it, they will unceremoniously spear it if it still has some life in it. By the time this happens, the animal usually will offer no response to the hunters, its sensory universe reduced to a haze of poison-induced pain, paralysis, and trauma.

For Ju/'hoan hunters the moment of the kill is one of neither elation nor sadness. When I asked one man what he felt when he cut an animal's throat, he replied that it felt no different from cutting bread. But this is understandable. It is hard to feel anything at all when overwhelmed by the almost postcoital sensory void that marks the end of a successful hunt. And while Ju/'hoansi do not speak of individual animals having spirits, they do not doubt that many animals have a powerful life force, in particular those animals with *n!ow*.

But even if individual animals' life forces resemble something like a spirit, it does not mean that they are subject to the same rules that govern human behavior. Different species also clearly have different norms and rules they live by. And one set of norms that are uniquely human as far as Ju/'hoansi are concerned are those relating to the sharing of meat.

13

Insulting the Meat

During the first couple of weeks I lived at Skoonheid I was shadowed by an intermittently sober older man who dived for cover whenever I turned around. Nervously, I asked !A/ae Langman about my stalker.

"Ah, yes. It's Jan Pumper," he told me. He then explained that my stalker was nicknamed "Pumper" because he was the only one who could reliably start the old diesel motor for the old farm borehole pump.

"His real name is ≠Oma //Amte," he added, "and, as he will tell you, Skoonheid is *his* farm."

After several weeks of checking me out, ≠Oma eventually decided I was safe to talk to. Before long we became friends of a sort.

Old ≠Oma was Skoonheid's most established resident, and in the months before I arrived there he had discovered hair-straightening cream. He had applied it to his skull every morning since. Like other Khoisan, his hair curled naturally into small, tightly knotted clumps. So, to achieve the tidy coiffure he desired, he applied a far greater quantity of hair straightener than the recommended dose and did so with far greater frequency than the instructions prescribed. An unwelcome side effect of this was that the skin just below his fringe would discolor, peel, and flake in dry weather and blotch in humid weather, giving him a slightly disturbing halo.

Once he had overcome his suspicions about me, he complained to me how difficult it was to maintain his straight hair and how unfair he thought it was that his hair should be so much more resistant to straightening than others'. While the general consensus at Skoonheid was that white people's hair made them resemble goats, ≠Oma took a different view. He felt by straightening his hair he would transfer some of the symbolic power exercised by the white farmers onto his aging scalp. This was particularly important, he explained, if he was to exert any authority over the new settlers at Skoonheid.

When Skoonheid was still a commercial farm, ≠Oma was its foreman and so the most senior of all the workers. Foreman was a position of some importance, because it channeled the authority of the white *baas* (boss). And on the Omaheke farms, remote as they were, the boss's authority was absolute.

"If you are foreman," ≠Oma explained, "then you are the eyes and the ears of the *baas* on the farm. You are the chief of the workers and are in charge when the *baas* is away."

Foremen were usually paid better than other workers. And if farmers bothered to provide any housing to their workers, foremen were also usually given the best of the housing available. Foremen also typically enjoyed privileged access to the main farmhouse and sometimes were invited to share a coffee with the farmer on his porch to plan the day's tasks. Foremen's wives often worked as domestic servants in the farmhouse, a position that also brought with it the reward of leftovers from the farmer's table.

But being a foreman came with clear costs. Foremen often became objects of mockery, malicious gossip, and mistrust. Other workers scathingly referred to them by the Afrikaans term *witvoets*, which translates as "whitefoots."

"They are *witvoets*," !A/ae Langman explained, because "even though their skin is red like ours, and they look like us, they are secretly white. There, hidden under their shoes and socks, they are *skelm-wit* [scoundrel white]. Like old ≠Oma."

When fighting broke out in farm compounds, as often as not the foreman was involved. And a fight between a foreman and other San workers could result in the wrath of a whip-wielding *baas* being visited upon the workforce.

"If a boss were to hit a foreman, it would be the same as him hitting himself, so he always hits the others," !A/ae explained.

Despite the material rewards associated with being foreman, Ju/'hoansi often declined the role. The social costs were too high. Only on a handful of farms, like Skoonheid, where most of the workers came from the same extended family and the foreman's perks were shared among them, was the foreman's role a tolerable privilege.

Before independence in 1990, ≠Oma had grown comfortable with his old life enclosed within Skoonheid's farm boundaries. He was similarly accustomed to the certainties of being foreman for a relatively predictable and benign white *baas*—one of the few who paid his workers reasonably and rarely resorted to abuse. And in time ≠Oma came to internalize this hierarchy. He embraced his leadership role and the authority his privileged status as foreman gave him.

When I arrived at Skoonheid in 1994, ≠Oma lived with his extended family in the simple but dilapidated two-room brick foreman's hut a short distance from the main farmhouse. It had been his home since he was appointed foreman a decade or so earlier. Since then he had built an outside cooking area, protected from the wind by two corrugated iron sheets. Pewter mugs along with a couple of blackened cooking pots hung from fencing wire, and a small fire burned in the sand. He'd also improvised a washing area with a single old tap from which he piped water directly from the old water tower in the main compound by means of an old cracked hose pipe.

≠Oma nervously welcomed the arrival of the two hundred or so other landless Ju/'hoansi who were deposited at Skoonheid in 1994. He was, after all, the foreman, and unlike the new settlers he had a house made of bricks to remind them of his status. But ≠Oma's attempts to impose his authority on the new settlers only won him ridicule. So he gave them home-brewed beer and offered them meat to impress them. And while the new settlers enjoyed the beer and meat and ate it without thought, as soon as the alcohol liberated their tongues they turned on him again, accusing him of trying to purchase their patronage, of trying to be their boss.

By the time I became friends with old ≠Oma, he was close to acknowledging that the other settlers would never afford him the respect he demanded. In a pantomime of his old duties as foreman, he still tended the remains of the main farmhouse garden. He watered and weeded its patchy scraps of lawn and raised cement-and-brick-bordered flower beds.

But his heart was no longer in it and over time the garden received less attention from ≠Oma than he gave his hair. ≠Oma grew similarly apathetic about the fate of his few remaining livestock. His former boss had gifted him a calf every Christmas and ≠Oma had assembled a large herd (by Ju/'hoan standards) of around twenty head of cattle by the time Skoonheid was sold to the government. ≠Oma then applied what remained of his material wealth to staying permanently drunk.

Within a year of Skoonheid coming under government control, ≠Oma's once-impressive herd of cattle had been reduced to a handful of bony, much-neglected heifers. Some had been secreted off in the night by cattle thieves who knew he'd be too drunk to notice. Others were sold off for ridiculously low prices in return for cash that was spent on hair cream and alcohol. In the end !A/ae Langman insisted that he look after ≠Oma's few remaining cattle on his behalf.

Eventually ≠Oma lost everything, including his life, to alcohol, leaving the small foreman's house at Skoonheid a ghostly mausoleum. A neighboring farmer often asked ≠Oma to help out when he had guests come to hunt on his farm. In exchange, ≠Oma would be rewarded with meat as well as some cash. An added perk of this work was the opportunity to quietly liberate the farmer of some of his booze. While the hunting parties were away, ≠Oma was said to raid the farmer's bar. But the farmer had cottoned on to ≠Oma's pilfering. To teach him a lesson the farmer was said to have spiked the brandy in the bar with some noxious chemical. ≠Oma underestimated the cunning of the farmer and the farmer underestimated ≠Oma's determination to gulp down the unpalatable mix in pursuit of a few hours of oblivion. ≠Oma never robbed his bar again. His corpse— along with those of several of his family members who also partook of the toxic brew—was dumped unceremoniously back at Skoonheid by the farmer the following day.

The mockery ≠Oma endured during the last few years of his lifetime was harsh but not unusual among Ju/'hoansi. It also was not directed only at *witvoets* but at anyone who became too self-important. It was one of the many social leveling mechanisms Ju/'hoansi used for enforcing the fierce egalitarianism that enabled their ancestors to make such a good living for so long in this desert. When talking about social leveling mechanisms, Ju/'hoansi still describe the feelings that motivate them to insult or mock others as jealousy.

When Ju/'hoansi still depended solely on hunting and gathering, good hunters needed a thick skin. For while a particularly spectacular kill was always cause for celebration, the hunter responsible was rarely praised. Instead, he and the meat he offered were routinely insulted. Regardless of the size or condition of the carcass, those due a share of the meat would complain that the kill was trifling, that it was barely worth the effort of carrying it back to camp, or that there wouldn't be enough meat to go around.

For his part, the successful hunter was expected to show great humility, to be almost apologetic when he presented the carcass and never to brag about his achievements.

Of course, everyone knew the difference between a scrawny kill and a good one, and even scrawny animals taste good. But everyone would maintain the farce and continue to pass occasional insults even while they were busy filling their bellies. Hunters never took the insults to heart and those dishing them out often did so through broad grins. This was a performance in which everyone played well-rehearsed roles. It was also a performance with a clear purpose, and beneath the lighthearted insults lay a sharp and potentially vicious edge. Its function was to enforce the "fierce" egalitarianism that underwrote Ju/'hoan social life.

One Ju/'hoan man offered Richard B. Lee a particularly eloquent explanation of why they did this. "When a young man kills much meat, he comes to think of himself as a chief or a big man, and he thinks of the rest of us as his servants or inferiors," Lee's informant stated. "We can't accept this . . . So we always speak of his meat as worthless. This way we cool his heart and make him gentle."[1]

The lighthearted insults and the hunter's theatrical humility also reminded everyone of the constant tension between self-interest and community interest that simmered below the surface of band life and that occasionally erupted into arguments. And for a hunter, especially one who was particularly skilled and energetic, this meant taking care not to be so successful that he stood out or, worse still, began to consider other people to be in his debt or himself to be in theirs.

"Insulting the meat" was one of many tricks Ju/'hoansi used to cool hearts, discourage arrogance, and tear down any potential hierarchies before they formed. But this kind of teasing was not only confined to good hunters. Nor was it always without real malice. No one was exempt from mockery and almost any opportunity was seized on to tease or laugh at others.

If insults prevented hunters from getting too big for their leather sandals, it also created an atmosphere in which sharing was second nature.

Gathered foods were not subject to any strict conventions on sharing. They were said to belong to the person who collected them and would be shared among those who slept at her fire. But since gathering trips were cooperative affairs, and knowledge of where to go and what was in season was shared, no individual household within a band ended up with significantly more to eat than any other. And if by chance one did, then those with less would visit others' fires.

Meat, by contrast, needed to be very carefully distributed for fear of invoking jealousy and anger. Even more so than tobacco, meat exercised sufficient power over foraging Ju/'hoansi to persuade them to forget their manners if and when they felt slighted. Omissions or errors in protocol when distributing meat could ignite resentments that burned even hotter and longer than heartbreak.

Distributing the meat of smaller kills posed few difficulties. Their meat was usually given to the very young and very old to eat. There was a certain logic to this. These animals were too small to share widely, so apportioning them to those who were not able to contribute food not only ensured that these people remained well looked after but also helped avoid jealousy.

Distributing the meat of larger kills was most difficult precisely because it provided more than enough meat to go around. A sudden surplus of the most valued of all foods tested the cohesion of communities otherwise bound together by the common experience of having just enough. For in surpluses, as Ju/'hoansi understood all too well, lay the roots of power and control. As a result, hunters took particular care in distributing meat strictly along customary lines.

The meat of any animal killed was always "owned" by the hunter whose arrow first struck home, even if that arrow was borrowed from another hunter. But the hunter's ownership was conditional. Not sharing the meat widely was inconceivable, not only because a single household would never be able to consume all of it before it spoiled, but also because doing so would spell the end of a band as a functional community.

The owner of the animal was responsible for butchering and subsequently distributing its meat. First shares were given to other hunters who accompanied him, his own household, his in-laws, and his immediate name relatives. Afterward he would also provide shares to others until all parts of the carcass were spoken for. Those who received meat from the first share would then be expected to redistribute their share in a similar pattern to the hunter. Because each step in the meat distribution process was jealously scrutinized by everyone, it was more or less certain that everyone got an appropriate share.

Before the formal appointment of two government-recognized Ju/'hoan chiefs after independence, the Ju/'hoansi had neither chiefs nor kings. No individual had the power to bind others to their decisions by any means other than their ability to persuade. Foraging Ju/'hoansi were textbook examples of "acephalous" societies: ones with no formalized hierarchies or established governance systems. Instead, they organized their relationships with one another according to a series of norms that were maintained by consensus rather than by any individual's or institution's authority.

The closest thing to institutionalized leaders among Ju/'hoansi were the two or three n!orekxausi (landholders) in individual bands. These were the individuals through whom the right to exploit individual n!ores (territories) were inherited. Usually translated as "owners" and "leaders" in English for want of better terms, the n!orekxausi themselves neither thought of themselves as leaders nor were they thought of as such by others. Beyond having the right to deny or grant permission to people from different bands to hunt within their *n!ore* or harvest its plant resources, *n!orekxausi* had no real powers to speak of. They had no formal role in resolving disputes; no role greater than any other in determining how, when, and where a band might move camp; and certainly no greater entitlement to any material resources than anyone else.

But the absence of formalized leadership roles did not mean an absence of leadership. In any band there were always individuals whose character, intelligence, ability, charm, or charisma made them more influential than others. But they tended to be especially cautious about exercising their influence for fear of provoking jealousy.

There are some historical examples of foraging Bushman leaders—like Tsemkxau, who killed the Gobabis magistrate in 1923—whose influence extended beyond the boundaries of their individual band. But their authority was almost always born of unusual circumstances and only ever flickered briefly.

———

By the early summer of 1994, events of national or international importance still generated little interest at Skoonheid, a place where the small town of Gobabis represented the edge of the known world. Recent experience had persuaded Ju/'hoansi here that there was little value in believing the promises of politicians whose voices would crackle and wheeze over the airwaves on the rare occasions that someone managed to coax an old radio to life.

Elsewhere in Namibia, election fever had taken hold. Ministers and MPs were busy mobilizing the rank and file of their respective parties to fight for their opportunities to maintain their erratic parliamentary attendance records and the associated perks of leadership. The euphoria of independence had not yet given way to the cynicism and uncertainty that would make future Namibian elections less celebratory. But as Namibia prepared for its second ever fully democratic election in November 1994, Skoonheid's Ju/'hoan population could scarcely have shown less interest. They had voted in the first universal election in 1989, supervised by the United Nations in the months before Independence Day, and as far as

they were concerned, life remained as difficult as ever. Back then they felt
that they were being asked to participate in a process they didn't fully
understand, to determine a future in which they felt they had little stake.
One of my Ju/'hoan companions, Baartman, explained that it was as if
they were voting "to choose a new boss" rather than being offered the
opportunity to become their own boss.

One afternoon in the run-up to the election, a small fleet of four-wheel-
drive vehicles decked out in the colors of one of the major political parties
rumbled through Skoonheid honking their horns. People dragged themselves up from where they were sitting and gathered around to see what
the commotion was about. But as soon as they realized that these were
political campaigners and, more importantly, had brought no food to
distribute, the crowd quietly dispersed.

The campaigners were at first bewildered and then irritated by the
Ju/'hoansi's lack of interest in what they had to say.

"Do you Bushmen not understand that we fought to win you freedom?"
one of the campaigners asked the two or three Ju/'hoansi who had not yet
bothered to move on. The small audience looked unimpressed.

I mentioned that another political party had recently visited Skoonheid
and that the audience had been much more attentive. But, I explained,
they had brought meat and soft drinks along.

"These people are stupid," one of the campaigners said with a shrug as
they unloaded a bundle of pamphlets, dumped them under a camel-thorn
tree, climbed back into their vehicles, and sped off in a flurry of dust,
hoping to find a more receptive audience elsewhere. Some of the settlers
shuffled over to examine the bundle.

No one at Skoonheid other than !A/ae Langman could read, and the
pamphlets did not have enough interesting pictures to hold anyone's
interest for too long. The pamphlets' paper was also too thick and glossy to
be used for cigarette papers, and so they were left abandoned where they
lay.

Many things contributed to the ongoing exclusion of Bushmen from
mainstream political processes in Namibia. Some of these were practical.
Bushmen represented only 2 percent of the total national population and
were almost exclusively confined to remote rural areas or scattered across

white-owned farms and communal areas where they were regarded as drunks, beggars, and household servants. They were treated as—and thought of themselves as—a marginalized, politically inarticulate minority.

Some blamed their exclusion from mainstream politics on the Old Time people like /Engn!au.

"They were weak, those Old Time people," I was told. "They were stupid and knew fuck-all about guns or cattle. And this is why we are now always under others who don't care what we say or think."

Everyone blamed the white farmers. "The Boers came here to waste the Bushmen," they said, "to steal our land, to steal our work, and to make themselves rich."

And everyone also agreed that the *Gobasi*—the "blacks"—were not much better. "They do not see the Bushmen. They just walk over us like we are sand under their shoes."

Everyone also agreed that while it was a good thing that the farmers could no longer beat them and cheat them with impunity as they had been doing a few years previously, the quality of the equality that independence brought was a pale imitation of what they considered real equality.

Legal hierarchies based on race or ethnicity are now a thing of the past in Namibia. The nation's new constitution and laws proudly proclaim everyone's equality regardless of their racial or ethnic identity. They also reaffirm every citizen's "fundamental rights" as enshrined in the United Nations' Universal Declaration of Human Rights.

Like the historical documents that inspired Namibia's new constitution— the Magna Carta, France's Declaration of the Rights of Man, the American Declaration of Independence, and the Universal Declaration of Human Rights—there is a notable omission from it. For while it asserts that "no persons may be discriminated against on the grounds of sex, race, colour, ethnic origin, religion, creed or social or economic status," it also reaffirms property rights and implies that material inequality is not only acceptable but also a natural and self-evident truth.

For the landless Ju/'hoansi in the Omaheke, by contrast, the most obvious and unacceptable form of inequality is material inequality. This is not an ideological position so much as a practical one. !A/ae Langman's older brother, Kan//a, put it this way to me soon after his arrival at Skoonheid in late 1995: "I don't know what this freedom is. As long as we have no land and no life on our own, we are nothing. We will always be under the Herero and Boers. They can do what they want . . . they can cheat us and hit us and we must just say, 'Yes, *baas*,' 'No, *baas*.' Even here the government administrator tells us she will chase us away if we don't do what she says."

Kan//a, like many others, simply couldn't imagine how it was possible for people to be "equal" in any fundamental sense if some were so much richer than others. To him material equality was a precondition for equality in other respects.

The kind of egalitarianism practiced by hunter-gatherers was not born of the ideological dogmatism that we associate with twentieth-century communism or even the starry-eyed idealism of New Age "communalism." Rather, it was the outcome of interactions between people acting explicitly in their own self-interest in a highly individualistic society. This was because, among foraging Ju/'hoansi, self-interest was always policed by its shadow, jealousy, and jealousy in turn ensured that everyone got their fair share.

Jealousy was the "invisible hand" of the Ju/'hoan social economy. Yet it exerted its influence very differently from the "invisible hand" famously imagined by Adam Smith in *The Wealth of Nations*. For Smith, man "intends only his own gain," but in doing so he is guided by an invisible hand "to promote an end which was no part of his intention." And this, according to Smith, is to promote the interests of society more effectively than man could, even if he had intended to. Smith believed that trade and enterprise in pursuit of personal enrichment and unburdened by regulatory interference ensured the fairest and most effective "distribution of the necessaries of life" and so advanced the interests of society. As much as the inequality associated with unfettered capital growth suggests that the reason Smith's hand is invisible is because it isn't there, the metaphor continues to be invoked by enthusiastic advocates of the free market and repackaged as trickle-down economics.

Yet, ironically, hunter-gatherer egalitarianism suggests that even if Smith's hidden hand is nonsense, his belief that the sum of individual

self-interests can ensure the fairest distribution of the "necessaries of life"
was right, albeit in a very different way from how he imagined it. For
hunter-gatherers the sum of individual self-interest and the jealousy that
policed it was a fiercely egalitarian society where profitable exchange, hierarchy, and significant material inequality were not tolerated.

Jealousy accounts for most conflict among hunting and gathering
Ju/'hoansi, just as it accounts for most conflict in places like Skoonheid.
It squats quietly in the shadows of Ju/'hoan social life, only occasionally
reminding everyone of its presence when people argue or fight. To confine
jealousy to the shadows, Ju/'hoansi emphasize the importance of good
manners and cheerful banter just as they go to considerable lengths to
avoid giving others cause to feel aggrieved.

———

Ju/'hoansi are not alone in their aggressive rejection of hierarchy. This
deep sense of egalitarianism is so widespread among hunter-gatherers that
it cannot simply be dismissed as an arbitrary cultural trait. Egalitarianism
played a role in ensuring that the Khoisan became the most stable population group in human history just as it must have played a role in enabling
Homo sapiens to expand so rapidly and easily at the expense of other
hominids elsewhere. And despite the fact that most of us live in economically stratified societies, there is good reason to believe that we remain as
uncomfortable with gross inequality as our hunting and gathering ancestors were. We may find that describing this instinct in terms of jealousy
somehow diminishes it, for we have learned to think of jealousy as a sin
rather than a social regulatory force capable of extraordinary things. Yet, as
much as modern human history has been shaped by the pursuit of wealth,
status, and power, it has also been defined by popular movements determined to flatten established hierarchies. And as much as we sometimes
find pleasure in others' success, we often find just as much pleasure when
we see the successful stumble.

The extent to which relative inequality still gets under our skin was well
illustrated recently by the various "Occupy" movements that sprung up in
global capitals after the economic upheavals that marked the end of the first
decade of the new millennium and still rumble on in various diffuse forms.

These movements were initially dismissed by their detractors for lacking a unified ideological platform. Interviews with "occupiers" yielded contradictory, speculative, and sometimes bewildering responses expressing a general dissatisfaction with the world and the urge to "eat the rich." But this was because the Occupy movement defined itself by standing against many things while standing for nothing in particular. In the end, this ensemble of discordant voices found episodic moments of harmony around the rallying call of "We are the 99 percent!"—a slogan that captured one thing they could all agree on: they were all angry about what they saw to be rampant material and social inequality.

What was particularly striking about the Occupy movement's focus on inequality was that few of the occupiers were particularly preoccupied with poverty in any absolute sense. Their beef was with relative poverty. In basic material terms, the countries where Occupy movements flourished are among the world's richest. Being among the poorest in any first world country now does not bear easy comparison with being among the poorest in the same country one hundred or even fifty years ago or with being among the poorest in a "developing" economy.[2]

———

Egalitarianism is often assumed to imply an absence of private property. And it is widely believed that because hunter-gatherers like the Ju/'hoansi were egalitarian, they had no sense of property ownership at all. If everything is shared equally, so the reasoning goes, then how can anything be owned? It is this idea more than any other that makes God-fearing free marketeers denounce communists and socialists as dangerous crackpots. This idea also continues to be glibly invoked by those who have claimed Bushman lands as their own across southern Africa. If the Bushmen have no sense of ownership, how could taking their lands be theft?

But as much as Ju/'hoansi may well nod in agreement with Karl Marx's belief that private property is a precondition for inequality, they would also find common cause with advocates of free markets in considering the absence of private property to be insane. Private property plays an important role in Ju/'hoan social life, because without it there would be no reason to share. For the Ju/'hoansi, the challenge of avoiding inequality did not require the abolition of private property; it just required thinking about private property slightly differently. As far as they and many other hunter-gatherers were concerned, private property in itself is not what's problematic—it's the desire to needlessly accumulate private property or to control its production and distribution.

In part this is a practical issue. With no permanent homes, the need to move camp as many as ten times in a year, and no option but to carry all their individual possessions when they did, having too much stuff was quite literally a drag for hunter-gatherers like the Ju/'hoansi. Men typically only ever owned their clothing, blankets, hunting kits, and a few small odds and ends, like musical instruments. Women only ever owned their clothing, digging sticks, and jewelry. Yet these objects were owned individually and absolutely. Theft from one another was considered unconscionable, but covetousness was considered natural. After all, if people did not own things and others did not covet them, where would the joy be in giving or receiving? And without the joy of giving and receiving gifts, how would one demonstrate friendship, respect, or love?

———

The act of giving or receiving a gift usually provided Ju/'hoan hunter-gatherers much more pleasure than the gift itself. This is true in most hunting and gathering societies. And while gift giving no longer plays the same important role it did when they still hunted and gathered, it still gives Ju/'hoansi great pleasure today.

Before they were dragged into the expanding settler economy based on labor exchange, gift giving was the only form of delayed exchange between Ju/'hoansi, and it didn't happen between just anyone. Gifts were given to reaffirm bonds between individuals and were always expected to be reciprocated, but never immediately, because doing so would have made it a trade. Over their lifetimes, foraging Ju/'hoansi usually developed many formal gift-giving relationships, which they called *hxaro* (generosity) partnerships. Most were within their individual bands or with people in neighboring bands, but almost everyone had gift-giving relationships with a few people from distant bands. Young Ju/'hoan adults usually had around twelve to fifteen gift partners, older adults double that number. Traditionally the most popular gift items were ostrich eggshell jewelry, arrowheads, spears, music instruments, and knives.

Nowadays, few Ju/'hoansi in the Omaheke have any *hxaro* partners at all. And in Nyae Nyae, people have far fewer *hxaro* partners and afford these relationships far less importance than they did in the past. But among hunting and gathering Ju/'hoansi living in small, mobile bands, gift-giving networks formed a spiderweb of invisible pathways along which various items moved, linking people to others across and even beyond Nyae Nyae. And because gifts received from *hxaro* partners would almost inevitably be regifted to another *hxaro* partner elsewhere, the movement of individual items described in real time the shifting movements of friendships that made up the broader Ju/'hoan social universe. These networks also meant that materials from beyond the Kalahari, like ironware and pottery, found their way into the isolated center of Nyae Nyae by the eighteenth century.

As much as it was impossible to hide a new gift in the close-knit world of a Ju/'hoan band, gift giving was done discreetly. Unlike in most farming and industrial societies, where gift giving can be as much a public demonstration of wealth and power as an act of affection, Ju/'hoansi gave gifts solely to reinforce friendships. The logic behind showing discretion when giving gifts was not to conceal the gift or the relationship but to ensure that the process did not give immediate cause for jealousy. Presenting a gift with undue fanfare would inspire the same sort of derision as a hunter bragging about his prowess. In presenting one another gifts, Ju/'hoansi were unconcerned with the equivalence of the gifts themselves. There was also no agreed way of measuring the respective values of, for example, an ostrich eggshell necklace relative to a leather blanket. But then again, in the world of Ju/'hoansi, the minute something became a gift, it became equal in value to all other gifts.

As in many other hunting and gathering societies, Ju/'hoansi felt comfortable asking others for things they wanted and usually expected their requests to be accommodated—a behavior anthropologists have referred to as "demand sharing." Demand sharing did not lead to a free-for-all that ended up undermining any sense of private ownership at all. Instead, demands for individual objects were usually—though not always—carefully considered and were often invoked either as part of an existing gift-giving relationship or sometimes to initiate one. And, just as frequently, gifts were often given in anticipation of someone's demand for a gift.

Anthropologists have often focused on the strategic benefits of gift giving and have proposed that hunter-gatherers like the Ju/'hoansi establish gift relationships specifically to expand the network of people they can depend on when times get tough. They have also pointed out how these relationships help individuals to build quiet influence in societies where there are no formalized leadership roles.

Among foraging Ju/'hoansi, gift-giving relationships certainly extended sharing networks that helped reduce risk. They also built strong bonds between people in different bands that ensured that they would help one another during tough times. But the intimate and private nature of these relationships always meant that these relationships were more affective than strategic, because socializing and visiting friends was for many Ju/'hoansi the single greatest source of joy in the world. As Thai Dam, one of /Engn!au's fellow Old Timers, explained, "If you have friends to laugh with wherever you go, even if you are hungry, you can have a happy heart."

Anthropologists have often been reluctant to write about amorphous ideas like happiness. Instead, in a reflection more of their own societies, they have tended to make sense of human motivations in terms of their strategic economic and material benefits. But well-established social networks built on strong, emotionally fulfilling relationships are widely recognized as one of the most important determinants of happiness. Psychologists, philosophers, and even animal behaviorists have long been aware that strong social networks generate contentment and that the social atomization that characterizes contemporary urban life is a path to misery. For Ju/'hoansi and other hunter-gatherers like them, these cooperative networks were underwritten by affection and maintained by jealous egalitarianism.

PART THREE

New Times

14

When Lions Become Dangerous

Twyfelfontein lies in a wide, open valley of broken red sandstone flanked by weathered hills and peaks. It looks like a place that only scorpions could call home. Yet it hosts a well-established population of desert-adapted rhino, elephant, giraffe, zebra, and even lion. When Africa and South America formed a single vast continent, this dry valley was the site of a shallow lake system. The lakes are long gone but water still bubbles up gently from a spring at the foot of the valley. Several hundred miles to the west of Nyae Nyae, Twyfelfontein is one of the driest parts of Namibia. As a result, this small spring has been a magnet for life here for thousands of years. Archaeologists have found evidence of human settlements dating back six thousand years, but it is almost certain that Twyfelfontein's human history stretches back much further.

Now a world heritage site, Twyfelfontein attracts a steady trickle of tourists. Some camp at the community-run campsite, but most stay at a fancy lodge nearby where they can wallow in a swimming pool, sip cold beer, and imagine what it must feel like to be truly thirsty in an environment like this.

It is not too hard to find giraffe, zebra, or elephant in the vicinity of Twyfelfontein if you have the energy, but the lions may as well be ghosts. They exist mainly as disembodied UHF blips emitted from the radio collars that have been bolted around their necks by the predator researchers keen on keeping tabs on their whereabouts. But there is one old lion in Twyfelfontein with very distinctive paw prints that is easy to find, even though he does not have a radio collar. That is because, like the giraffe and warthog standing just behind him, he is a petroglyph carved into a flat panel of red sandstone.

At first glance all the animals carved into this rock panel appear as they should. But on closer inspection there is something wrong with the lion. Like domestic cats, lions have eighteen claws. Four on each of their hind paws and five on each of the forepaws, although the small fifth-thumb claws on their forepaws sit high above the ankle and serve no obvious purpose. This means that when lions leave paw prints in the sand, these only show four distinct toe prints. The Twyfelfontein lion's head and torso are presented in profile but each of its paws have been carved in the shape of paw prints. And on each paw print there are five very distinct claws where there should only be four. As if to ensure that this anomaly doesn't go unnoticed, the artist also went to the trouble of carving five additional toe prints in orbit around the brush at the tip of the lion's tail. The reason for this is because this is not a picture of an ordinary lion but of a shaman that has transformed himself into a lion.

Lions appear infrequently in the thousands of Bushman rock art tableaux elsewhere in southern Africa. Yet, before the arrival of farmers determined to protect their livestock, lions along with humans were the most obviously successful, adaptable, and widespread of all local predators. There were few habitats where the social and versatile lions could not make a good living. Along with humans, they sat comfortably at the top of the food chain.

No wild lions roam the Omaheke now. The only lions left in this part of the Kalahari are those that dreamlessly pace back and forth behind the wire-mesh fences of a local predator sanctuary. Despite this, most Ju/'hoansi in the Omaheke are still reluctant to refer to lions by the proper Ju/'hoan word for lion, *n!hai*. Instead they refer to them as *ju'm*. Using the real word for lion, *n!hai,* I was warned, was dangerous, because "a lion might think you are calling it to kill you." Why specifically did they use the word *ju'm*, then, I inquired of /Engn!au. What else did it mean?

"When you say *ju'm*, it sounds like you are saying the word for human, *Ju,* and this confuses the lions if they hear it," he explained. "But," he added, the reason Ju/'hoansi referred to lions as *ju'm* was because "some lions are also humans."

Over and above the possibility that a lion may be a human, Ju/'hoansi considered lions to be among the most humanlike of all animal-people.

The similarities were obvious. Lions lived in extended family groups and had distinct territories that often overlapped individual Ju/'hoan bands' territories. Also like people, lions were social and affectionate with one another, liked to sing in the night, and loved to eat meat. Ju/'hoansi were quick to note there were many big differences as well. Male lions were often bullies, think nothing of killing other lions' young, and were very hierarchical. And of course, among lions, females were hunters too.

Some Khoisan peoples, like the Hai//om, who lived adjacent to the great Etosha salt pan far to the west of Nyae Nyae and whose ancestors were almost certainly the artists responsible for Twyfelfontein's petroglyphs, considered lions to be their closest kin in the animal world. Unlike the lions in Nyae Nyae, the lions in Etosha lived in large territorial prides that preyed on the herds of game that flock to Etosha's waterholes in the dry seasons. Hai//om considered the lions to be co-owners of their territories. Despite the Etosha lions' reputation for aggression, Hai//om oral histories tell of a peaceful accord with them. They also speak of how it is easy for a male human hunter to be seduced by a lioness and persuaded to join their world as a lion-person and how many shamans could transform into lions at will—hence the Twyfelfontein petroglyph with its humanlike digits. The Hai//om's kinship with lions was grounded in the obvious similarities between the species and the fact that lions lived in far greater numbers around Etosha than they did in places like Nyae Nyae.

Ju/'hoansi did not have quite the same intimate relationship with lions as Hai//om. But they too considered lions to be tolerable neighbors on account of a timeless accord that enabled them to peacefully share water, space, and meat with each other. The Ju/'hoansi's accord with lions, like that between the lions of Etosha and the Hai//om, was in essence a non-aggression pact grounded in the shared knowledge that both lions and humans were perfectly capable of killing each other. Thus lions would not hunt people and people would not hunt lions. Tsemkxao ≠Oma of the /Gautcha eloquently explained the fundamental logic of the pact to Elizabeth Marshall Thomas in the 1950s. He explained that where lions were hunted, they were dangerous to people. But where lions were not hunted, they were not dangerous to people. To maintain this accord, Ju/'hoan hunters occasionally left a small portion of an animal they had killed as a share for the lions if they were nearby. Likewise, once lions had enjoyed a good feed from a kill, they occasionally let Ju/'hoansi approach and take a portion of the carcass for themselves. In practice, chasing lions off a kill when they are too full to put up a fight was pure opportunism and something done only by the most experienced Ju/'hoan hunters. Hunters in eastern Africa regularly did this too, but Ju/'hoansi described it as an act of sharing.

The peaceful accord between Ju/'hoansi and lions in Nyae Nyae did not survive John Marshall's efforts to persuade the Ju/'hoansi to begin farming cattle in the 1980s. The arrival of nearly a hundred slow, docile, meaty beasts in Nyae Nyae proved too difficult for the local lions to resist. After all, their accord was with the Ju/'hoansi, not cattle. The /Gautcha community was the first beneficiary of the cattle fund set up by John Marshall in the mid-1980s. In 1987 the /Gautcha community lost nineteen head of their small herd to lions despite having taken careful steps to protect them. When other villages were also provided with cattle, lion raids increased and Ju/'hoansi grew increasingly worried about a species with which they had coexisted for millennia. Some demanded that the Nyae Nyae Conservancy issue them guns. But others were profoundly disturbed by the idea of hunting the lions. If people continued to fight with lions, they reasoned, going into the bush to hunt or gather would become dangerous.

Wildlife officials in Tsumkwe refused to help, so Ju/'hoansi took matters into their own hands to protect their livestock. One man speared a lion to death as it clung to the belly of his cow. Another shot and killed two lions with poisoned arrows. Another village that participated in the livestock program attracted so much attention from lions that the villagers decided to abandon both their cattle and their village and move to the relative safety of Tsumkwe.

The conflict with the lions came to an abrupt end after Nyae Nyae's lion population collapsed in the 1990s, after the arrival of nearly two thousand Herero on Nyae Nyae's southern border. These Herero were much more experienced cattlemen than the Ju/'hoansi and, like generations of farmers before them, they considered lions to be vermin.

———

Nyae Nyae's southern boundary is marked by a large and furious-looking "veterinary" fence. It runs for several hundred miles in a ruler-straight line from east to west until it slams into the border with Botswana. Its current function is to control the movement of animals and in doing so prevent the transmission of livestock diseases. Its unspoken purpose—when it was erected, at least—was to stop the free movement of people. Marking the boundary between "Bushmanland"—centered on Nyae Nyae—and Hereroland to the south, the fence bisects what was once the territorial heartland of the Nyae Nyae Ju/'hoansi.

Today there are thousands of acres of rich grassland and healthy acacia forest on the Nyae Nyae side of the fence. But on the Hereroland side much of the grassland has been replaced by miles of sand and desert scrub punctuated by a few disconsolate trees under which gaunt, dry-uddered cattle whisk flies from their eyes.

The area immediately south of the fence is called G/am by the Ju/'hoansi and Gam by everyone else. G/am is the site of a permanent waterhole. It was once the heart of a Ju/'hoan band's *n!ore* and, in dry winter months, hosted several other Ju/'hoan bands from *n!ores* that had only seasonal water sources. By the 1950s the waterhole at G/am was used by a handful of adventurous Herero and Botswanan farmers, who, having struggled to find adequate water and grazing on the Botswana side of the border, used it periodically as a seasonal cattle post.

With good water and rich vegetation in the adjacent *omiramba*, G/am was once prime hunting territory not only for the Ju/'hoansi but also for other predators. When I first visited there in 1994, the plains around G/am were still home to a free-running pack of African wild dogs, many hyenas, and occasional leopards and cheetahs. It also formed part of the range of several young male lions and a solitary scowling patriarch whose face bore the scars of battles with younger males that periodically tested his strength.

Now, nearly a quarter of a century later, G/am has been transformed from a remote waterhole into a dusty rural hamlet with its own simple amenities and, since 2013, electricity generated by a solar array secured in a razor-wired compound. Most of the hamlet's 1,800 residents are Herero repatriated to Namibia in 1993 after nearly a century of exile in Botswana. Several Ju/'hoansi still live in G/am. They herd Herero cattle and do odd jobs in return for milk, porridge, alcohol, and small change.

There is also no obvious sign of the predators that once thrived in the bush around G/am save the occasional cackles of hyenas at night and the odd paw print in the sand. Nor for that matter is it easy to find any obvious traces of the kudu, oryx, springbok, eland, and hartebeest that they used to prey on. Instead the desert sand near G/am is patterned with the spoor of cattle, goats, dogs, and people.

The fate of G/am's predators was similar to that of Europe and America's wolves when they too were forced to share their worlds with farming peoples.

———

The Herero were once the most powerful of precolonial Namibia's peoples. Their oral historians tell of how they migrated from the Great Lakes region of eastern Africa "many hundreds of years ago," eventually arriving in Namibia with their cattle sometime around the seventeenth century. Once there, they displaced established hunter-gatherer populations and claimed much of the central spine of the country as their own. As pastoralists they were highly mobile, and as their herds expanded they extended east and west across Namibia in search of new grazing and water. Some Herero took their cattle northward and eastward up the *omiramba* that led into the Omaheke and beyond into Nyae Nyae. But there was little water, and the Ju/'hoansi there were far from welcoming. The Herero, for their part, took the view that these Ovakuruha (First People) were more dangerous than others they encountered and that these areas were best avoided.

But as the nineteenth century drew to a close the Herero had more to worry about than unwelcoming Ju/'hoansi in Nyae Nyae and the Omaheke. Not only had a plague decimated their cattle wealth but the Germans, who had established a foothold for themselves on the Namibian coast a few years earlier, were now beginning to behave as if they were in charge.

While Britain, France, Holland, Portugal, and later King Leopold II of Belgium were carving up Africa among themselves during the first three quarters of the nineteenth century, Prussia and Bavaria were too busy squabbling over how to consolidate the German Reich to think about grabbing some African colonies for themselves. So it was only after German unification in 1871 that the significance of being left out of the largest land grab in human history dawned on them. The first chancellor of the new Reich, Otto von Bismarck, was skeptical about the value of colonies. But the German press and public were not. So he bowed to public pressure and the German colonial project began in earnest.

In 1882 a German guano tradesmen named Adolf Lüderitz purchased a stretch of Namibia's bleak southern coastline from a local chief. Two years later Bismarck offered him state protection, thus staking formal claim for what soon became Deutsch-Südwestafrika: German South-West Africa. The other colonial powers sniggered quietly among themselves. As far as they were concerned, the Skeleton Coast's only value was as a place to abandon mutinous ship hands in the certain knowledge that they would starve if they didn't die of thirst first.

The Germans set about using their coastal territory as a springboard to launch themselves deeper into southern Africa's interior. After forging several additional treaties with various local chiefs, several of whom were Herero, they declared the entire coast from the Kunene River on the Angolan border in the north to the Orange River in the south a German protectorate. Within a decade their influence had spread as far inland as Gobabis. But German colonial ambitions were not satisfied by merely having a firm foothold in Namibia.

In 1903 the Kaiser resolved that it was time to extend German sovereignty into the lands of the then dominant Herero. To this end he dispatched ten thousand of Germany's finest *Schutztruppe* to South-West Africa under the command of General Lothar von Trotha, a man with a simple approach to dealing with those who stood in the way of his and Germany's colonial ambitions.

"I wipe out rebellious tribes with streams of blood and streams of money," Trotha proclaimed. "Only following this cleansing can something new emerge."

Trotha quickly engineered a war. Following a series of skirmishes and a siege in which he rained cannon and mortar fire on Herero in their Waterberg heartland, Herero resistance broke. But Trotha did not consider his work done quite yet. He wanted South-West Africa "cleansed" of Herero and so he initiated what is widely regarded as the first systematic program of ethnic genocide of the twentieth century.

"The Herero must leave the land," he demanded. "If they refuse, then I will force them to do it with the big guns. Any Herero found within

German borders, with or without a gun, will be shot. No prisoners will be taken. This is my decision for the Herero people."

Under a hailstorm of German mortar and cannon fire and pursued by a cavalry of *Schutztruppe*, the Herero fled into the vast waterless Kalahari in the hope of reaching Bechuanaland and British protection three hundred miles to the east. Hundreds followed the Eiseb Omuramba that led them through G/am and into Botswana. Herero oral histories lament the many hardships they endured as they fled across the desert, leaving a trail of corpses behind them. Those Herero who remained behind were either put to the sword or herded into grim concentration camps, the most notorious of which was Shark Island. On this single guano-bleached outcrop off the Namibian coast, an estimated four thousand Herero men, women, and children starved to death. For their part, the Germans gathered the corpses for science, with the pioneering eugenicist Dr. Eugen Fischer being the principle beneficiary of this grim harvest. Dr. Fischer made extensive use of this material in his magnum opus, *Principles of Human Heredity and Race Hygiene*, which he published in 1921. Fischer's book proved popular in postwar Germany and won him a number of high-profile fans, none more so than Adolf Hitler, who found inspiration in its pages while kicking up his heels in Landsberg Prison following his failed putsch in 1923. Such was Hitler's admiration for Fischer's views on racial purity that, once he had assumed the German chancellorship, he immediately appointed Fischer to the prestigious post of rector of Berlin University.

After Namibia achieved its independence from South Africa in 1990, the new government invited the descendants of Herero who fled to Botswana to return to Namibia. Many accepted the offer.

The Herero returnees were allocated G/am as a resettlement area, largely because there was nowhere else in Namibia where so many people could be accommodated. With the returnees came their cattle, the animals by means of which they expressed their wealth, identity, and status. Tradition dictated that Herero should never sell cattle inherited through their paternal line. These cattle embodied their ancestors. To sell them for profit was to prostitute their lineage. To consume them merely for pleasure was tantamount to cannibalism. These animals could be slaughtered only to mark solemn occasions that materially transformed a lineage: a marriage, a birth, a coming of age, or a death. Cattle inherited through the maternal line or purchased could be given away or exchanged, but as a rule people were reluctant to do so. And among the community of Herero returnees that had spent eight decades living in poverty as exiles in western Botswana, the sanctity of their tradition was no laughing matter. For these immigrants, who were determined to restore their ancestral roots in Namibia and had little else of value, their cattle meant everything.

But once the first two thousand head of their cattle had cleared quarantine, the returnees were confronted by a serious problem. The lions and other predators in G/am cared little for Herero lineages or tradition.

To make matters worse, the arrival of the Herero and their cattle in G/am coincided with the start of a three-year drought that sucked the life out of the northern Omaheke. Government and aid agencies mobilized to drill new boreholes for them, but as a young herdsman explained, "Cattle cannot eat water." In a single short year, grasslands were picked clean by thousands of hungry cattle long before anyone even dared mention the word "drought." The Herero's goats climbed into the lower limbs of the camel-thorn trees to pluck dark moist leaves from between their branches, and the cattle abandoned their vegetarianism to suck phosphates from the dried bones of fallen comrades, gnaw on twigs, or eke imaginary sustenance from brightly colored plastic bags, discarded clothing, and other refuse.

Many starved. Others were poisoned by the green leaves of the *gifblaar* (poison leaf) and the flowering bulbs of the *slangkop* (snake's head). These deep-rooted plants are well adapted to drought and rise like floral sirens from the soil in spring whether it has rained or not. As the drought wore on, those cattle that survived ceased wandering in search of grazing and instead waited hollow-eyed in the hope that their masters would conjure up some greenery from the soil. Their masters in turn loitered at ministerial extension tents waiting for word of when the trucks bearing bales of alfalfa that the government had promised would arrive.

And as they waited, lions, hyenas, and other predators helped themselves. Far fewer cattle were actually killed by predators than died of disease, starvation, or eating poison plants. But Kalahari predators are not particularly fussy about where their meat comes from, and they happily scavenged any carcasses they encountered. Finding predator footprints in the sand led the Herero to conclude that the lions were killing their cattle.

The Herero immigrants were accustomed to the uncertainties of life in this desert. But like others frustrated by problems far beyond their control, they conjured up proximate and manageable causes for their misfortunes. In G/am it was the predators, rather than the rain gods, that became the locus of their frustrations.

In the Herero settlers' minds the dangers posed by the predators assumed mythological proportions, amplified by the roars of the lions and the whoops of the hyenas that filled the night air. But hunting predators without appropriate permits is illegal in Namibia. So the Herero set about protecting their herds in secret. Where fresh lion, hyena, or leopard tracks were found, the animals were quietly tracked down and then shot. But the main approach they took to managing the predator problem was far less discriminate. They simply poisoned the carcasses of dead animals and left these for the predators—and anything else that stumbled across them, from jackals to vultures—to consume.

In eradicating local predators, the Herero settlers were doing something that farming peoples across the globe had done since the invention of agriculture. And that involved reconceptualizing elements within it in terms of the benefits they offered or the risks they posed. Unwelcome elements, like lions, wild dogs, and hyenas, were classified as pests.

———

Now, two decades after arriving in G/am and with their predator problem dealt with, the Herero still covet the rich grasslands of Nyae Nyae and occasionally cut holes in the veterinary fence to sneak their cattle into Nyae Nyae. The Ju/'hoansi have had to rely on police intervention and assistance from a local legal charity to protect their lands, but even with their help stopping the trespassing has proven difficult. Nyae Nyae is far too large an area for the small local police contingent to patrol, and few Ju/'hoansi are willing to testify against the Herero or even report these incursions when they happen. A number of recent inexplicable illnesses and deaths in Nyae Nyae have been attributed to Herero witchcraft, and this has persuaded all but a few of the Ju/'hoansi to keep their mouths firmly shut.

As far as the Ju/'hoansi are concerned, Herero witchcraft is just another illustration of the contempt that Herero have shown Ju/'hoansi ever since they first encountered one another.

"When the Herero see Ju/'hoansi, they just see nothing," explained a *n!orekxausi* of a southern Nyae Nyae village. "They just think we are animals in the bush drinking wildebeest milk. To them it is nothing to take our land and our blood." In the past, when Ju/'hoansi resisted Herero intrusions, retribution was often brutal. These conflicts took place far from administrative centers, and few were ever reported to authorities. One of the few incidents that ever attracted the attention of the authorities was a case in 1947 where twenty-four Herero men were found guilty of butchering and then defiling the corpses of two adult male Ju/'hoansi, two adult female Ju/'hoansi, and seven Ju/'hoan children in revenge for the death of a Herero boy who was killed by a poison arrow. One Herero oral historian told me how his ancestors thought nothing of killing Ju/'hoansi and other Bushmen whenever the opportunity arose. He took the view that the German genocide and later the suffering that the Herero experienced under apartheid was God's way of punishing them for all the Bushmen they had killed.

To the Ju/'hoansi, the threat of Herero witchcraft had obvious similarities to the fate of G/am's lions. Poisoning and witchcraft were both means of delivering death by deception, and no Ju/'hoan doubted that Herero considered Ju/'hoansi to be no more deserving of life than any other form of "vermin."

The relationship between Herero and Ju/'hoansi in G/am and Nyae Nyae was typical of the kinds of relationships that evolved between established hunter-gatherer populations and farming peoples whenever they encountered one another, from the Americas to Southeast Asia. Wherever these encounters occurred, farming societies expressed their derision for hunter-gatherers in similar terms. They used words like "wild," "savage," "dangerous," "animal-like," and "primitive" to refer to the hunter-gatherers and to justify their genocide and the conscience-free colonization of their lands.

15

Fear and Farming

There was a biblical quality to the Herero repatriation to G/am. This fact was latched onto by a local "prophet," a man appropriately called Josepha. He had a "hotline" to God and for a negotiable fee could also cure AIDS, reduce your blood pressure, issue a bespoke curse, and procure magical remedies that would empower prisoners awaiting trial to outtalk magistrates and thus avoid lengthy sentences. Some considered Josepha to be a con man, but others took the view that he was indeed a conduit to the Christian god. He told me how the Herero returnees at G/am were nothing less than the ancient Israelites returning to the Promised Land after enduring so many decades roaming in the wilderness.

Whether Josepha had the hotline to God that he claimed or not, there was more to his comparison of the Herero returnees with the fabled Israelites than a sense of biblical destiny. Both were communities of subsistence farmers trying to carve out lives in marginal environments where their ability to deal with predators and other pests could be the difference between success and failure. And, as subsistence farmers, both communities were far more vulnerable to famine, chronic nutritional privation, and environmental shocks than hunter-gatherers.[1] Both communities also believed humans to have been created by God in His image and to have been granted a divine mandate to tame and shackle an otherwise hostile wilderness. This was because both communities were the progeny of the Neolithic Revolution—the extended moment in time during which groups of people in different parts of the globe adopted farming and in doing so reconfigured their relationships with the natural world and ushered in the Anthropocene. For if our physiology is a legacy of our hunting and gathering past, much of what we do and how we think about our place in the world stems from our relatively short history as farmers.

No one can be certain quite what persuaded the first groups of hunter-gatherers to abandon hunting and gathering and commit themselves to a life of toil in the fields.

It is unlikely that the originators of the Neolithic Revolution shared a spontaneous epiphany and suddenly set their minds and bodies to the problem of domesticating various plant and animal species. This transition must have happened over many generations. It is also almost certain that the first farmers did not consciously embrace agriculture so much as inadvertently become dependent on it as a result of a convergence of climatic and environmental factors.

Whatever the immediate catalysts were for this change—and there must have been many—the shift from hunting and gathering to farming occurred independently in several different places. Populations in and around the Tigris and Euphrates floodplains were the first to transition from hunting and gathering to agriculture around 10,000 years ago when they began to cultivate grains and pulses and to domesticate sheep, goats, and pigs. Then, around 8,000 or 9,000 years ago, foragers in the Yangtze and Yellow river basins in eastern Asia started to farm rice, millet, pigs, and silkworms. They were followed over the course of the next five thousand years by New Guinea highlanders—who domesticated bananas and sugarcane—and Native Americans, who began to cultivate corn, beans, and manioc. And finally, perhaps 4,000 years ago, people living in central and western Africa began to cultivate sorghum, yams, and palms.

Wherever it became established, agriculture spread far and fast beyond its points of origin. Because domesticated plants and animals thrive under a relatively narrow range of environmental conditions, agriculture first spread latitudinally. And as it spread, progressively more plant and animal species were found to be suitable for domestication. At the same time, those species that had already been domesticated became incrementally more productive as farmers, sometimes unconsciously, selected the strains

that suited them best. Six thousand years after the first farmers planted
fields in the Fertile Crescent, agriculture was the dominant form of economic
activity throughout Europe and central Asia.

Around 12,000 years ago, cyclical shifts in the orientation of the earth's
axis brought the last ice age to an end. Its departure was marked by several
thousand years of climatic volatility capped off by a millennium of rapid
global warming that left the planet almost 5 degrees Celsius (9 degrees
Fahrenheit) warmer and considerably wetter than at any point in the
preceding 120,000 years.

For the Khoisan and others living in subtropical latitudes, these climatic
shifts must have been challenging, but they did not pose an existential
threat. However, for hunter-gatherers in the northern hemisphere, where
the end of the ice age catalyzed far-reaching environmental changes, this
would have been a very difficult time: many of the plants that they traditionally used to fill their bellies disappeared as the climate transitioned to
warmer and wetter conditions, rendering much of their locally acquired
botanical knowledge redundant. At the same time many once prolific
mammal species in Europe, Australasia, and the Americas fell into terminal
decline. Larger mammals, like mammoths, saber-toothed cats, and short-
faced bears, that were particularly well adapted to colder conditions,
perished.[2] And as keystone species, their disappearances catalyzed other
changes to their environments. The disappearance of mammoths in Siberia
and Alaska resulted in the resurgence of woodlands (which the mammoths
had previously pruned and cleared), which led to further temperature rises
because the forest trees' dark leaves absorbed more solar radiation than the
dull khaki grasses that once dominated the landscape. And these changes,
in turn, created a range of entirely new habitats in which different, better-
adapted plant and animal species thrived.

It is unlikely that northern hemisphere hunter-gatherers would have
been able to get by on only fifteen hours of work per week during this
period. Famines would almost certainly have been more frequent, and
entire communities must have perished on occasion. To survive during
this unpredictable time would have tested the limits of their resilience and

resourcefulness. Unable to rely only on established food sources, hunter-gatherers navigating rapid climatic and environmental change would have had to experiment with new ways of making a living. So where Ju/'hoansi in the twentieth century saw little point in exposing themselves to the dangers of hunting big, dangerous animals like elephants for food, hunter-gatherers trying to survive changing climates and environments may well have taken risks that they previously wouldn't have considered to be reasonable. Risks like hunting mammoths.

Hunting dangerous creatures like mammoths in turn would have required that groups of people find new ways of cooperating with one another and working as teams. It would also have required them to experiment with new and often complex ways of processing unfamiliar plants in order to make them more palatable and easier to store. This is likely the period when they worked out that pounding otherwise indigestible grains like wheat or toxic tubers like cassava into fine powders, mixing them with water, and then cooking them might make them edible.

Confronting the problem of scarcity in a once benevolent environment also would have challenged the hunter-gatherers' sense of cosmic order. Where deities and spirits once interacted with people as moral equals, people now looked to them for help. There is good evidence to suggest that a series of giant limestone pillars (a construction of a scale usually associated only with farming societies) decorated with carvings of wild animals in Göbekli Tepe in modern-day Turkey was constructed by hunter-gatherers just before or during the transition to agriculture. Among the ruins archaeologists found traces of wild grains and nuts as well as the bones of gazelle, wild cattle, and wild pigs. But they found no evidence of the domesticated animal species that characterize early Neolithic archaeological sites nearby. The site has been dated to around 9600 BCE, several centuries before agriculture really took off, suggesting that here, at least, hunter-gatherers began to adopt some of the cultural forms that would in time help them embrace the possibility of manipulating their environments to help their survival.

It is also likely that this transition to agriculture was pushed along by a far greater emphasis on food storage by hunter-gatherers, whose confidence in their environment's providence would have been severely dented by climatic upheavals. Whereas they were once certain that their environment would always be able to deliver something of use, they must have started to worry that if they had food today, there was no guarantee that there would be food the following day, week, month, or year. In circumstances like these, it is hard to sustain an immediate-return economy, and they would have gone to much greater efforts than they had in the past to preserve or store foods for later consumption. This practical measure alone would have started to transform the way hunter-gatherers experienced and understood time, because in storing surplus foods their economic efforts became increasingly focused on meeting future as much as present needs.

At the same time, the environmental and climatic changes in the northern hemisphere created just the right conditions for a few plant species in localized geographies to generate unusually abundant yields. In the Fertile Crescent, the progressive shift to a warmer climate transformed what had previously been a cold steppe ecosystem into a warm savanna ecosystem in which wild grains like barley and wheat as well as legumes and pulses thrived, yielding far more food than other sources.

Hunter-gatherers are opportunists. So when a particular plant or animal species presents itself in unusual abundance, they make use of it. And if by chance the food source responds well to accidental interventions—maybe the inadvertent pruning of a tree to gain access to a fruit or nut—there is no reason to think that hunter-gatherers would not intentionally intervene that way in the future.

If the manketti trees, so important to the hunting and gathering Ju/'hoansi in Nyae Nyae, had become even more prolific as a result of a climatic quirk, or become more productive as a result of pruning, the Ju/'hoansi may have gradually increased their dependency on them, built permanent homes nearby, chased off other animals with a taste for nuts, and begun to manage and nurture the trees. And if this happened over a period of several generations, it would have helped them develop a more detailed knowledge of manketti husbandry and harvesting. It might also have suggested to them that some other Kalahari plants might be responsive to a similar treatment.

If evolutionary success is judged on the basis of a species' ability to reproduce, then aiding the expansion of Homo sapiens over the past ten millennia was a golden ticket. The plants and animals that became staples for farmers are now among those that future archaeologists will conclude dominated the earth along with humans during the Anthropocene. Cattle, goats, sheep, dogs, cats, poultry, rice, wheat, and maize are now ubiquitous even in habitats where they could never have survived without the assistance of humans.

Today's intensive farming techniques are extraordinarily productive.[3] Now fewer than 2 percent of Americans employed in agriculture are able to feed everyone else in the United States—and have plenty left over for export. But the productivity of modern farming techniques conceals just how precarious life was for small-scale farmers less than a century ago and how precarious it remains for subsistence farmers in many developing countries today. This is particularly true for subsistence farmers in more marginal environments—people like Herero pastoralists and Kavango millet farmers on the fringes of Nyae Nyae.

Both hunter-gatherers and farmers are susceptible to short-term "seasonal" food shortages and occasional famines. Just as hunting and gathering Ju/'hoansi grumble about losing weight in the late dry seasons, so rural subsistence farmers everywhere expect to go hungry for the period when food stored from previous harvests runs low but new season crops are not ready for harvest. Among both farming and hunting and gathering societies, seasonal weight loss at these times of year can stretch to as much as 7 or 8 percent of body weight—more than enough to impact on their fertility and sense of general well-being.

But over longer periods of time than a single seasonal cycle, farming societies were much more likely than hunter-gatherers to suffer severe, recurrent, and enduring famines.[4] Hunting and gathering is a low-risk way of making a living. Hunter-gatherers hedge their bets by relying on many different potential food sources and so can capitalize on an environment's own dynamic responses to periodic droughts, floods, and other climatic anomalies. The 125 different edible plant species utilized by Ju/'hoansi in Nyae Nyae all have slightly different seasonal cycles, respond differently to different weather conditions, and occupy specific environmental niches.

Some are more drought-resistant than others, some are more responsive to excessive rainfall, some cope better with exceptional cold, and others with exceptional heat. This means that when the weather proves unsuitable for one set of species, it is likely to benefit another. When you add hunting into the mix, this hedge becomes even more successful. While a severe drought will drastically reduce the total yields of some of the most important food plants in the Kalahari, it also usually makes hunting and scavenging easier, because animals' conditions decline, they become less alert, and they congregate closer to permanent water points or scarce food resources. Thus, among the foraging Ju/'hoansi, meat typically made up a larger proportion of people's diets during "lean months" than in good ones.

But in agricultural societies that depend on only a few staples, when there is not enough rain or rivers run dry, then harvests inevitably fail. And if a harvest fails and insufficient contingency has been made by setting aside food from the previous season or by having a sufficiently sophisticated exchange network to procure food from elsewhere, then famine is inevitable. This doesn't only apply to droughts. Most farmed plant species tend to be quite fussy and sensitive to pests. They only do well when they have just the right amount of rain at precisely the right time, just the right soil, and just the right amount of sunshine. Too much or too little of any of these may not necessarily result in a famine, but it will lead to a disappointing harvest.

As important, the amount of work farmers have to do tends to be inversely proportional to the favorability of the elements. If there is not enough rain, not only will crop yields be lower, but a farmer will have to work even harder to produce anything at all. Similarly, because most agricultural societies have until recently relied on only a small number of specialized crops or animals, a single disease outbreak can be catastrophic as it spreads rapidly through densely planted fields or herds of livestock living cheek by jowl. Just such a catastrophe, the rinderpest (morbillivirus) epidemic of the late nineteenth century, still looms large in the collective memory of the Herero just south of Nyae Nyae and shapes the almost pathological fear of livestock diseases throughout southern and central Africa.

An infectious viral disease like measles with a mortality rate of nearly 90 percent among cattle populations with no immunity, the rinderpest scythed its way through the herds of southern and eastern Africa's pastoralists during the 1890s. Also carried by wild animals like buffalo, giraffe, and warthogs, the rinderpest spread rapidly across the continent. Having already caused catastrophic famines in Ethiopia and Tanzania, the rinderpest reached the Kalahari in 1896. Within six months, two-thirds of all Herero cattle perished and the Herero economy imploded. With their cattle wealth destroyed, Herero social structures, which were so intertwined with the health of their cattle, began to collapse, and once rich and powerful families found themselves suddenly as "impoverished as Bushmen." To make matters worse, the arrival of the rinderpest was followed by a rapid succession of human plagues that found willing hosts in the immune system–suppressed bodies of malnourished Herero. These included typhoid, malaria, and anthrax, the latter most likely nurtured by the piles of rotting cattle flesh that littered the countryside. To contemporary Herero oral historians unwilling to assign blame for their exile to the capriciousness of their precolonial leaders or the overwhelming power of German cannons, if it wasn't for the rinderpest, the Herero would never have capitulated to the Germans or been the victims of the first great genocide of the twentieth century.

Livestock perishing in biblical numbers as a result of plagues like the rinderpest was not the only viral peril farmers faced. Living in such close proximity to increasingly intensively farmed animals meant that some livestock diseases adapted to human hosts. Our historic love affair with beef brought us tuberculosis and measles, and our hankering for bacon and chicken wings ensures that every once in a while we are hit with terrifying new strains of influenza. These diseases hit early Neolithic populations particularly hard, because they were on the whole poorly nourished compared to hunter-gatherers. This was not only due to occasional poor harvests but because their diets tended to be dominated by only one or two usually carbohydrate-rich crops that produced systemic vitamin and mineral deficiencies.

The vulnerability of agricultural societies to famine, disease, and natural disasters meant that the expansion of the Neolithic was punctuated by catastrophic societal collapses. Genetic histories of modern European populations point to just such a series of catastrophic collapses that coincided first with the Neolithic expansion through central Europe around 7,500 years ago and then later with the Neolithic expansion into northwestern Europe about 6,000 years ago. These collapses may have been caused by disease. The mortality rates associated with them were between 30 and 60 percent, a proportion roughly equivalent to mortality rates associated with the Black Death that stalked Europe in the fourteenth century. But the early Neolithic populations in Europe were small and spread out. This would have made it hard for plagues to be transmitted widely. Rather, it's more likely that these deaths came about as a result of unsustainable farming practices, an overreliance on a small number of plant and animal species, and a couple of years of unfortunate weather—perhaps a sustained drought, too cold a winter, flooding, or a combination of all three.[5]

If hunter-gatherers like the Ju/'hoansi maintained an unyielding confidence in the providence of their environments, then Neolithic farmers' lives were fraught with fear: fear of droughts, blights, pests, thefts, raids, strangers, famines, wars, and eventually taxes. So when harvests didn't fail and all was well, farmers celebrated their good fortunes often by sharing the rewards of their labor in the form of sacrifices and tributes to often capricious gods.

As vulnerable as they must have felt, Neolithic farmers did not consider themselves to be completely at the mercy of the gods. They had a strong sense of themselves as being at least partially the authors of their own destinies. If they did things right, they could minimize the risks that fed their fears. This meant pleasing the gods in the conduct of their day-to-day life but above all it meant working hard to make the land productive. In this sense they assumed some of the responsibilities of their creator, as if deputized to complete their work on earth, a motif common to many of the organized religions that emerged out of agricultural societies. But where gods created universes, humans worked on smaller canvases, like homes, gardens, villages, pastures, and dams—spaces where the forces of nature were kept at bay and in which the wild was made tame.

It is no coincidence that agricultural metaphors pepper the holy texts of the great religions. Judeo-Christian texts in particular are littered with parables and stories in which fields, farmers, domestic animals, harvests, and shepherds take center stage. And as if to remind us of the fears associated with agricultural disaster, the eventual fate that awaits humankind according to the Christian Bible is a harvest in which the "wheat of the blessed will be gathered into God's storehouse and the chaff of the damned cast into eternal fire" (Matthew 3:12).

Where hunter-gatherers considered themselves to be part of their environments, farming societies saw their environments—or at least parts of them—as something separate from themselves, something manipulable. Once humans conceptually separated themselves from their environments in this way, it made sense that they started to reorganize and reclassify the world around them in terms of their ability to exert their control over it. To them, all the world was a "wild" and "natural" and often dangerous space when left to its own devices. And while farmers recognized that they depended on their ability to harness natural forces, they also took the view that where nature intruded unbidden into domesticated spaces, it became a pest. Unwanted plants growing in a plowed field became weeds, and unwanted animals partial to a farmers' grains or preying on his livestock were declared vermin. The conceptual separation farming communities made between the natural/wild and the human/cultural worlds was so widespread that for a long period social anthropologists believed it was a human universal.

But the conceptual separation of the human and natural worlds was rarely absolute. All farmers understood that land left untended and uncared-for would inevitably be rewilded. They also realized that some wild lands and some wild animals were more resistant to domestication than others. In the Fertile Crescent, where many plant and animal species were appropriate for domestication, the division between nature and culture became deeply embedded over time. But in the tropics of Africa, South America, and eastern Asia, only a handful of local plants and even fewer animals were domesticable. As a result, many of these societies acquired most of their protein from hunting and so often viewed their animal neighbors in a way similar to that of hunter-gatherers.

Modifying, constraining, and controlling an environment requires lots of work—far more so than hunting and gathering. Fields need to be cleared, furrowed, and fertilized even before seeds are planted. After that, seedlings need to be watered, weeds weeded, and growing plants protected from hungry birds, insects, and—in places like the fringes of the Kalahari—hungry elephants. And finally, crops need to be harvested and facilities created for their storage and preservation, by which time the annual work cycle begins again. Over and above this, farming also makes numerous secondary demands on people's time. So when work in the fields is done, tools need to be made and mended, and farm structures built or maintained. And on top of all that, farmers need to perform ordinary everyday tasks, like looking after infants, preparing food, and maintaining their homes. Just as importantly, because farming generates harvests season-ally, storage vessels and systems also need to be built and other foods have to be preserved for consumption until the next harvest.

The almost universal belief now that hard work is a virtue is perhaps the most obvious of the Neolithic Revolution's many social, economic, and cultural legacies. There are few societies on earth where work is not consid-ered as fundamental a part of our humanity as our desire to reproduce or our need for companionship. In many societies it defines who we are and almost everywhere it dominates politics. In advanced economies, the airwaves are packed with the rhetoric of politicians and ordinary people alike invoking the virtues of "strivers" and "working families" and decrying the laziness of "shirkers" and "freeloaders." And in most less-developed economies, consultants and experts of all kinds spend their energy devel-oping policy briefs and grand plans to create jobs. Almost everywhere full employment remains an ideal for politicians of all shades, among whom fears of rising unemployment invoke the specter of electoral defeat. It is no wonder, then, that John Maynard Keynes believed that our desire to solve the "economic problem" was not only "expressly evolved by nature" but was the sum of "all our impulses and deepest instincts." He just failed to recognize that economics became a problem only with the transition to agriculture and that our preoccupation with solving this problem was a consequence of our ancestors' having created it in the first place.

If the agrarian equation between hard work and prosperity is an enduring legacy of the Neolithic Revolution, it is not the only one. For the additional demands of labor, coupled with increased productivity, laid the conceptual foundations of an economic model that inspired the likes of da Gama and Dias to sail south and still shapes our ongoing preoccupation with productivity and trade. It did so by making hard work into a virtue and transforming time into a commodity, objects into assets, and systems of exchange into commerce.

16

Cattle Country

It is difficult to ignore the life-size statue of a bull that stands sentinel on a ten-foot-high redbrick plinth at the town limits of Gobabis, the dusty capital of Namibia's Omaheke Region. The bull faces eastward, looking longingly toward the savanna, while his impressive testicles point downward to white lettering proclaiming this to be CATTLE COUNTRY.

Appropriately for a region now scarred by tens of thousands of miles of barbed-wire fences, the statue was surrounded until recently by a protective halo of razor wire. This security measure was installed following the casual castration of the bull late one night by children from the local high school. That the town council acted so determinedly to protect the bull's testicles from further molestation was no surprise. Gobabis remains a racially divided town in many ways. But the one thing that unites Gobabis's two dominant groups, the white Afrikaans-speaking ranching community and the pastoralist Herero, is their shared love of cattle. Both were equally outraged by the emasculation of their bull and set aside their differences to save its gonads from further harassment.

The statue on the plinth is of a white Brahman, a cattle breed for which Gobabis is now internationally renowned. The dewlap that hangs like a rough-cut leather blanket from the bull's chin and neck and the large hump that squats above its shoulders show that the Brahman is the product of a different lineage from many of the cattle breeds most familiar to Europeans and Americans. Brahmans are hardy and tolerant of heat, and they are resourceful foragers when grazing is poor. Introduced to Namibia in the 1950s, the white Brahman has been carefully interbred with other cattle breeds in the hope of creating a hybrid particularly well adapted to the challenges of Kalahari life.[1]

All cattle trace their ancestry from a species of prehistoric long-legged mega-cattle called aurochs, the subjects of the mesmerizing life-size rock paintings in the Lascaux cave's Hall of the Bulls in southwest France. The last known auroch died in 1627. But, around a quarter of a million years ago, vast herds of auroch grazed plains stretching across Europe, Asia and northern Africa. They became so successful and widespread that in time they evolved into several geographically distinct breeds. One of these breeds, the *Bos taurus*, which spread from northwestern Africa through Europe, was the species domesticated by early farmers in the Fertile Crescent. Its genes still run strong in many European cattle breeds like the Aberdeen Angus, the Friesian, and the Iberian fighting toro. The genes of another subspecies of auroch, the *Bos indicus* (sometimes referred to as zebu), which were domesticated in central Asia around eight thousand years ago, are responsible for the distinctive physical characteristics of breeds like the Brahman, with their fatty humps and regal dewlaps.

The cattlemen's eventual conquest of this part of the Kalahari may have taken place many millennia after the first farmers in the Fertile Crescent sowed their first seeds, but it is very much part of the same chapter in human history. The story of this conquest helps us to make sense of how and why the Neolithic Revolution expanded far beyond the places it began, eventually converging on the Kalahari some ten millennia later. It also reveals the extent to which so many of our contemporary social, cultural, and economic institutions were shaped by the legacy of the agricultural revolution.

———

Early Neolithic farmers had one massive advantage over hunter-gatherers. When the stars were in alignment, the weather favorable, the pests subdued, and the soils still packed with nutrients, farming was very much more productive than hunting and gathering. This enabled farming populations to grow much more rapidly than hunter-gatherers and sustain these growing populations with less land.

But even the most hardworking early Neolithic farmers learned to their cost that the same patch of soil could not keep producing abundant harvests year after year. Some worked out that circulating crops and leaving fields fallow helped restore productivity, but for most the progressively declining soil productivity required that they find new land to cultivate every few years. Early herders made even greater demands on land than horticulturalists. Where an acre of land planted with wheat in the Fertile Crescent might have generated enough grain to feed a large extended family for a year or more, the same acre of land would be unlikely to sustain a single goat, let alone a herd, for more than a month or two. So, as farming populations grew, so did their demands for space.

Early Neolithic farmers wanting to grow their way to prosperity had only a few options available to them. With necessity spurring the need for invention, the challenges of farming awakened in them a willingness to embrace technical innovation. Where hunter-gatherers' technologies had been gradually refined over hundreds of generations to meet timeless challenges, farmers were confronted by the need to develop new tools to meet novel challenges ranging from irrigation to the chemistry of food preservation. Thus, the early Neolithic saw the invention and widespread use of a whole range of transformative new technologies, like hoes, spades, ceramics, bricks, metalwork, and, in time, the wheel.

The development of new problem-solving technologies was not an overnight process. It depended on the incremental accumulation of experience and knowledge blended with occasional moments of innovation, luck, and plenty of experimentation. Inventing some great new technology was hardly a viable option for already emaciated people contemplating an anemic field of failed wheat.

Where successful hunter-gatherer societies maintained their egalitarianism by avoiding surpluses and the social pressures they placed on them, successful farming societies did the opposite. At first, surpluses offered some security against the risk of famine and disaster. Surplus food safely stored might mean the difference between life and death in a bad year. But in time farmers came to see surpluses as tangible rewards for their labor, which developed in them a sense that they had "earned" their rewards. They were also tantalized by the idea that sufficiently large surpluses might eventually purchase them freedom from a life of toil in the fields.

The development of new technologies and methods to preserve foods enabled farmers to create tangible "wealth" even if they didn't think of it in precisely those terms. And in storing food they were also storing labor. For as much as a basket of grain represented the prospect of several satisfactory meals in the future, it also represented the sum of effort that was required to fill it, from the preparation of the field and planting of the seeds to the threshing of the harvest. And because of this, labor itself came to be thought of as something that could be exchanged.

Inevitably the Neolithic Revolution spawned myriad different systems of exchange to enable the flow of surpluses between people. And while all systems of trade and exchange developed by farming societies ultimately enabled the movement and accumulation of physical goods, they also dealt with other, less tangible facets of human life like prestige, love, access to the heavens, and luck. Those societies that developed the most effective systems for creating, managing, and distributing surpluses grew the fastest and became the most influential. And inevitably others began to adopt their successful ways.

Regular surpluses enabled a much greater degree of role differentiation within farming societies. Initially these roles would have almost been all agricultural related: priests to pray for good rains, fighters to protect farmers from wild animals and rivals, toolmakers to provide implements, builders to provide accommodation and food storage, and butchers to process livestock products. Societies that became productive enough to support many more people than were needed to work in the fields became highly differentiated and saw the emergence of tradesmen, priests, mongers, accountants, and specialist artisans. Here surpluses were transformed into debt, wealth, and money, and, for those who controlled their distribution and circulation, power.

———

The spread of farming was unlikely to have been driven solely by adventurous farmers inspired to find new territories just for the hell of it. In some places the expansion would have been organic and prompted by incremental population growth over successive generations. But the largest and most dramatic expansion were almost certainly driven by competition for resources, because where there was no room for growth, the only other option was to find new productive land.

The aggressive expansion of Neolithic peoples is revealed in the archae-ology and genetic history of early Neolithic societies as well as more recent documented history. Comparisons of DNA extracted from the skeletons of Europe's early farmers with the DNA of Europe's various hunting and gathering peoples shows that farming did not spread because hunting and gathering populations were persuaded to adopt agriculture by their more productive neighbors.[2] Instead it shows that hunting and gathering populations were typically displaced by aggressive farmers seeking new lands. While the genetic data offers only a soft-focus picture of the history of the Neolithic expansion, it suggests that Neolithic farmers expanded from the Middle East into Europe around nine thousand years ago following a maritime route through Cyprus and the Aegean Islands. Once estab-lished in the south of mainland Europe, farming peoples expanded farther westward and northward, eventually coalescing into a series of distinct agrarian societies. And if the evidence of how hunter-gathers in the nine-teenth and twentieth centuries were treated by farming peoples is anything to go by, it's almost certain that this process involved a lot of bloodshed.

The spread of farming across Africa followed a similar pattern to that of early Europe. But in Africa's case it resulted in the descendants of a single distinct human lineage colonizing almost all of central and southern Africa over a period of two thousand years. This population group is now referred to as "Bantu," a linguistic term derived from the root word *ntu* (people) in the 650 or so closely related modern Bantu languages. Up until recently, hypotheses about the timing and routes of the Bantu expansion relied on an incomplete patchwork of unreliable oral historical, linguistic, and archae-ological evidence. Now genetic affinity studies have helped establish a clearer picture of the Bantu expansion.

These studies point to the verdant Cross River valley on the Cameroon-Nigeria border as the likely epicenter of Africa's own Neolithic Revolution. With no domesticable grain species like wheat or corn, the first farmers there focused their energies on cultivating yams. Even though they did not have access to as diverse a set of domesticable plant species as farmers in the Fertile Crescent, Africa's Neolithic population grew rapidly and from around seven thousand years ago expanded northward and westward. The descendants of this migration formed what linguists now refer to as the Niger-Congo language group.

Then, beginning around 5,500 years ago, one of the Niger-Congo groups, the Bantu, expanded eastward, following savanna corridors between rain forests. In doing so they laid the foundations for a series of distinct social, cultural, and economic dynasties. The expansion happened in two phases. The first flowed eastward toward the Great Lakes region in Africa's Rift Valley around three thousand years ago. It was here that Bantu were introduced to new technologies and other domesticated plant species by other farming peoples with Asiatic roots. The Bantu expansion flowed southward, with groups breaking off and settling pretty much everywhere that was not hostile to agriculture, like deserts and rain forests.

———

Around 850 CE, the Bantu expansion ground to a halt near the banks of the Great Fish River in what is now South Africa's Eastern Cape Province. By this time Bantu in different parts of the continent had coalesced into hundreds of fluid yet distinct peoples, each with their own particular customs, dialects, and laws. But because they shared similar languages, technologies, and economic practices with their neighbors, these groups merged and split over time, creating a succession of new communities, civilizations, and kingdoms.

There is no reason to believe that Khoisan didn't live in many of the areas of southern Africa that we now associate almost exclusively with Bantu peoples: countries like Malawi, Mozambique, and Zambia. But if Khoisan ever did live there in large numbers, they left few obvious archaeological traces beyond some rock art panels. Genetic studies reveal traces of Khoisan ancestry in the DNA of people living in these countries now, but not as much as one might expect if these populations had merged.

However, in some other parts of southern Africa now associated almost exclusively with Bantu civilizations and societies, there are more obvious signs of Khoisan history. Beyond a wealth of archaeological sites predating the Bantu expansion and the hundreds of galleries of rock art and petroglyphs in South Africa, Zimbabwe, and Namibia, Khoisan in southeastern Africa inscribed their presence deep into the cultural memories of some Bantu peoples like the Zulu and Xhosa, South Africa's two most powerful civilizations during the early colonial era. As much as the Zulu and Xhosa peoples were almost certainly as contemptuous of hunter-gatherers as other pastoralists, the interactions between them and Khoisan populations were intense and enduring enough for the Zulu and Xhosa to integrate some of the click consonants peculiar to the Khoisan languages into their languages.

The cultural and linguistic influence of Khoisan on peoples like the Zulu and Xhosa raises some interesting questions that remind us of the limitations of what we can infer from genetic research. They also raise the possibility of other, more unexpected linkages between Khoisan and other peoples. By the time Europeans landed on the Cape, many Khoisan there roamed the plains with herds of fat-tailed sheep and cattle in tow. And like their Bantu neighbors to the north, they were dedicated, affectionate, and diligent herdsmen who named their cattle individually. In the absence of any concrete data, the established presence of Khoisan-language-speaking herders in southern Africa in the second millennium has led to much theorizing. Some have argued that these Khoisan groups vacillated between herding and hunting and gathering. Others have postulated that these herding populations were immigrants from eastern Africa. For others the simplest and easiest explanation is that some of the Khoisan groups that lived in close proximity to Zulu and Xhosa adopted herding by way of a sort of cultural osmosis.

Recent genomic studies of the descendants of the cattle-rearing Khoisan, most notably the Nama of South Africa's Western Cape Province, reveal a small component of their ancestry is the result of direct gene flow from eastern African peoples like the Masai. Significantly, some of these genes relate to the ability to process lactose—and so the ability to consume large quantities of cow's milk. This raises the possibility that a small group of Afro-Asiatic pastoralists from eastern Africa migrated southward with their livestock hundreds of years in advance of the main Bantu expansion. This group was then assimilated into a Khoisan hunter-gatherer population that subsequently adopted a quasi-pastoralist lifestyle and moved into the Cape, laying the foundations for a distinct herding tradition among several Khoisan groups.[3]

Archaeology indicates that the pioneers of the Bantu expansion probably reached the fringes of the Kalahari sometime between 1,500 and 1,200 years ago. This is also roughly when geneticists calculate the first— and in many cases the only—distinctly Bantu genetic markers entered the gene pools of some San in the central and eastern Kalahari.[4] And to these pioneers the Kalahari must have appeared an inhospitable place, so much so that they were not tempted to venture beyond its fringes. The same geological and climatic quirks that enabled the Khoisan to flourish there for nearly a hundred millennia made it distinctly hostile to the early ambassadors of the Neolithic Revolution. To the north of the central Kalahari lay the last of the great Kalahari wetlands, the Okavango Delta. At first it must have looked appealing to farmers, like a great floodplain fringed with papyrus. But it soon proved otherwise. The patchwork of reed beds and sandy islands were infested with tsetse flies, mosquitoes, and disease-bearing parasites that were hostile to livestock and humans alike. And the waterways that connected them were patrolled by territorial hippos and some very big crocodiles. To this day the soils in the delta still frustrate even the most sophisticated agriculturalists armed with the latest irrigation technologies, specially selected seeds, and fertilizers.

So instead farmers established small villages on the edges of the Kalahari, where they grew crops and raised cattle. Bosutswe in eastern Botswana was one such village. It was established around 700 CE and was settled almost continuously until the sixteenth or seventeenth century. Glass beads, copper jewelry, and clay artifacts unearthed by archaeologists point to the links between places like Bosutswe and the Bantu civilizations that established complex city-states in places like Mapungubwe in South Africa and Great Zimbabwe at the turn of the first millennium. But for all its long history, Bosutswe, and villages like it, would have remained remote provincial outposts and their inhabitants would have looked eastward beyond the sunrise for trade, inspiration, and news.

Over the millennium that followed, the residents of villages like Bosutswe must have ventured occasionally into the desert. During sustained periods of good rainfall it would have been hard to resist. Brief summer rains produce a sea of long green grass interspersed with hardwood forests. But every time they did so, a dry cycle inevitably kicked in. In response they fled the desert, perished where they were, or surrendered to circumstances by abandoning their herds and adopting the ways of those who had been living in the desert successfully for millennia: the Bushmen. Again, it is the DNA of Khoisan that provides the best evidence of these incursions. A marker in the genes of some Ju/'hoansi points to a single significant Bantu incursion twelve hundred years ago that was sustained enough for strangers to do what they do when they don't fight: they make children. But the precision of this marker also points to the brevity of this genetic incursion and the fact that it ultimately ended in failure. The Bantu disappeared within a very short period of time and left few obvious material traces of their presence or the livestock they brought with them. Markers in the genes of other Bushman groups living closer to farming settlements, like the G/wikhoe of the central Kalahari or the Hai//om of northwestern Namibia, show much more recent and extensive evidence of gene flow with Bantu from places like Bosutswe.

In the end, the challenge of finding enough water for cattle in the Kalahari, like so many obstacles that stalled the advance of agriculture and commerce, was cracked by technology. By midway through the nineteenth century, the pressures of an ever-expanding European colonial presence across southern Africa had already forced some pastoralist peoples to try their luck herding along some of the Kalahari *omiramba* and in areas like Ghanzi, where a limestone ridge cut through the sand overburden, creating a series of easily accessible natural wells. But as abundant as the grazing was, there was seldom enough water in the dry seasons to make permanent settlement in much of the Kalahari a serious option.

But as difficult as it is to find, there is much more water in the Kalahari than the Bantu who wanted to graze their cattle there in the nineteenth century could ever have imagined. It is secreted in giant aquifers beneath tens and sometimes even hundreds of feet of sand. As inaccessible as most of this water was to those who could dig with only their hands or simple shovels, it was not beyond the reach of the Industrial Revolution's engineers. Over the course of the nineteenth century, drilling technology moved in leaps and bounds. Simple percussive drills that could hammer narrow holes into the ground had been in use since the 1800s in Europe and America (and many centuries earlier in China). These cleverly geared machines were powered first by hand, later by horse, and eventually by steam. They could drill over three hundred feet into the ground and had already been used to open up much of the midwestern United States to farmers. These drills were first brought to South Africa by miners in the mid-nineteenth century but were quickly adopted by farmers. And within a few years they were replaced by the even more powerful rotary drills, which cut rather than hammered their way into the earth and were powered by the ever more versatile and portable internal combustion engines.

With the ability to drill for water in even the driest parts of the Omaheke, the fate of many Ju/'hoansi was sealed. For as much as they were able to drive out small groups of Herero wanting to make use of a handful of waterholes, they could only be a nuisance to well-resourced and well-armed farmers, soldiers, and policemen determined to claim this land for themselves and their livestock.

———

For Ju/'hoan women in the Omaheke, the crunch of rotary drills cutting through the sand in pursuit of water during the 1930s and 1940s portended much more than just the arrival of farmers and their cattle.

When they still foraged independently, Ju/'hoansi, like most other well-documented hunter-gatherers, defined gender roles very clearly. But they were adamant that gender differences were no grounds to assert the superiority of one gender over the other. Individual charisma, strength of character, persuasiveness, common sense, and humility were much more important factors in an individual's influence within a band than his or her genitals. Both men and women could be healers and both could be *n!orekxausi*, the holders of inheritance rights to any particular territory.

Traditionally Ju/'hoansi also did not make a tremendous fuss about weddings or, for that matter, divorces. While monogamy was the norm amongst Ju/'hoansi, people occasionally entered polygamous relationships. These raised few eyebrows, even though to most Ju/'hoansi the idea of having two or more spouses and sets of in-laws to deal with at any one time sounded horrible. Parents sometimes took an active role in discussing the suitability of a union but were never in a position to overrule the wishes of their children. Ju/'hoansi were also not particularly prescriptive about what constituted a "good" marriage beyond the fact that it should be loving, a man should provide meat, and a wife should gather. Violence was considered an obvious and sensible reason for a woman to abandon a man, and infidelity by either party was likewise seen as a good reason for a couple to split. Unburdened by the pressures of conforming to any established rules beyond the gender roles that existed outside of marriage and with no single partner wearing the trousers, many Ju/'hoansi cheerfully maintained monogamous relationships until death. And when a couple divorced, the emotional turmoil of the event was rarely if ever amplified by a sense of social failure.

Gender equality in hunter-gatherer societies also just made sense in terms of the practicalities of making a living. Men and women both played important roles in food provision, and it was plainly obvious that when making decisions about when and where to camp, both men and women offered perspectives that needed to be taken into consideration.

Traditional Ju/'hoan views on gender relations, however, would not endure long after the arrival of white farmers.

White farmers in the Omaheke desperately needed Ju/'hoan labor, and the kind of laborer they wanted was male. A Ju/'hoan laborer's female dependents might be given some domestic tasks to do, but more often than not they were simply expected to sit in the workers' compounds and not make trouble. In the early days of white settlement, Ju/'hoan women occupied themselves by gathering. But since they were not able to move between camps on the farms, all bush foods within a reasonable distance of the workers' compounds were quickly exhausted. And, just as importantly, farmers now provided them with bags of cheap and easy-to-make carbohydrate-rich corn porridge, so they often had just about enough to eat. With no productive roles on the farm other than making babies, minding children, and preparing meals for their families, Ju/'hoan women found themselves suddenly marginalized even within their families. More than this, they became dependent on males for food in their bellies and places to stay. Farmers had no reason to accommodate "stray" women with no clear links to their laborers.

Another problem was that white farmers, like the Herero, had their own particular views about appropriate roles for Ju/'hoan women that were often spiced up by fantasies regarding their sexual availability. Several farmers in the Omaheke informed me without batting an eyelid that "Bushman girls" were incapable of resisting a male's sexual advances when they were "on heat" or that they were required to make themselves permanently sexually available to Ju/'hoan men.

Some farmers took Ju/'hoan women as secret concubines and "paid" for the sexual favors they received with food or clothing. In rare instances unlikely and ultimately doomed love affairs blossomed. Some Ju/'hoan women and girls were raped by farmers, knowing that they were powerless to do anything about it. The evidence of these liaisons is still scattered throughout the Omaheke in the form of individual Ju/'hoansi with blue or green eyes, straight hair, big noses, and pale skin. And in almost every event—in particular during apartheid—farmers never acknowledged paternity. Instead, pregnant and sometimes nursing mothers would be hastily removed to places where the evidence of the farmers' indiscretions would not be around for their wives, their families, or government authorities to see. Under apartheid, interracial sexual liaisons were not only socially unacceptable, they were illegal. For Ju/'hoan women in Herero villages things were arguably even worse. It was not unusual for Herero men to regard Ju/'hoan women as little more than sexual objects. Rape was commonplace and sexual favors were often exchanged for alcohol or food, as still often happens today.

Herero and white farmers' views on gender roles were also a product of the Neolithic Revolution, a process that sowed the seeds of modern patriarchy.

With the shift to agriculture, gender roles changed dramatically. Tasks immediately related to production probably played only a minor role in this transition. In productive terms alone, subsistence farming does place a slightly higher value on male brawn simply because of the energy input involved in some farming-related tasks. Thus, societies with roots in "plow agriculture," which required significant upper-body strength, are typically more patriarchal than those that prepared their fields with equipment like hoes that were wielded just as effectively by women as men.[5]

But making a living from farming involved much more than hefting heavy rocks and digging furrows. It involved many tasks in which strength did not really make a meaningful difference—tasks like toolmaking, food storage and preparation, livestock herding and rearing, sowing seeds, and harvesting. There was plenty of work for everyone regardless of gender.

With an increased workload came an increased emphasis on making babies, who in time could also be put to work. The increased demands for infant care meant that women focused on jobs that could be undertaken while nursing at or near the home, like processing cereals, making clothing, preparing food, and mending tools. This resulted in the development of the almost universal association of women with domestic spaces and men with outside "public" spaces in agricultural societies. In and of itself, this wouldn't make a difference if it were not for the increased productivity that farming created and the risks and fears that haunted farmers' dreams.

Increased productivity also meant larger, denser communities. And larger, denser communities enabled more complex, often hierarchical social institutions to manage behavior, distribute resources, and manage risks. Tethered to their domestic duties, women typically had fewer opportunities to participate in ever more important public spaces. At the same time competition between households, villages, or even coalitions of villages for resources like land placed a far higher premium on the distribution of resources and correspondingly the ability to organize, lead, and project influence whether by means of persuasion or, as often as not, the ability to make war—a task to which men were far better suited. And the locus for the evolution of social life to do this was inevitably the male, public world. As a result, over time, while the male-dominated public realm grew in importance and complexity, women remained largely confined to their homes, where they had no option but to exercise their influence indirectly through their male kin.

In all farming societies, social and political power was ultimately shaped by the flow of goods and resources between people. Among Africa's pastoralists, like the Herero, cattle became the primary form of wealth and the number of wives a man had became the primary expression of that wealth, with women being exchanged for cattle in the form of a brideprice. Among European and Asian societies, exchange relationships became increasingly characterized by more symbolic tokens representing credit and debt—which, by the time da Gama and Dias sailed around the Cape—had taken the form of coinage. And, like the cattle the farmers brought with them, the introduction of money into places like Nyae Nyae would also pose extraordinary challenges to the Ju/'hoansi.

17

Crazy Gods

In July 2003, G/au ≠Oma¹ died while out checking his guinea fowl traps. It was a while before anyone realized he was missing, as he was known to take his time when he wandered into the bush beyond Tsumkwe's litter-ridden town lands. Like many other Ju/'hoansi in Nyae Nyae, he had been suffering from a virulent, drug-resistant form of tuberculosis that had been slowly transforming his lungs into a spongy mess of blood and mucus. But unlike the many other Ju/'hoansi in Nyae Nyae to die from TB, G/au's death was "news." Over the next few weeks obituaries for G/au were published in esteemed publications across the world. These included the *New York Times* and the *Washington Post* in the United States, the *Telegraph* and the *Times* in the UK, and most major non-English papers in mainland Europe and Southeast Asia.

This was because for much of the 1980s G/au was a bona fide, honest-to-God global movie star whose name and picture appeared in lights above cinemas from Los Angeles to Laos. The source of his fame was one of the most unexpected box office hits of all time, *The Gods Must Be Crazy*, produced by a small South African company called Mimosa Films. Originally made for an Afrikaans-speaking South African audience, it broke local box office records in 1980, the year of its release. It was subsequently dubbed into English and released internationally. First shown on only a few art-house screens in the United States, the movie soon started to play to full theaters as its reputation spread by word of mouth. Within a year it went mainstream and for a period would become the highest-grossing foreign film in American cinema history, where it remained on general release for three years. The surprise hit also attracted record audiences in France, Hong Kong, Taiwan, China, and Japan.

Keen to capitalize on its success, the film's writer, producer, and director, Jamie Uys, quickly penned a sequel. A clumsy rehash of the original, the sequel didn't do well and Uys sensibly retired from the movie game to spend his millions and wonder at precisely why his god had been crazy enough to make a low-budget comedic adventure with a Bushman lead generate such extraordinary box office receipts. With Uys out of the game, others picked up the baton and G/au subsequently starred in a series of increasingly bizarre spin-offs produced specifically for the East Asian market. This resulted in the release of a largely unwatchable trilogy: *Crazy Safari*, *The Gods Must Be Funny in China* (financed by the then avowedly communist government in Beijing), and *Crazy Hong Kong*.

The success of *The Gods Must Be Crazy* owed as much to Jamie Uys's undoubted skills as a director as it did to the fact that G/au, despite never having seen a movie before, was a natural big-screen performer. But it was the film's basic conceit—poking fun at modernity by portraying it from a hunter-gatherer's perspective—that lay at the heart of its appeal.

The Gods Must Be Crazy follows the adventures of a Ju/'hoan character, Xi, played by G/au, as he journeys in search of the "edge of the world" to return an unwanted gift to the gods. The unwanted gift in question is a glass Coke bottle that was carelessly lobbed out of the window of a light aircraft flying high above the "remote" Kalahari, where Bushmen (according the story's avuncular narrator) "live in complete isolation, unaware there are other people in the world." The bottle is discovered by Xi, who takes it to the village to show to his family. Intrigued by this strange object, they quickly discover dozens of uses for it, from curing leather thongs to bashing tubers and making music. "It was harder and heavier and smoother than anything they'd ever known," explains the narrator. "It was the most useful thing the gods had ever given them, a real labor-saving device."

The problem was that there was only one Coke bottle. Soon "everybody needed it most of the time." In a world where there was plenty of everything and everything was always shared, scarcity in the form of an empty Coke bottle raises its ugly head and acquisitiveness, jealousy, and conflict follow close behind.

In case the audience might misinterpret this unsubtle subtext, the first ten minutes of the film are presented in documentary form. It contrasts the peaceful lives of the Bushmen with those of harried urbanites. As the narrator explains, the Bushmen "must be the most contented people in the world. They have no crime, no punishment, no violence, no laws, no police, judges, rulers, or bosses. They believe that the gods put only good and useful things on the earth for them. In this world of theirs, nothing is bad or evil . . ."

"Only miles to the south," the narrator continues, "there's a vast city. And here you find civilized man. Civilized man refused to adapt himself to his environment. Instead he adapted his environment to suit him. So he built cities, roads, vehicles, machinery. And he put up power lines to run his labor-saving devices. But he didn't know when to stop. The more he improved his surroundings to make life easier, the more complicated he made it."

Perhaps it was because the film was so intentionally lowbrow, packed as it was with obvious homages to the physical comedy of Buster Keaton and Charlie Chaplin, that the subversive message of the opening lines was cheerfully guffawed at by white South Africans, Americans, and others who in other circumstances frothed about the dangers posed by "Reds" and the "toxic" ideology of socialism.

Despite the fact that the film was arguably the most engaging—and certainly the most entertaining—portrayal of "primitive affluence," it did not win praise from anthropologists. Most struggled to see it as a work of fiction any less caricatured than the representations of American or European life in pretty much every other film playing concurrently with it when it was released in mainstream American cinemas in 1984: films like *Indiana Jones and the Temple of Doom* and *The Terminator*. Richard B. Lee was "appalled by its bald-faced misrepresentation of the contemporary San." He added that "to say that there are San today who are untouched by civilization is a cruel joke. The !Kung [Ju/'hoansi] San of Namibia where the film was made, have been subject to 25 years of forced acculturation and 10 years of wholesale recruitment into the South African army."[2]

Although it would be neither the first nor the last time that anthropologists would struggle to come to terms with the frothiness of Tinseltown publicity, their criticisms of Uys's willingness to merge fact and fiction in the film's promotional material were more pointed. Uys often claimed in interviews that he "found" G/au in the "remote bush" and that G/au had only ever seen one white man, a missionary, before Uys appeared. This was nonsense. Even setting aside the fact that there had been whites living in Nyae Nyae since McIntyre set up shop in Tsumkwe in 1961, G/au was working in the kitchens of the small school project at Tsumkwe when Uys first met him. Another criticism that anthropologists leveled at the film was that in showing people of all races and backgrounds engaging with one another as equals, it presented an idyllic view of a region still in the vise grip of a vicious apartheid regime. They were right, of course, but many others took a far more positive message from it. And that was that a racially and ethnically tolerant world was not only possible but infinitely more desirable than apartheid.

Despite the anthropological outrage, I am yet to meet a Ju/'hoan who didn't enjoy the film or who considered the representation of Ju/'hoansi in it as offensive. It was so popular in Tsumkwe that it was shown on an almost permanent loop on the TV in the Tsumkwe Self Help shop for nearly a decade.

After his film career came to an end, G/au preferred to keep to himself. I met him in 1998 when I was helping a film crew from Sony Pictures cast a Ju/'hoan child actor for a role in a big-budget Hollywood movie about Namibia's wild desert horses that would later be given the ultimate indignity of being released straight to video. I'd tracked him down to ask him if he would help explain what life on a film set was like to a young girl from Tsumkwe who was invited to join the cast.

I was also a little starstruck and brought him a bottle of Coke as gift. He accepted it without blinking.

By then G/au was living in a whitewashed brick house just off the main road in Tsumkwe. Even though it was relatively new, it already seemed threadbare. And like most other Tsumkwe Ju/'hoansi with brick and mortar houses, he spent very little time inside of it. Instead he preferred to live and sleep under the shade of his porch, using the interior mainly as a glorified storeroom.

G/au was born in Botswana but moved to Nyae Nyae as a child when there was no border fence between the two countries. He grew up in a village a few miles to the east of the giant baobab, the Holboom, before moving to Tsumkwe in the 1970s. Now that he had "retired," he lived more or less permanently in Tsumkwe. But, as he reminded me, pointing to his broken-down Toyota, for several years he was one of the only Ju/'hoan with his "own wheels" and so he could go to the bush to hunt anytime he wished. Beyond the vehicle, the bare cement walls of his house, and some assorted gadgetry, there was little to distinguish his life from those of others in Tsumkwe. He had acquired several cattle, but they hadn't done well: he wasn't a diligent herdsman and the lions had eaten most of them, he explained.

I asked him whether it was true that he was paid only $2,000 USD for his role in the original movie. G/au rattled off a surprisingly detailed account of his payments for *The Gods Must Be Crazy* and the sequel. These did not amount to a great deal, but it was closer to ten thousand dollars than two, and considerably more than that if the monthly "pension" he received from Uys's company, Mimosa Films, was taken into account.

But did he feel ripped off by Uys? I asked. After all, *Gods* made millions of dollars for Uys and his partners and that wouldn't have happened without him. He shrugged. Uys, who had died a couple of years previously, had been "his good friend" and "they had traveled far together." I later learned that G/au's financial affairs were still handled by Uys's former partner at Mimosa Films.

The only thing he had to say about his money was that having more than others meant that everybody was always accusing him of selfishness and demanded food, blankets, alcohol, and sweets from him all the time. So much so that he would sometimes just "walk into the bush to hide from them."

I asked about the film's publicity material and the story Uys often told about him never seeing a white man before he encountered Uys. Again he said he didn't mind. It was all part of the fiction of the film, as far as he was concerned—and, as fictions went, Uys's PR material was far less outlandish than that of some of the movies he'd subsequently starred in.

I would have liked to ask him more, but for some reason G/au and I didn't bond in the way I had hoped. Perhaps it was because I couldn't quite translate the character from the film into the person who was sitting in front of me. Perhaps it was because G/au had had enough of fans offering adulation and anthropologists telling him he should be outraged by his treatment by Mimosa. So we talked briefly about the girl and the plan for the movie. He said he knew who she was and promised to talk to her before the plane was sent to pick her up and fly her to the movie set just outside of Swakopmund on Namibia's coast.

I didn't bother chasing him down again on future visits to Tsumkwe. But we greeted each other cheerfully enough on the few occasions we ran into one another before his death. On our very last meeting, at the entrance to the General Dealer, he told me that he had recently been baptized by an Australian missionary who brought a swimming pool to Tsumkwe and "threw him in." He said that he felt better as a result of it and expected that his spirit would ascend into heaven when he died rather than loiter in Tsumkwe, making mischief among the living.

He died not long afterward. He was the first of several Ju/'hoan and Hai//om I knew who would find spiritual salvation in the church, only to drop dead a few months later.

The anonymity of G/au's death and the fact that he had died from a disease associated with poverty made me regret that I had not made more of an effort to learn his story, which now will forever be overshadowed by Xi's.

———

If G/au's dunking in a portable pool ensured that his spirit wouldn't linger around to haunt Ju/'hoansi living in Tsumkwe, then fictional Xi's ghost almost certainly still does. It reveals itself in the sometimes too obvious disappointment of tourists who arrive in the town expecting to see cheerful hunters in leather underpants casually skinning kudu carcasses or chattering groups of women carrying bags of veld food. Xi's ghost also loiters in the Nyae Nyae "Living Museum," a tourist village twenty miles north of Tsumkwe where bewildered visitors can salvage a little of their fantasy if someone is around to show them a grass hut, gather some food, and demonstrate a few tracking tricks in exchange for cash. But Xi's ghost is busiest in a village called Nhoma, just outside the conservancy, where an arrangement with the onetime owner of the Tsumkwe Lodge has led to the establishment of a better-organized tourism experience where great care is taken to maintain the illusion of traditional hunter-gatherer life.

This has been done courtesy of a dummy village built strictly for this purpose.

All these initiatives are to procure money that will be spent almost as soon as it is acquired. Beyond commercial hunting, craft sales, and the harvesting of devil's claw (*Harpagophytum procumbens*, a medicinal plant), there are few other goods or services Ju/'hoansi in Nyae Nyae have to offer except unskilled labor. And with not much call for paid unskilled labor in Nyae Nyae, this means that if they want paid work, they have to go elsewhere. But in a country where employment hovers around 50 percent, leaving Nyae Nyae with few marketable skills to find a job in a world where they have few kin connections is not considered a sensible prospect.

But thanks to Xi's ghost there is one set of "jobs" that the Ju/'hoansi are uniquely positioned to exploit: that of being "performing Bushmen."

Den/ui is usually one of Nyae Nyae's liveliest villages. It is home to more than eighty people, including one of Nyae Nyae's most famous hunters, the legendary /Ui N!a'a, a man renowned in Nyae Nyae for the beauty and muscularity of his legs. But when I head to Den/ui to visit / Ui in November 2015, the village is nearly deserted. Whole clusters of huts are empty and in poor repair, with thatch falling from their roofs in ungainly clumps and leaves littering sand that is undisturbed by footprints.

/Ui explains that, aside from his immediate family and a handful of others, everybody who lived in Den/ui had gone to Erindi, Namibia's largest "private game reserve," and were only expected to return in the rainy season. They are the second or third village to have done so. At Erindi they are expected to live "traditionally" in a grass village established for the benefit of Erindi's guests. And at the end of each month—and out of sight of the tourists—they are paid a nominal fee for their time. Erindi, for its part, has granted their resident "Bushmen tribe" a mystical new name: "CwiCwi." The reserve also warn its guests that visits to the Bushmen are "subject to San Community movements," because they are "a nomadic culture . . . [who] live solely off the land." The Ju/'hoansi in turn are required to wear their traditional leather aprons and are forbidden to either solicit or accept tips from the guests.

/Ui declined to go to Erindi because he had no interest in leaving Den/ui. He also makes a reasonably good living in Nyae Nyae hunting, guiding tourists, occasionally assisting film crews, and working as a tracker with the department of wildlife.

Others in Nyae Nyae have also been whisked off to another similarly Disneyfied destination, a farm and wildlife sanctuary near Windhoek called N/aankuse, famed for its tame carnivores and its patronage by Angelina Jolie and Brad Pitt. Ju/'hoansi preferred N/aankuse to Erindi: the pay is better, they provide hospitality training, and its cognate foundation offers education to the children who go to stay there in addition to running a small medical clinic for Ju/'hoansi in Hereroland.

Every Ju/'hoan I meet who has spent time at either of these lodges complains about the experience. But complaint comes easily in Nyae Nyae, and scattered in among the moans is a palpable sense of pride that people should come from all over the world to see them, even if it means that they have to parody themselves. Yet every year, after hearing of the experiences of others who have performed at Erindi or N/aankuse, other Ju/'hoansi line up to take their places. And they do it because their recent history as hunter-gatherers is their only real "asset" in a world where brands often exert greater power than the things they represent. Few have a sense of why or how exactly they became a cultural brand, but they certainly don't mind it.

Xi's ghost haunts Nyae Nyae in other ways too. It is now nearly impossible for strangers to take photos of Ju/'hoansi in Nyae Nyae without being harassed for cash. There is a palpable sense that anyone and everyone from outside Nyae Nyae, in particular white foreigners, are harvestable. This is because most white visitors are obviously very wealthy. Few if any ever show up in Tsumkwe without fancy four-wheel drives, coolers packed with beer and meat, clean clothes, and fancy cell phones. As a result, the sound of a camera's shutter anywhere within earshot is now likely to generate demands for cash and much scowling if it is not paid.

———

One of the most powerful scenes in *The Gods Must Be Crazy* occurs toward the closing credits of the film. It shows Xi abandoning a bundle of cash that is soon scattered by the wind like dry fallen leaves. In publicizing the film, Uys claimed that G/au did exactly this when he received his first payment as an actor, with the result that Uys purchased a dozen cattle for him instead. Uys's story was untrue. G/au was like most other Ju/'hoansi in Nyae Nyae at the time: they may not have understood a great deal about money, but they had no doubts about the fact that it was valuable and that it was capable of exerting tremendous power over people. They also knew that this power was far from straightforward, and—like the Coke bottle in the movie—every benefit that money brought carried in its shadow some kind of cost.

The money earned by the Ju/'hoan cast of *The Gods Must Be Crazy* was significant by local standards. But it was a pittance compared to what the Ju/'hoansi who were in the process of being recruited into the South African Defence Force while the film was being shot would soon earn.

Before the arrival of the military in 1979, the only money that trickled into Nyae Nyae came from government and church projects. But the quantities of cash disbursed were so negligible and the number of direct beneficiaries so few that both the cash and the products that were purchased with it—mainly food, tobacco, and blankets—were instantaneously absorbed into the broader community.

There are no obvious analogues among other peoples for what happened in Nyae Nyae, where—following the recruitment of almost every able-bodied male Ju/'hoan between the ages of eighteen and thirty-five into the South African army—in a little over than six months Tsumkwe went from being largely moneyless to being swamped with cash.

By the time the first Ju/'hoan recruits donned their khaki military fatigues, South African military authorities had already accepted the principle of equal pay for equal work for all its recruits, although it would take several years before it was rolled out. Previously military pay was rationed according to race. White soldiers earned more than Indian and mixed-race soldiers of the same rank, who in turn earned more than black soldiers. But prosecuting an escalating war against an "enemy" that was fighting for racial equality, among other things, risked turning manpower the South Africans depended on into a mutinous liability and persuaded them that "de-racializing" military salaries was a priority.

Throughout the military occupation of Nyae Nyae, around 150 Ju/'hoansi out of a total adult population of some 1,000 people served in the South African army at any one time. All who joined up pocketed the equivalent of $600 USD every month in addition to various combat bonuses. This translates into around $2,000 USD per month by 2015 standards. All of this income was disposable. No Ju/'hoansi in Nyae Nyae had regular overheads like rent, school fees, or a utility bill. Additionally, because the military also provided military families in Nyae Nyae with food rations in the form of maize porridge, oil, sugar, and meat, they also didn't have to spend much on food. Despite this, only a few soldiers saved any of their money. Many blew the bulk of their salaries within hours of being issued them by the paymaster general in cash-stuffed brown envelopes. With the bottle shop usually the first stop after the paymaster's truck, many Ju/'hoan soldiers recall paydays when they awoke in the night to discover they were penniless, with nothing to show for the preceding month's soldiering.

Not all their money was squandered on alcohol. Clothing, blankets, crockery, knives, hardware, farming implements, batteries, and all manner of bric-a-brac sold well in Tsumkwe's small shops. Many soldiers also purchased "luxury" items like radio–cassette players. Some of the more sober soldiers purchased motor vehicles. But these were not sturdy enough to handle Nyae Nyae's unforgiving roads combined with the Ju/'hoansi's often improvised driving skills. Most ended up rusting wrecks on the roadside.

As much as Ju/'hoan soldiers sometimes resented the demands placed on them by their families, they usually gave a good proportion of their money away. With military salaries streaming into almost every Ju/'hoan household in the early 1980s, money became not only an agent of change but also one of the only means of interacting with the powerful external forces that were exerting an ever more profound influence over their lives. Yet, even though there was plenty of money coming in, its impact confounded the economic principle that states that the scarcer something is, the more valuable it becomes. Because in Nyae Nyae, the more money people made, the more valuable it seemed to become. Those with the most money became the most preoccupied with it, and those with the least, the most dismissive of it. Unlike other objects and gifts that circulated among Ju/'hoansi, money claimed a power that existed independently of the giver and receiver. And this power was amplified by the fact that pretty much everyone from outside of Nyae Nyae obviously fetishized it to the point that there were very few areas of their lives into which money didn't intrude.

The sudden influx of cash also raised a lot of questions among the Ju/'hoansi for which there were no obvious solutions. Should money be shared like meat or food or private property? And if so, how much and with whom? Was it an appropriate *hxaro* gift?

In much the same way that there is no clear consensus on the answers to these questions in highly industrialized economies, the Ju/'hoansi didn't reach a consensus either. In an echo of the left-right divide that shapes political affiliation in many industrialized economies, most Ju/'hoansi in Nyae Nyae with little or no cash income considered it an obvious obligation on those with money to share it widely and evenly, but most of those who made good money increasingly took the view that it was theirs to dispose of as they wished.

In the absence of any established norms for dealing with or redistributing money, the influx of cash generated many problems. Jealousy alone, which had been so successful at maintaining a delicate egalitarian balance in band life, was clearly not up to the job. In the maelstrom of misunderstanding, loans were misinterpreted as gifts and gifts as loans. Accusations of selfishness, profligacy, and theft flew everywhere, and almost everyone in Nyae Nyae ended up being offended by or upset with someone else. In this poisonous atmosphere, the alcohol many purchased with their cash— ironically, to help them forget these same problems—ignited a thousand drunken brawls.

These problems rumbled on as a source of misery in Tsumkwe for the duration of the decade that the military ran things there. The stress they caused was further amplified by other problems, like the continuing dependency of most Ju/'hoansi in Tsumkwe on food handouts from the administration; the administration's plans to transform Nyae Nyae into a game reserve; and the profound existential anxieties provoked by a sense that the world around them was changing at a much faster rate than they could keep up with. The only really positive thing was that the Ju/'hoan recruits in Nyae Nyae did not see nearly as much frontline action as Bushman soldiers in other regiments. Then, in 1989, when the South African military packed up and left Bushmanland under United Nations supervision, the military salaries dried up as suddenly as they had appeared.

When this happened, remarkably little was left to show of the millions of dollars that had been pumped into this small community over the preceding decade. Even though some soldiers had invested in cattle and cars, most of their earnings ended up in the pockets of the various traders who had set up shop in Tsumkwe to scavenge off the military's largesse. And with no military salaries to leech off of, all but a handful of the traders packed up what was left of their wares and headed off in search of opportunities elsewhere.

This sudden departure of the military was a retrenchment on a scale that would have been lamented as an economic disaster in other parts of the world. Yet in Nyae Nyae it was greeted with more relief than anxiety. Some imagined that the problems they associated with soldiers' money might disappear.

Today, much less money flows into Ju/'hoan hands in Nyae Nyae than did during the period of the military's presence. Now money comes into the community via the conservancy in the form of salaries for the dozen Ju/'hoansi employed directly by it and in the form of the annual cash dividend realized mainly through the sale of elephant hunting rights. Several Ju/'hoansi in Nyae Nyae also have government jobs. Some are interesting: a lucky few are paid to DJ at the small Ju/'hoan-language radio station, teach in the schools, or track down errant elephants with the nature conservation. Most jobs, though, are dull and menial, like collecting rubbish, cutting bushes on the roadside, or scrubbing floors. Tourism, craftmaking, and occasional film projects also realize some cash, but not enough to rely on. By far the most important source of money now is the state pension for over-sixties, which is equivalent to around $50 USD per month. Given that no one of pension age in Nyae Nyae is of a generation that cared about remembering birth years or counting, their ages on the ID cards that were issued at independence are often uninformed guesses, and so pension eligibility is a bit of a lottery.

So as much as money is a vital part of the economic jigsaw in Nyae Nyae, very little money is actually "made" there. Rather, Ju/'hoansi see it as something that comes in from the world beyond Nyae Nyae and, once spent, magically returns to where it came from. Ju/'hoansi are also much more used to money than they were during the military period. People still are jealous of those with lots of it but accept that it belongs to a different sphere of exchange from gifts and food. Except among the small but growing number of Ju/'hoansi who have embraced temperance as part of their pact with the evangelical churches, paydays and pension days remain a drunken free-for-all marked by singing, dancing, and eating interspersed by squabbling and moments of clumsy, occasionally bloody violence.

Yet, even if Ju/'hoansi are used to money, it remains a mysterious force full of apparent contradictions. Why, they wonder, are some forms of work more valuable than others? Why do prices always rise for no obvious reason? And where does the money come from in the first place?

As perplexing as these questions are, money now generates less confusion than it did during the military presence. After decades of trying to make sense of the cash economy, most Ju/'hoansi have simply accepted that there are no straightforward answers to their questions about it and so they don't waste time trying to find them.

———

Old /Engn!au was the only Ju/'hoan I ever met to propose a theory of sorts about where money came from. He expressed it in the form of a story about his favorite character, the trickster jackal. In his stories the trickster jackal was presented as a mythological Ju/'hoan everyman who survived by his wits. Simultaneously a jackal and a human, he was a creature of the First Times, the period when human and animal identities were in a constant state of flux. But the First Times that the jackal lived in were not the same as those of most other traditional Ju/'hoan "stories of the beginning." For this jackal lived in a First Times where white farmers and Herero were in charge.

/Engn!au's money story went like this:

Jackal had been riding his donkey and grew tired. He decided to stop and cook some meat. When the meat was stewing in his pot, he saw some Herero coming toward him. Quickly he covered the fire with sand so they could not see it.

When the Herero arrived he said to them, "Look, you black people, this is a magic pot. It doesn't need a fire to cook food. You must just hit it three times like this."

Jackal grabbed his whip and hit the pot three times. *Tca-tca-tca!* Then he opened it and showed the Herero that the meat was still sizzling hot.

"I will sell you this magic pot for one thousand dollars," said Jackal.

"That is a wonderful pot," the Herero conceded. So they gave Jackal a thousand dollars, took the pot, and left.

When the Herero had walked for a while, they grew hungry. So they put some raw meat in the pot and hit it three times with a whip. But when they opened it, they saw that the meat was raw. So they hit the pot again. But the meat was still raw.

"We have been tricked!" they shouted. "This jackal, this Bushman, he is a crook." So they went back to find Jackal. When Jackal saw them coming, he was scared. So he quickly took the money they had given him for the pot and hid it in his donkey's anus.

When they reached Jackal, the Herero said, "Jackal, this pot is not magic. Take it and give us our money back!"

"I can't," replied Jackal. "This pot is yours now. Anyway, I have already spent the money."

But just as he said this, the donkey farted and all the money tumbled from its backside. For a second Jackal was terrified, but then he smiled.

"Look at this donkey," Jackal said to them. "It's magic because you feed it grass and it will shit money. If you buy this donkey from me for a thousand dollars, it will shit more money for you!"

"Ah, this is a magic donkey!" agreed the Herero. So they gave Jackal another thousand dollars. And, with the donkey in tow, they went away again. As soon as they were gone, Jackal fled with the money.

/Engn!au was adamant that he was no Ju/'hoan Aesop and that he was not in the business of dispensing wisdom by metaphor. He also insisted that none of his many stories were allegorical and that it was pointless asking him what they meant because they didn't mean anything. "They are just stories," he said.

When it came to most of his tales, this made perfect sense. Teasing any kind of underlying message out of traditional Ju/'hoan folktales seemed impossible anyway, and, as /Engn!au would point out, doing so would be dishonest.

Unlike his other stories, the elements of this one—that money is created by magic; that it is acquired through trickery and deceit; that it inspires greed, violence, fear, possessiveness, and anger; and that it often appears to come from assholes and is covered in shit—do not require tremendous reinterpretation to find meaning in it.

But the most striking thing about this particular story is that it is the only one of the many stories of the First Times that /Engn!au and others told me that resonates powerfully with life beyond the Kalahari. I suspect that this is because it deals with an element of their recent experience that is now near universal. It is also because this story was pregnant with allegorical opportunities that can be applied to so many different situations. For instance, if we substitute "subprime mortgage" (or any number of other purchases on easy credit) for "magic pot"; "mortgage-backed security" for "donkey"; "promised returns" for "donkey shit"; "Wall Street bankers" for "Jackal"; and "everyday dupes" for "the Herero," then you have most of the key elements needed for retrospective analysis of the subprime financial crisis that began in 2007. You could just as easily equate the magic pot with a moribund economy that fails to deliver growth no matter how hard it is whipped, and the donkey with a central bank "quantitively easing" magical money from its rear. The possibilities are almost endless.

If /Engn!au's story of a magic pot can be read as an allegory of a convoluted financial crisis, then it is not surprising that most of the questions about money that continue to perplex Ju/'hoansi and others on the fringes of the world economy also perplex most people in advanced monetized economies. Most people in modern economies would consider themselves competent users of money, even if they don't have a great deal of it. Many also consider themselves competent in the art of making money. But only a select few would be able to provide cogent answers to questions like where money comes from, what determines its value, and what economic growth is. Similarly, only a select few would feel confident to explain inflation, bond yields, interest rates, monetary policy, market volatility, or how any number of increasingly convoluted derivative financial instruments actually work. And among those who consider themselves qualified to answer these questions, few agree on what the answers are. If they did, and if economics were a hard science, then developing economic policies with predictable outcomes would be a much simpler enterprise.

The Promised Land

//Eng's hands are still busy. Recently she and her husband started to make rope bridles for horses and donkeys. They assemble them from scratch by plaiting plastic fibers carefully unpicked from discarded maize porridge sacks. When I visit her in April 2014, several bridles, complete with bits, nose bands, cheek pieces, and reins, hang from the branch of a tree outside her home. She tells me that she has already sold a few of them to Herero. But this morning she's been busy knitting hats for my children.

During the mid-1990s, //Eng was the most energetic participant in the hat-knitting project I helped a group of Skoonheid's mothers to set up. //Eng and others poured aeons of accumulated creative energy and artistry into the hats, producing multicolored designs of great beauty, complexity, and symmetry. Their skills baffled and awed others who could not imagine how such complex designs could be created without the rudimentary mathematical skills needed to count stitches or the literacy needed to map designs on paper beforehand. When I asked //Eng how they managed it, she explained simply that the hats created themselves and that the patterns do the counting for them.

But it is the "green fingers" at the ends of //Eng's hands that have been busiest. She takes me to see her vegetable garden, conscious that when I came to stay the previous November, Skoonheid was a dust bowl, having been mauled by the worst drought since 1994. But on this visit her garden, carefully protected from cattle by a wooden fence, is like nothing I have ever seen in the Kalahari. It is a riot of greens, pastels, whites, purples, and oranges. She leads me through a patch of corn that cranes over us, each stem bending under the weight of ears that will soon be ripe for picking. Beyond them, neat rows of onions poke out of the red Kalahari sand.

There are also prickly pears, green beans, papayas, and most impressively pumpkins. Still green and surrounded by a sea of leaves and fading yellow flowers, //Eng's pumpkins are still growing. They are already the size of the wheels on my truck.

Since the drought broke in late December, the rains have been good. Now nearly every household at Skoonheid has a vegetable garden. And everyone else's garden is also looking impressive. But only //Eng's is spectacular. She still cannot abide being idle, but others' idleness bothers her less than it used to. She does not have any bad words to say about her fellow settlers, even those who lounge in her compound while she works.

"Life is good now, /Kunta," she explains. "We are blessed at Skoonheid."

Skoonheid now has a settled and peaceful feel to it. Whereas twenty years ago it was little more than a bleak refugee camp plagued by hunger, violence, and insecurity, it has slowly molded itself into a village, a community, and a home. And as if to signal their approval of this development, the gods have sent fewer droughts and better rains.

Other changes at Skoonheid from the time I first lived there are equally profound. Once hostage to almost weekly brawls and stabbings, Skoonheid became a "dry" community in 2011 following the example of !A/ae "Frederik" Langman, who in 2007 was formally recognized by the government as the "chief" of the Omaheke Ju/'hoansi—a decade after he was chosen by the community to fill the role. Energized by their newfound temperance, the community demanded that the single entrepreneurial brewer of homemade beer at Skoonheid shut up shop. They also insisted that if anyone in the community still wanted to get drunk, they would have to go to Epukiro, some twenty miles away, and drink there. Much of the community also followed !A/ae's example by adopting the "path of Jesus." Now they cheerfully sang Christian songs, shared prayers, and occasionally even assembled to "speak in tongues" like the groups of young Afrikaner missionaries who come to preach at Skoonheid every once in a while.

The central area of the resettlement camp now comprises six rows of small, simple concrete brick houses arranged in orderly lines like a surreal mini-suburbia in the middle of nowhere. There are also new water towers and pumps for the borehole, powered by several large solar panels that follow the sun as it moves across the sky. Some of the houses have water piped directly to them. Some also have electricity now that Skoonheid has been linked to the national grid.

Beyond the infrastructural developments, most here are no richer financially than they were one or two decades ago, but they are much more content. There are a few projects on the go. Women like //Eng make beaded jewelry for an outfit that supplies the souvenir shops in safari lodges and a few of the men have discovered joy in metalworking, welding basins and water tanks in one of the old farm sheds. But these projects don't earn anyone much of a living and no one is working with any great urgency. But since the settlers have been persuaded that no one will be able to chase them from their homes, they feel secure enough to take on seasonal work on farms when it suits them or when they need cash. Some have even become specialists. My adoptive brother //Kallie, who has a special understanding of horses, works on a fancy stud farm near Windhoek, while his young nephew Jacobus, who speaks passable English, is now a "Bushman Guide" on a safari farm far to the south.

Most Ju/'hoansi at Skoonheid still depend on government rations and handouts. The German embassy in Namibia also donated two or three head of cattle to most households at Skoonheid a couple of years ago. But many of these died in the drought of 2013. No one minded, because it meant that for a few months, as they worked through the carcasses of the dead cattle, everyone had meat to eat.

But even if most people at Skoonheid are satisfied with their lot, they are acutely aware that they are among the lucky few. There are now more than twenty resettlement projects with Bushman beneficiaries spread across Namibia, of which Skoonheid is the most established and by far the best resourced, thanks to the effort of NGOs and a visit by the president in 2007 that resulted in a rush of investment. Riddled with problems and never large enough to provide more than a semblance of security, the resettlement farms cater to fewer than 5 percent of Namibia's landless Bushman population. For most other Bushmen in Namibia—and in neighboring Botswana—life remains very difficult. For while some have managed to complete school and make a go at life in a New Time world, they collectively remain the worst off of southern Africa's people by an eye-watering margin.

And as if to remind us of this, while //Eng and I admire her pumpkins, word reaches us that there has been another fatal stabbing at what is now the Omaheke's single largest Bushman settlement, the sprawling township of Epako. The victim and the murderer, we learn, are a Ju/'hoan father and son who were squabbling over something while drunk.

"Why do so many of the murders involve people killing their own family?" I wonder aloud.

"Kill a member of your family?" replies //Eng. "Why, who else would you want to kill?"

Epako Township still has the same curious mix of authoritarian order and dystopian entropy typical of most other apartheid-born townships in Namibia and South Africa. It lies about two and a half miles to the east of Gobabis, a safe distance from what were once the "whites only" areas of the town where Epako's inhabitants were once expected to trudge daily to clean white homes, look after white children, and provide manual labor in white-owned shops, garages, and businesses.

The township is organized around a series a blocks of decaying single-room housing built in the 1960s and '70s and some newer housing built since independence. Groups of blocks in turn form "sections" established for different ethnic groups under apartheid. The obsession with maintaining "cultural" difference that preoccupied apartheid's planners meant that separating people on the basis of race alone was not enough. They also wanted to make sure that people of different cultures didn't interact too much either. Despite the fact that there are no longer any rules regarding who can settle where in this township, each section still has its own distinctive cultural atmosphere.

The Herero and Damara sections are the largest, but there are also sections for Ovambo and Tswana. Where the Herero section is fairly orderly and shows off its relative wealth in the form of occasional satellite dishes, the Damara section has a more improvised feel to it. There are more donkey carts than cars, more inverted paint tins than plastic chairs. There are no gardens to speak of in Epako, although most households take the trouble to rake the dust in their yards. There is no Bushman section.

Two decades ago only two Ju/'hoan families lived in Epako. They squatted in makeshift shelters on the edge of the township. Back then Ju/'hoansi avoided the township if at all possible. They considered it a dangerous place. A place for the *Gobasi*—"black people." But by the late 1990s, as more and more farmers cleared their lands of "excess" laborers, the Ju/'hoan population of Epako began to grow steadily. The first arrivals occupied the no-man's-land between the Herero, Ovambo, and Tswana sections in an improvised neighborhood they christened "Please-Do-Not-Fight." But as ever more Bushmen with nowhere else to go trickled in, Please-Do-Not-Fight became cramped and volatile. And so, on the northern edge of the township, a new shantytown began to emerge out of the sand. A disorderly array of hastily improvised dwellings linked by a spiderweb of rutted sandy paths, this shantytown was referred to by all as the Plakkersdorp—"Tin Town."

By the turn of the new millennium, the Plakkersdorp still maintained an air of impermanence. It played host to a transient population of fewer than a hundred or so Ju/'hoansi at any one time. For most of them the Plakkersdorp was no more than a single stop within a broader network of temporary residences that extended through the farms and beyond into Hereroland.

Now, a decade and a half later, the Plakkersdorp is no more—not because it has disappeared but because it has been rechristened and become something altogether more permanent. It is now known to everyone as Kanaan (Afrikaans for Canaan), the Promised Land. Kanaan now hosts a population of over three thousand people. Around half are Ju/'hoansi. The remainder of households are made up of other rural poor also washed up from the Omaheke's ever more efficient and businesslike commercial farms.

Even if Kanaan has a chaotic feel to it, it is not as disorderly as the Plak-kersdorp was. The Gobabis town council has done its best to impose a semblance of order on it by demarcating individual plots and using a bull-dozer to cut a grid of sandy thoroughfares. Every house in Kanaan is improvised from scrap gathered in and around the town. The high-spec houses here are cobbled together from pieces of corrugated iron torn from the walls of a defunct factory in the east of town. But corrugated iron is at a premium, and most have to make do with other materials like plastic sheeting, hardboard that loses its shape after a couple of summer storms, clay, wood from the acacia forests that once surrounded the town, and anything else that is ready to hand. Recently a Dutch town twinned with Gobabis donated twelve freestanding "dry" toilets to Kanaan that have been distributed about the settlement.

Hunger is a perennial problem in Kanaan, and it finds its expression in distended bellies, scabies, tuberculosis, and a range of other ailments. Just as in Tsumkwe and Skoonheid, the state pension scheme is the main source of cash income for Ju/'hoansi in Kanaan. But there are fewer eligible pensioners in Kanaan, and with so many mouths to feed, pension money rarely stretches beyond a few days. Kanaan's residents are not eligible for the same external support offered in the resettlement areas. They view places like Skoonheid as swanky neighborhoods occupied by the privileged few.

Kanaan's residents employ a range of enterprising strategies to survive. A few have unskilled or semiskilled jobs in town. Others get along by begging, borrowing, and doing casual work for their marginally wealthier neighbors in the Herero and Damara sections. Almost everyone in Kanaan wants a job and the security it brings, but with youth unemployment in Namibia at nearly 60 percent and Gobabis's economy flatlining, few have a realistic chance of finding one.

In the meantime, the Ju/'hoansi in Kanaan form a class of their own at the base of the urban food chain and, like powerless people everywhere, vent their frustrations on one another. Drunken fights are a daily occurrence in Kanaan and stabbings are frequent enough to invite no real surprise.

———

I am careful about where I leave my truck when I visit Kanaan these days. The Ju/'hoansi's stories about the predatory *taranoa* have made me paranoid. In OshiHerero, *taranoa* means "watch me carefully." It is the local slang for the gangsters who lord over Epako's underbelly.

Many of Epako's younger men find camaraderie and purpose by traveling in packs and preying on others. They loiter at the informal beer halls eyeballing passing foot traffic. Occasionally they strut and shout at members of other gangs or try to persuade passing schoolgirls to "show them some love." Epako's most established gang, G-Force, is multiethnic and draws on a core group of boys who attended the local secondary school together a few years back. Pitted against them are the Skoonmakers (the "Cleaners"), a mainly Damara-speaking gang that has a reputation for hassling the more isolated households of the Herero section. And then there is the Herero section gang, the Skoffels (the "Shufflers"). They happily harass everyone.

Most of the gangsters in Epako, though, are more feathers than claws. But occasionally things turn nasty. Groups of unemployed young men with knives, alcohol, and the searing November heat do not always mix well. The Skoonmakers are the most feared of the township gangs these days. Last time I was there, there was gossip about how they had castrated a G-Force boy before throwing his mangled testicles to the township dogs.

All the gangs pick on Ju/'hoansi. Ju/'hoan pensioners now travel in packs for safety on pension day or have to sneak back home with their money or the food they purchase to avoid being robbed. And Ju/'hoan women and girls complain that they have to run a gauntlet of rapists and perverts lurking in the grasslands beyond Kanaan where they go to pee at night.

As nervous as Ju/'hoansi in Epako are of the *taranoa*, they have not yet formed any gangs themselves. But whenever I visit Kanaan, barefoot Ju/'hoan children who know only of township life gather in my wake. Dressed in rags, they are skinny and hard and don't bat an eyelash when I reject their demands for cash. There is a predatory confidence to their scavenging, a confidence that a decade ago would have been unimaginable. In a few short years this generation of streetwise Ju/'hoan kids will be forming gangs of their own.

Occasionally the children will wander into Gobabis's town center, which is organized around an incongruous palm-lined four-lane main road that launches itself eastward into the heart of the Kalahari and westward toward Namibia's capital, Windhoek. Beyond the main road, the bulk of the town is made up of a patchwork of dusty plots with brick-built houses with corrugated iron roofs. To many of Epako's residents this dismal suburbia represents a vision of prosperity. For the braver and hungrier Ju/'hoan kids, it represents an adrenaline-filled, guard-dog-dodging, razor-wire-fence-jumping opportunity to steal food or clothing from washing lines when begging outside of the Shoprite or Shell service station yields too few rewards.

———

Gobabis's economy is sustained by the repeat custom of local ranchers buying wholesale goods at local shops to take back to their farms. Almost all of its shops are located on a half-mile-long stretch of the main road. There are several small bakeries; hardware stores offering tools, salt licks, car parts, diesel generators, borehole pumps, skinning knives, and ammunition; butchers; street vendors selling single cigarettes and cell phone credit; budget clothing retailers; and a private medical practice painted garish pink that backs directly onto the town cemetery and has separate entrances for different "qualities" of customers. There are garages and low-cost supermarket franchises. Recently, Gobabis welcomed a couple of "China Shops" set up by entrepreneurial Cantonese immigrants. These are packed with cut-price umbrellas, tents, toys, cell phone chargers, and televisions with rip-off brand names like "Soni" and "Penisonic" that are as likely to burst into flames when they are plugged in as they are to work.

But only a few of Epako's residents can afford to purchase more than basics in Gobabis's shops. As elsewhere, these shops depend on their ability to seduce customers into making impulse buys, or, if they have a job, offer them easy terms of credit. Garish advertising posters promising fulfillment if only they can afford to purchase the right kinds of hair extensions, athletic shoes, cell phones, or sugary drinks and shelves stacked with colorful products often result in customers leaving a shop having purchased something different from what they intended. Sometimes this leads to muttered accusations of sorcery as they try to make sense of whatever malicious force it was that muddled their minds.

Despite their worries about the shopkeepers' sorcery, most of Epako's residents think of these businesses as crucibles of aspiration. But to most of Kanaan's Ju/'hoan population they are symbols of a universe from which they remain largely excluded.

Unlike in the resettlement camps, there is a sense of disquiet among Ju/'hoansi in Kanaan. For although Kanaan may be marginal, it is not remote, and no one here ever falls prey to the illusion that their hunger has anything to do with a scarcity of food. Within easy walking distance of Kanaan are nearly half a dozen shops with shelving that groans under the weight of food and wholesalers' warehouses in which tons of maize, sugar, flour, and other products lie stacked on pallets.

This small-town environment is much more abundant than the bush ever was, but if you don't have money, it is far from provident. And the Ju/'hoansi here wonder why it is that they must continue to live on the edge of starvation when there is so much food nearby.

The Ju/'hoansi in Kanaan have a good point about food, one that resonates far beyond the rutted paths that spider through their "promised land." For the first time since the Neolithic Revolution we live in an era where more than enough food is produced for everyone on the planet to eat well. We produce so much food that around 440 pounds of food per person currently alive ends up in landfills every year—enough again to adequately nourish another five billion or so of us for a year. This has been the case for some time and most of us are better nourished than the average person at any time since the development of farming.

This Kanaan is not the economic promised land John Maynard Keynes imagined in 1930. It's hard to know what he would make of a people who once embodied the most elusive elements of his Utopian vision now broken on the rack of the economic forces he imagined would bring about his own Canaan. But Keynes viewed capitalism as an ugly means to an ultimately beneficial end. He believed that without it the "economic problem" could never be solved.

In outlining his vision of the future, Keynes differentiated between what he considered our "absolute" needs and our "relative" needs. Absolute needs were the basic elements of a satisfactory life. To his mind this probably included enough food, clean water, comfortable housing, properly managed utilities, universal health care, an effective transportation infrastructure, and so on. He contrasted these with relative needs, which he considered to be those that "satisfy the desire for superiority" and that we embrace "only if their satisfaction lifts us above, makes us feel superior to, our fellows."

Keynes believed that technological advances and improved productivity would ensure that our absolute needs were met with the minimum of effort, because much of the work that needed to be done would be automated like the robotic arms in a car factory. When our absolute needs are all so comfortably met, Keynes argued, our sense of what is truly important would change organically and we would learn to recognize that "avarice is a vice, that the exaction of usury is a misdemeanour, and the love of money is detestable."

Keynes's sense of what our absolute needs are was based on his vision of a good life—a vision born of the wonders of the Industrial Age and the more traditional comforts of college life in Cambridge. Now defining absolute needs is less a question of asking what we need or want than it is a question of understanding the limits of what is possible. We live on a planet that now feels very small and crowded, and no one ever imagined a Utopia that cannibalized its own future. It's simply not possible for everyone to have the same energy and resources footprint as an American or a European.

For most of us living in the world's richest countries, our absolute needs are almost universally met, and if resources were more evenly distributed among the population, they could arguably be met several times over. We are adequately nourished and live in warm homes packed with all sorts of enterprising gadgetry and comforts. And all of this stuff is imported or produced by the roughly one in ten of us who are employed in agriculture or manufacturing. The rest of us expend our productive and creative energies in the ever more expansive services sector, leaving some to wonder whether there is any point at all to what they do. As much as it is easier for some people to blame globalization, immigration, or any number of fantastical conspiracies for the decline in manufacturing jobs, the truth is that increased productivity and technological advancement are the real culprits. And it is not just jobs in manufacturing that are being impacted. A recent study by Oxford economists reckons that nearly half of existing U.S. jobs will be at risk from automation and computerization within the next two decades. These include most jobs in transportation and logistics, "the bulk of office and administrative support workers," and a "substantial share of employment in service occupations where most U.S. job growth has occurred over the last few years."[1]

Yet, even so, we still seem a very long way away from embracing Keynes's Utopia. Mainstream economists and governments alike—on both the left and the right of the political spectrum—remain preoccupied with maintaining growth on the one hand and reducing unemployment on the other while debating about how much of our hard-earned wealth should be put to the common good and how much we should be able to squirrel away for ourselves. Few politicians seem willing to engage with the real challenge: the need for us to adjust to the reality of living in a post-work world.

When Marshall Sahlins wrote about hunter-gatherers pursuing a "Zen road" to affluence by having few needs easily met, he was invoking a similar set of attitudes to those that Keynes hoped would prevail in a world where people's absolute needs were adequately met. Keynes was of the view that our innate desire to solve what he referred to as our "real problems—the problems of life and of human relations, of creation and behavior and religion" would be enough to distract us from any residual instinct to work.

But Keynes was unusual among economists in his view that our productive instincts are secondary to our spiritual ones. Most other economists consider work to be the elemental particle of human sociality and economics the science of interpreting and manipulating the ever more complex forms arising out of these interactions. This view of human nature, which underwrites the free-market capitalism championed by Keynes's critics, also lay at the heart of Karl Marx's critique of the free market. Marx, like generations of economists before and since, believed that human nature was to spontaneously and creatively produce in a manner that is conducive to social and individual satisfaction. To him the urge to produce was the essence of humanity, and his anxieties about capitalism had their roots in his belief that capitalism robbed people of the profound fulfillment that came from producing things. Marx's communist Utopia, in contrast to Keynes's post-labor Utopia, was one in which everyone continued to work but was liberated to seek a more profound fulfillment from their work by owning the "means of production."

The evidence of hunting and gathering societies suggests that both Marx and neoliberal economists were wrong about human nature: we are more than capable of leading fulfilled lives that are not defined by our labor.

But if this is so, then why is it proving so hard for humans to embrace abundance the way hunter-gatherers did?

In part it is because hunter-gatherers' "primitive affluence" was neither a mind-set nor the economic expression of any particular ideology: there is no "manifesto of primitive communism." Their economic perspective was anchored in, among other things, their confidence in the providence of their environment, a hunter's empathy for his prey, an immediate-return economy, and indifference to the past and the future, and reaffirmed by social relationships shaped as much by jealousy as affection.

It is also because there is another, more fundamental obstacle in the path to achieving Keynes's vision. For the hunter-gatherer model of primitive affluence was not simply based on their having few needs easily satisfied; it also depended on no one being substantially richer or more powerful than anyone else. If this kind of egalitarianism is a precondition for us to embrace a post-labor world, then I suspect it may prove to be a very hard nut to crack.

Few Bushmen anywhere in southern Africa are able to easily meet their absolute needs today. In nutritional terms at least, most are worse off than they were as hunter-gatherers, plagued by the physical and social ailments we associate with poverty. And, of course, what they think of as their absolute needs now are very different from what they were when they hunted and gathered.

But even among the few Ju/'hoansi at Skoonheid whose absolute needs are met and who have been as surprised as they are pleased by recent developments at the resettlement camp, there is still a broader sense of dissatisfaction. And it is not only that they continue to endure the paternalism of others and are straitjacketed by their prejudices about Bushmen. It is because they consider the distribution of resources—most significantly land—to be grossly iniquitous. The jealousy that once regulated band life has now been projected onto a broader canvas—one that reflects a much wider-lived reality that includes events and people who live beyond their immediate horizons.

Namibia has an exemplary record of governance since independence. There have been problems, but these have often been more a function of capacity and resources shortfalls rather than bad intentions. Yet Namibia, like its neighbors South Africa and Botswana, remains among the top five most unequal countries in the world. This inequality is not, as has so often been the case in the world's "developing" economies, the result of the actions of a corrupt, kleptocratic class so much as a function of the nature of economic growth. But the net result is a massive concentration of available wealth in relatively few hands and a pronounced and obvious underclass making up half the population, with the Bushmen sitting at the bottom of the pile.

Even for those Ju/'hoansi at Skoonheid, inequality remains a burning issue, and one in which they find common cause with others in the bottom half of the economic pile everywhere else in the world. And if Ju/'hoansi are unable to accept a life of adequacy while others have much more, it suggests that Keynes may have put the cart before the horse. Perhaps the only way for us to embrace the abundance that has by and large already arrived is to find a way to deal with the inequality that inspires jealousy and anger as much as the impulse to work hard enough to keep up with or even overtake the Joneses.

———

Five years ago the Ju/'hoansi considered cell phones to be impossible luxuries. But back then phones only worked in the cities, and the Herero and others who wore them so prominently on their belts outside of town did so only to impress their peers or persuade eligible young women that they were going places. When night fell at Skoonheid or Tsumkwe, the nocturnal soundscape was made up of laughter, chatter, arguments, the hooting of owls, the whir of insects, and the howls of jackals.

Now this soundscape is punctuated by the chirps of cell phones followed by often shouted conversations between phone owners unaccustomed to speaking at a normal volume to people who are far away. With wireless companies installing cell phone towers in remote areas across Namibia and developing special airtime packages to make phone ownership accessible to all but the very poorest, it is a technology that Ju/'hoansi have grasped with surprising speed. At more prosperous places like Skoonheid, there are fewer households without access to a cell phone than with access to one. And even in Nyae Nyae, while much fewer Ju/'hoansi own phones, and fewer still live close enough to the cell phone towers in Tsumkwe to get reception, there is a pervasive sense that these gadgets are now an essential part of life. Despite the fact that most adult Ju/'hoansi have no schooling, the semiotics of remembering a phone number and the routine menus of cell phones pose surprisingly few problems. They do, however, affect the choice of phone. In Gobabis a Chinese phone that costs as much as a large bag of maize porridge and has a rechargeable flashlight built in is by far the most popular.

Five years ago, if I needed to ask a friend in Tsumkwe or Skoonheid a question, it involved a complicated relay of person-to-person messages or traveling several days to get there. Now, sitting in my office in Cambridge, I text them, call them, or, in some cases, message them on Facebook. What is more, there is a small but growing presence of young (mostly male) San from both Botswana and Namibia on various forms of social media. Some use it as a political platform. But most, like their contemporaries in places like the United States, use social media to share selfies, post links that reaffirm their worldviews, and laugh at video clips of cats.

For these young men and women the idea of sharing their lives on the Web is not as big a leap as it may at first seem. Among foraging Ju/'hoansi there was no such thing as public space, just as there was no such thing as private space. Almost all social life took place in the open. Everybody in a band knew everybody else's business. Even now Ju/'hoansi in permanent settlements live most of their lives in public. Their huts or houses, if they have them, are used for little more than storing clothes and other valuables. For younger people having to cope with education systems and jobs that place such an emphasis on working alone, the digital community provides some comfort.

With some young Ju/'hoansi embracing the digital revolution in a manner that a few years ago would have seemed unimaginable, it is no surprise to discover that there are no Old Time people like /Engn!au living in Kanaan. There are now just old people. The last generation of Ju/'hoansi in the Omaheke to experience life as hunters and gatherers has disappeared. And when I ask now about what the difference between New Time people and Old Time people is, I get the sense that I am increasingly regarded as an Old Time anthropologist. When I ask about the difference between Ju/'hoansi and others, the first thing I am told is that Ju/'hoansi are "poor" and others are "rich."

For the Ju/'hoansi, the old certainties that enabled their grandparents to live in the present have long gone. They now narrate their past as a story of marginalization that began with the theft of their ancestral lands. They are also now preoccupied by the future. Most Ju/'hoansi in Kanaan don't believe that their lives will change for the better, but they all have hope. Some of them recently moved to a new resettlement farm near Gobabis. Parents talk about what might be possible if their children are able to complete school, even if they don't know yet how to persuade them to stay there. They remind me that everyone in the world is a New Time person, because where parents once guided their children, now parents often depend on their children to guide and help them come to terms with new technologies and new ways of interacting.

And Ju/'hoan children dream of all sorts of things their parents didn't have. They dream of owning their own vehicles, having somewhere to call home, and always having food in their bellies. But they are not convinced that this will happen. The only thing they are certain of is that the world will be different ten years from now, just as things were different when their parents and their grandparents before them were young. For them impermanence, unpredictability, and change are imminent in almost every aspect of their lives.

If in becoming New Time people Ju/'hoansi have accepted that their lives are shaped by the unpredictable eddies and currents of an ever-changing world, then they might take some comfort in the idea that we are on the cusp of a new age in which we will no longer be hostage to the economic problem and in which the productive mind-set that the Neolithic Revolution nurtured will no longer be fit for purpose. Doing so will require that we learn to be more like the Ju/'hoansi's immediate ancestors, embrace the affluence we have created, and recognize value in things other than our labor. Working a whole lot less might well be a good place to start. And it may well be that millennials—a group in the first world who have known nothing but abundance and who seem increasingly inclined to seek out work that they love rather than persuade themselves to learn to love the work they find—will lead the way in doing this.

Further Reading

The most interesting and up-to-date material on subjects raised in this book appears in academic journals publishing original research. In the age of Internet connectivity it is easy enough to track down and access good research even if it is sometimes shoved behind paywalls. The further reading suggested here is for the most part widely available and accessible to a general rather than an academic audience. I've organized it into broad subject areas loosely aligned to key themes in the book.

Keynes's Utopia and the Original Affluent Society

John Maynard Keynes's vision for an economic Utopia forms part of a large corpus of written work and commentary by arguably the most illustrious economist of his generation. "The Economic Possibilities for Our Grandchildren," published as part of an anthology (John Maynard Keynes, *Essays in Persuasion*, New York: W. W. Norton, 1963, pp. 358–73), it has only recently begun to receive much serious attention. Robert and Edward Skidelsky's *How Much Is Enough?: Money and the Good Life* (New York: Other Press, 2012; New York: Penguin Books, 2013) offers a good introduction to Keynes's optimistic vision for the future and offers some interesting ideas on how we might achieve something resembling it.

A dig through any anthropological library will reveal a substantial literature dealing with "primitive affluence." Even if the idea is no longer embraced as enthusiastically as it once was in mainstream social anthropology, Marshall Sahlins's *Stone Age Economics* (New York: de Gruyter, 1972), remains as compelling as it was at the time of its publication. Sahlins is one of cultural anthropology's most insightful meta-theorists. A cursory Internet search will reveal how widely Sahlins's ideas have been appropriated by all sorts of different groups, from "primitivists" idolizing our Paleolithic pasts to New Age economists.

Among the more interesting recent anthropological contributions to the discussion on primitive affluence are David Kaplan's **"The Darker Side of the 'Original Affluent Society,'"** published in the *Journal of Anthropological Research* 56, no. 3 (Autumn 2000): 301–24, and Nurit Bird-David's essay **"Beyond 'The Original Affluent Society': A Culturalist Reformulation,"** *Current Anthropology* 33, no. 1 (February 1992): 25–47.

Anthropological Literature on the Bushmen

It has often been joked that more academic articles and books have been written on the Bushmen than there are Bushmen alive. While this is, of course, hyperbole, the academic literature on the Bushmen is almost uniquely rich and has generated an enormous amount of secondary commentary.

Much early anthropology on the Bushmen was shaped more by colonial prejudices than any sustained engagement with Bushman populations. Isaac Schapera, an anthropologist at the London School of Economics, produced the first comprehensive anthropological overview of the Bushmen in his book *The Khoisan Peoples of South Africa: Bushmen and Hottentots* (London: Routledge, 1930). The book is somewhat dated and hard to get hold of outside of academic libraries. But it has some wonderful pictures and is in itself a fascinating milestone in anthropology's evolution.

A much more useful overview of the various Khoisan peoples is Alan Barnard's *Hunters and Herders of Southern Africa: A Comparative Ethnography of the Khoisan Peoples* (Cambridge, UK: Cambridge University Press, 1992). It documents what Barnard refers to as "deep structural" linguistic and cultural continuities among the various Khoisan peoples. Another of Barnard's works worth mentioning is a volume he produced documenting the history of anthropological research among Bushmen, *Anthropology and the Bushman* (Oxford, UK: Berg, 2007). For those interested in a broad overview of all major anthropological work on Bushmen up to 2006 and the big debates in the field of Bushman anthropology, Barnard's work is an invaluable introduction. It also includes a massive bibliography.

Mathias Guenther's *Tricksters and Trancers: Bushman Religion and Society* (Bloomington: Indiana University Press, 2000) also deals with

Bushmen as a broader cultural group. It's a rich and detailed synthesis of Bushman religious beliefs and ritual distilled from his own research and an exhaustive review of the academic literature. It is dense, thorough, and intellectually challenging.

Most of the classic ethnographies on Bushmen have focused on the Ju/'hoansi (as detailed below). There are a few notable exceptions, none more so than George Silberbauer's monograph of the G/wikhoe of the Central Kalahari Game Reserve in Botswana, *Hunter and Habitat in the Central Kalahari Desert* (Cambridge, UK: Cambridge University Press, 1981). Silberbauer spent more time living and working in the field than any other twentieth-century Bushman ethnographer and did so in one of the toughest and driest parts of the Kalahari in part in the capacity of the Bechuanaland Protectorate's "Bushman survey officer." It is my favorite ethnography.

The Ju/'hoansi

Richard B. Lee's *The Dobe Ju/'hoansi* (Belmont, CA: Wadsworth, 2013) was originally published under the title *The Dobe !Kung*. Lee has updated and revised it periodically since it was first published in 1984. It is now in its fourth edition and remains a staple of undergraduate anthropology courses. Distilled from a larger, wordier monograph—*The !Kung San: Men, Women, and Work in a Foraging Society* (Cambridge, UK: Cambridge University Press, 1979)—it is an accessible and articulate introduction to the Ju/'hoansi's traditional hunting and gathering way of life as well as the transitions they have had to endure over the last half century. Lee writes with a clarity that is rare in anthropology. The book is rightly considered a classic.

Lorna Marshall's two ethnographies on the Ju/'hoansi, *The !Kung of Nyae Nyae* (Cambridge, MA: Harvard University Press, 1976) and *Nyae Nyae Kung: Beliefs and Rites* (Cambridge, MA: Peabody Museum of Archaeology and Ethnology, 1999), also occupy a special place in the anthropological canon. While her writing is more workmanlike than Lee's, as an ethnographic record of Ju/'hoan life in Nyae Nyae before they came into sustained contact with others, her books are without equal.

A general introduction to the varied work of the Harvard Kalahari Research Group (and some others) is *Kalahari Hunter-Gatherers: Studies of the !Kung San and Their Neighbors*, edited by Richard B. Lee and Irven DeVore (Cambridge, MA: Harvard University Press, 1976). It includes essays by different researchers covering many aspects of Ju/'hoan life, including early child development, spatial organization, and animal behavior.

A member of the original Harvard team, Megan Biesele still works in the Kalahari. Rated locally as one of the best Ju/'hoan speakers in the anthropological community (I am rated among the worst), she is best known for her monograph on folklore and religious practice, **Women Like Meat: The Folklore and Foraging Ideology of the Kalahari Ju/'hoan** (Johannesburg: University of the Witwatersrand Press, 1993). It is a complex book dealing with a complex subject but well worth the effort of reading for those keen to get a sense of the Ju/'hoansi's cosmic landscape. Another of Biesele's books, **Healing Makes Our Hearts Happy: Spirituality & Cultural Transformation Among the Kalahari Ju/'hoansi** (New York: Simon & Schuster, 1997), coauthored by Richard Katz and Verna St. Denis, shows how traditional shamanic practices have assisted the Ju/'hoansi to make sense of the changing world around them and is a testament to how cultural forms can be reimagined and reinvigorated to cope with changing circumstances.

For those interested in Nyae Nyae's history, Robert Hitchock and Megan Biesele's jointly authored **The Ju/'Hoan San of Nyae Nyae and Namibian Independence: Development, Democracy, and Indigenous Voices in Southern Africa** (New York: Berghahn, 2010) provides a no-frills overview of the recent history of Nyae Nyae and the evolution of Ju/'hoan community organizations.

One of the most unusual but most illuminating of the books on the Ju/'hoansi is Marjorie Shostak's **Nisa: The Life and Words of a !Kung Woman** (New York: Vintage, 1983). *Nisa* is a biographical ethnography charting a Ju/'hoan woman's life through the period of extraordinary change visited on the Ju/'hoansi during the late twentieth century. Shostak also wrote an intensely personal sequel, **Return to Nisa** (Cambridge, MA: Harvard University Press, 2000), published posthumously. It documents a journey to reconnect with Nisa in 1991 after Shostack was diagnosed with the breast cancer that would claim her life in 1996.

Popular Books on Bushmen

The popular literature on Bushmen and Ju/'hoansi is more substantial than Laurence van der Post's various works, like *The Lost World of the Kalahari* and *The Heart of the Hunter*, and Elizabeth Marshall Thomas's *The Harmless People* and *The Old Way*.

The veteran UK journalist Sandy Gall published a sober account of the historical tribulations of southern Africa, *The Bushmen of Southern Africa: Slaughter of the Innocent* (London: Pimlico, 2001). Documenting a research trip he undertook in the late 1990s in which I introduced him to the likes of Old /Engn!au and !A/ae Langman, he draws heavily on the excellent historical work by the likes of Robert Gordon and others to produce an eloquent history of the Bushmen's dispossession combined with some contemporary reportage.

Few other popular books on the Bushmen have managed to reproduce either the poetry and eloquence of van der Post's work or the sensitivity and empathy of Elizabeth Marshall Thomas's. An exception to this rule—because it combines the poetry of van der Post with the honesty and empathy of Marshall Thomas—is Willemien Le Roux's *Shadow Bird* (Roggebaai, SA: Kwela Books, 2000). Le Roux grew up in the Kalahari and spent all of her adult life with Bushmen in Botswana's Ghanzi District, the Okavango Delta, and beyond. *Shadow Bird* is a partially biographical collection of short stories, each based on the lives and stories of the people she lived and worked with. It is gritty, perceptive, empathetic, and beautifully written.

With much of her life's work focused on helping Bushmen find their own voices and represent themselves, Le Roux was also the driving force behind the development of the cultural and oral history book *Voices of the San* (Roggebaai, SA: Kwela Books, 2004), coedited with Alison White; it is a compilation of hundreds of commentaries made by individual Bushmen from a range of language communities, organized thematically and combined with photography and artwork documenting their lives and history.

Perhaps the only other book by an anthropologist working with Bushmen that carries real emotional weight was penned by Hans Joachim Heinz, a notorious philanderer (at one time he was married to three women while living with a fourth), former (and much reformed) Nazi soldier, entomologist, and anthropologist. The story of his love affair with a !Xo woman, Namkwa—*Namkwa: Life Among the Bushmen* (Boston: Houghton Mifflin, 1979)—is poignant, honest, and vivid. I became friends with Heinz when he was in his eighties and over the course of three years filmed hours of interviews with him. He was hacked to death in 2001 while he slept on the verandah of his small house on the banks of the Thamalakane River near Maun in Botswana.

Representing Themselves: San Writers

Perhaps the most obvious omission in the vast literature on San are San writers. This is primarily a function of the fact that literacy levels in San communities remain very low as a result of an education system that makes few accomodations for the particular needs of San learners. Be that as it may, every year even more San manage to make it through school and some through university. Some have written about San issues in academic publications and coauthored papers with others. Only one, to my knowledge, has written a book: Kuela Kiema, a Kua from Botswana—*Tears for My Land: A Social History of the Kua of the Central Kalahari Game Reserve, Tc'amnqoo* (Gabarone, Botswana: Mmegi Publishing House, 2010). It's worth a read but very hard to get hold of, having only been distributed locally in Botswana. Recently Job Morris, a young San activist from Ghanzi in Botswana, led a collaborative initiative to develop the San Youth Network (https://sanyouthnetwork.wordpress.com), an online initiative through which young San activists contribute articles on matters relevant to them.

There are also numerous development reports, maps, and oral history databases to which San have contributed directly, as well as volumes of oral history, like *Voices of the San*. Many of these have emerged out of development partnerships like the Kuru Family of Organizations, the Kalahari Peoples Fund, and the Nyae Nyae Development Foundation. Perhaps the richest recent tradition of self-representation among San comes in the form of artwork. San artists' work has been exhibited globally and now graces some of the world's premier exhibitions. Projects like the **Kuru Art Project** in D'kar, Botswana (http://www.kuruart.com) continue to produce—as they have since the early 1990s—works of great beauty and power from a wide range of San artists much more comfortable with artistic rather than written represention, producing a corpus of work that is articulate, cathartic, and empowering.

History, Archaeology, and the "Great Kalahari Debate"

The "Great Kalahari Debate" kicked off in 1989 following Edwin N. Wilmsen's publication of a long and complex book, **Land Filled with Flies: A Political Economy of the Kalahari** (Chicago: University of Chicago Press, 1989). A combative and difficult read, *Land Filled with Flies* argued that the work of Richard B. Lee and others was built on a foundation of sand. The publication of *Land Filled with Flies* kicked off a heated and often acrimonious debate that played out in the leading anthropology journal, *Current Anthropology*, over a number of years. Wilmsen accused Lee and colleagues of incompetence. Lee and colleagues in turn accused Wilmsen of exaggeration, willful misinterpretation, and fabrication. Readers interested in the debate would do well to skip the debate itself and read Alan Barnard's summary in *Anthropology and the Bushmen*. As controversial as it was, Wilmsen's work nevertheless brought a valuable new perspective to Bushman anthropology and encouraged researchers to pay more attention to the complex historical forces that shape the contemporary Bushmen's world.

Perhaps the most important work to emerge in the wake of the debate was Robert Gordon's **The Bushman Myth: The Making of a Namibian Underclass** (Boulder: Westview, 2000), coauthored in its second edition by Stuart Sholto Douglas. It is a grueling and dispiriting read, as it documents in often terrifying detail the brutality suffered by Bushmen in Namibia and beyond at the hands of others.

For a simpler and less harrowing but no less thorough historical overview of Bushman history, see **The Bushmen of Southern Africa: A Foraging Society in Transition** (Athens, OH: Ohio University Press, 2000), coauthored by Andy Smith, Candy Malherbe, Mat Guenther, and Penny Berens.

Rock Art

Bushman rock art has inspired a substantial literature. David Lewis-Williams is almost certainly the best-known writer in the field. He was the first academic to argue that Bushman rock art was not crudely representational but formed part of a rich symbolic tradition. He has written many books. Of them the best introductions to his approach are the recently published *The Mind in the Cave: Consciousness and the Origins of Art* (London: Thames & Hudson, 2004) and a pocket guide, *San Rock Art* (Auckland Park, SA: Jacana, 2011).

For those interested in looking at the art itself, Patricia Vinnicombe's very expensive *People of the Eland* (Johannesburg: Wits University Press, 1976) is a good place to start, even if it is very heavily focused on South African rather than Namibian rock art.

Tsodilo Hills is now a world heritage site and much more accessible than it was just over a decade ago. Much writing on Tsodilo is confined to sometimes obscure academic journals. Fortunately a recent volume, coauthored by Alec Campbell, Larry Robbins, and Michael Taylor, *Tsodilo Hills: Copper Bracelet of the Kalahari* (Lansing: Michigan State University Press, 2012) offers a wonderful introduction to the archaeology of the Hills. It also serves as a guide for those wishing to explore the hills for themselves.

Human Origins and Genetics

Despite the Khoisan's unique interest to geneticists, no books have yet synthesized the ever-growing corpus of genetic work on them over the last decade. But this is not to say that there is very little information out there. While the majority of important discoveries and hypotheses have been published in major journals like *Nature* or *Science* and ever more on open-access platforms, they have also been widely picked up in mainstream publications from popular science magazines to newspapers. For those interested in following up on this, a number of papers by the leading genetic researchers in the field have been referenced in the endnotes—people like Professor Sarah Tishkoff at the University of Pennsylvania and Carina Schlebusch at Uppsala University.

There is, however, a growing popular literature looking more broadly at human evolution and the extraordinary new insights offered by advances in genetic research. Perhaps the best known are Stephen Oppenheimer's *Out of Eden: The Peopling of the World* (London: Constable & Robinson,

2004) and Spencer Wells's *The Journey of Man: A Genetic Odyssey* (New York: Random House, 2003). Both are excellent introductions, although, with genomic research moving so fast, these are both already a little out of date.

Martin Meredith (a historian and journalist rather than a geneticist) recently published ***Born in Africa: The Quest for the Origins of Human Life*** (New York: PublicAffairs, 2011). It is relatively up-to-date and very accessible.

For those interested in hunting and the role of meat and fire in human evolution, Richard Wrangham's monograph ***Catching Fire: How Cooking Made Us Human*** (New York: Basic, 2009) is a fun and provocative read. Plenty has been written about the role of hunting in human development. Robert Ardrey's ***The Hunting Hypothesis: A Personal Conclusion Concerning the Evolutionary Nature of Man*** (New York: Atheneum, 1976), while dated, outlines the main ideas still shaping research in the field today. Donna Hart and Robert W. Sussman offer an interesting counterperspective on the human-as-hunter evolutionary narrative in ***Man the Hunted: Primates, Predators, and Human Evolution*** (Cambridge, MA: Westview, 2005). They argue that our experience as prey rather than as hunters or scavengers shaped who we are today.

There is surprisingly little written by anthropologists about what hunters do and feel when they hunt. A committed hunter, Rane Willerslev's ***Soul Hunters: Hunting, Animism, and Personhood Among the Siberian Yukaghirs*** (Berkeley: University of California Press, 2007) offers a unique insight into Siberian hunters' empathetic relationships with their prey. It also offers readers a sense of how the practice of living off the land shapes people's sense of self and the world around them.

Louis Leibenberg, a South African evolutionary biologist, has dedicated much of his life to studying tracking. His book ***The Art of Tracking: The Origin of Science*** (Cape Town: New Africa Books, 2012) articulates his belief that speculative hypotheses about animal behavior inferred from tracks demand the same intellectual and creative skills needed to be a physicist or a mathematician. The book, which includes some of Liebenberg's own painstakingly detailed artwork, is a refreshing take on a subject as old as our species. It is available free on the website of his organization, CyberTracker.org.

The Neolithic Revolution

The Neolithic Revolution not only created work for farmers but also jobs for writers, many of whom have written extensively about the extraordinary transformations wrought by the transition to farming. Like the literature on ancient hunter-gatherers, many of the "big ideas" about the Neolithic Revolution were developed without the benefit of contemporary genetic studies. For those seeking the most up-to-date work, it will be necessary to browse the academic journals.

Perhaps the most famous recent work on the impact of the Neolithic Revolution is Jared Diamond's much-vaunted *Guns, Germs, and Steel: The Fates of Human Societies* (New York: W. W. Norton, 1999). He described the Neolithic as "the worst mistake in the history of the human race." More recently Diamond published *The World Until Yesterday: What Can We Learn from Traditional Societies?* (New York: Penguin, 2012), in which he compares "tribal" peoples' lifeways with those of "modern" peoples. The book is typically broad-ranging and explores matters from violence to obesity. While it has much of merit, his distinction between tribal and modern societies is too general for most anthropologists and a number of his assertions don't mesh, in particular with evidence on hunter-gatherers and farmers. It is still a worthwhile read.

Others, like Yuval Noah Harari in his recent bestseller *Sapiens: A Brief History of Humankind* (New York: HarperCollins, 2015), have taken a similar line to Diamond in *Guns, Germs, and Steel*, casting the Neolithic Revolution as an inevitable if unfortunate turn in our collective history.

Stephen Mithen's weighty but readable *After the Ice: A Global Human History, 20,000–5000 BC* (London: Weidenfeld & Nicolson, 2003), offers an insight into the factors that likely drove the Neolithic Revolution. It's also a treasure trove of interesting historical detours.

While not particularly rigorous scientifically, Calvin Martin Luther's eulogy to hunter-gatherers, *In the Spirit of the Earth: Rethinking History and Time* (Baltimore: Johns Hopkins University Press, 1993), is one of the most poetic and engaging invocations of the implications of the transition from hunting and gathering to farming on our species. Another similarly poetic and important work is Hugh Brody's *The Other Side of Eden:*

Hunters, Farmers, and the Shaping of the World (New York: North Point, 2000), which addresses the question of how hunters and gatherers ended up losing out to farmers. The book draws heavily on Brody's own substantial work among the Inuit.

Exchange and Sharing

Anthropologists have long been fascinated by exchange and sharing. It has been one of anthropology's most productive specializations, resulting in some truly original work.

The hypothesis of delayed- and immediate-return economies was developed by the now retired London School of Economics and Political Science professor James Woodburn. His ideas are neatly captured in his essay **"Egalitarian Societies,"** published in *Man, the Journal of the Royal Anthropological Institute* 17, no. 3 (September 1982): 431–51. Another very good essay reflecting on hunter-gatherer egalitarianism is Richard B. Lee's **"Reflections on Primitive Communism,"** published in *Hunters and Gatherers*, vol. 1: *History, Evolution and Social Change* (Oxford, UK: Berg, 1988), edited by Tim Ingold, David Riches, and James Woodburn.

Of all the anthropologists to have worked with Ju/'hoansi, Polly Wiessner has produced the most sophisticated work on exchange. She was also responsible for unlocking some of the systematic mysteries of the *hxaro* gift system. Wiessner is the most prominent of the researchers to have worked among Ju/'hoansi, one whom the rest of the anthropological community wish had written a full ethnography. Regrettably, her work is also only available in academic journals, although there are plenty of references to it in anthropology textbooks and course materials. A good introduction to her work is an essay titled **"Risk, Reciprocity and Social Influences on !Kung San Economics"** that she published in *Politics and History in Band Societies* (Cambridge, UK: Cambridge University Press, 1982), edited by Eleanor Leacock and Richard B. Lee.

Current Issues

There is no single publication available for those interested in keeping up to date with current issues faced by Bushmen. San in both Namibia and

Botswana remain the worst of all the region's peoples by a significant margin on pretty much every available indicator. But, more so than ever before, Bushman-related issues now reach the national press through English newspapers like the *Namibian* in Namibia and *Mmegi* in Botswana that are available online and have searchable archives.

In addition to newspaper reports, there is a fairly substantial academic and applied literature dealing with issues including land rights, social discrimination, education, and development. Among the anthropological community, Robert Hitchcock has the most illustrious applied publication record.

Another excellent resource on contemporary issues is the NGOs working with San communities and organizations. The Legal Assistance Centre (LAC) in Namibia is now the most active following the effective collapse of the San organizations that blossomed during the late 1990s. The Land, Environment & Development Project has conducted numerous studies available on the LAC website (http://www.lac.org.na/pub/publications.php). These include the European Commission study that I led between 1998 and 2001, *The Regional Assessment of the Status of the San in Southern Africa*. It's the most comprehensive study of its kind, taking three years to complete and conducted in six different countries. It is long and often technical but very informative if now a little dated. A very detailed update of the Namibia volume edited by my colleague and friend Ute Dieckmann was published in 2013 and is also available free on the LAC website.

The most widely covered issue facing Bushmen in the last twenty years was the illegal relocation of G/wikhoe, G//anakhoe, and Bakgalagadi from Botswana's vast Central Kalahari Game Reserve. The publicity generated by this event hinged almost entirely on the efforts of the UK campaign organization Survival International. It's a long and complex story and at its roots lie the forceful and paternalistic approach taken by the Botswanan government to its Bushman citizens. A great deal has been written on the issue in both the academic and mainstream media. A particularly good overview was written by Julie Taylor, then a doctoral student. It includes references to many other articles that interested readers may wish to follow up on. See Julie Taylor, **"Celebrating San Victory too Soon?: Reflections on the Outcome of the Central Kalahari Game Reserve Case,"** *Anthropology Today* 23, no. 5 (October 2007): 3–5.

Kalahari Geology, Ecology, and Geography

The Kalahari and the Okavango Delta are the subjects of numerous coffee-table books replete with images of swirling dunes, charging elephants, and dust-caked lions. They are also the subject of hundreds if not thousands of technical surveys, Ph.D. theses, and articles by geologists, students, environmentalists, and others. Remarkably, though, there are few major publications that deal with the Kalahari's geological or environmental history as a whole. For those interested in the geology and geography of the Kalahari, David S. G. Thomas and Paul A. Shaw's *The Kalahari Environment* (Cambridge, UK: Cambridge University Press, 1991) is the best place to start.

There is a growing and ever more detailed literature on indigenous plant use in southern Africa. Sadly, much of it is confined to esoteric journals and research by those seeking to commercialize the trade in some of these resources. An exception to this is Arno Leffers's *Gemsbok Bean & Kalahari Truffle: Traditional Plant Use by Ju/'hoansi in North-Eastern Namibia* (Windhoek: Gamsberg Macmillan, 2003). It's a beautifully presented compendium of the various plants commonly used by Ju/'hoansi.

Namibian History

Since independence in 1990, Namibia's historiography has grown massively. Numerous monographs and articles have been published, in particular with regard to its recent colonial past. Marion Wallace and John Kinahan's *A History of Namibia: From the Beginning to 1990* (New York: Columbia University Press, 2011) offers a lucid and engaging overview of Namibian history from prehistoric times to the postcolonial era and provides a wealth of references for those interested in reading further.

For those interested in Namibia's early colonial history, David Olusoga and Casper W. Erichsen's *The Kaiser's Holocaust: Germany's Forgotten Genocide and the Colonial Roots of Nazism* (London: Faber & Faber, 2010) provides a harrowing account of the first genocide of the twentieth century.

Film and Photography

Bushmen and Ju/'hoansi in particular have been popular filmic subjects ever since Laurens van der Post's six-part series, *The Lost World of the*

Kalahari, was first broadcast on the BBC in 1956. And as with some popular literature, the fantasy has often appealed far more to filmmakers than the sometimes gritty reality of contemporary life for many Bushmen. I have advised on, watched, or winced through a number of documentaries that were unapologetic in their presentation of a mythical Bushman world.

John Marshall's magnum opus, *A Kalahari Family* (2001), is nothing short of epic. It adds a powerful, visceral, and sensitive parallel narrative that breathes life into his mother's and sister's work. The film is accessible through academic institutions and is available for purchase (for an eye-wateringly expensive sum) at Documentary Education Resources (www.der.org).

The Foster Brothers Productions film *The Great Dance: A Hunter's Story* (2000) focuses on !Xo hunters in the south-central Kalahari in Botswana. It beautifully documents a hunt by running and captures the extraordinary empathy between hunter and hunted. It is so eloquently filmed that the sometimes bizarre commentary only marginally detracts from the movie as a whole.

Bushmen are a staple of safari lodge–style coffee-table books and glossy posed postcards in southern Africa. This mythology still clearly sells well. Most of the commercial images of them available online—hunting and gathering in traditional gear—are staged and lifeless, although they are evidently still in demand. Be that as it may, there are some wonderful photographic books about Bushmen by journalists and others. Paul Weinberg, a South African photographer, documented life in Nyae Nyae on and off and produced a powerful photographic record of a period of tremendous change; some of the images are included in this book. Weinberg has published his photos in several different volumes and exhibited them widely. Weinberg's *Once We Were Hunters: A Journey with Africa's Indigenous People* (Amsterdam: Mets & Schilt, 2000) and a more recent retrospective, *Traces and Tracks* (Johannesburg: Jacana Media, 2017) contains much of his best work. Work by some other photographers—like Adrian Arbib, who contributed some pictures for this book—are only available online but well worth looking up (http://arbib.photoshelter.com/gallery-collection/Namibia-San-Bushmen/C0000_nDaC.4Qsdg).

Acknowledgments

There are too many people—Ju/'hoansi, colleagues, friends, Namibian officials, family, and others—who have helped one way or another in shaping the ideas presented in this book for me to thank them individually. To all of you, I hope that the book does sufficient justice to your assistance. Failing that, I will buy you a drink.

Others have helped in the immediate challenges of turning a series of disparate ideas into an actual book. I'm especially grateful to Olivia Judson for assisting me to develop the initial proposal; Fleur de Villiers for her forthright advice; Michelle Fava for the wonderful maps and encouragement; and my parents for their help with the manuscript. I'm also grateful to the editorial team at Bloomsbury, as well as my literary agency, Greene & Heaton in London. I also owe a debt of gratitude to Megan Laws, Adrian Arbib, Sheila Coulsen, and Paul Weinberg for granting me permission to use some of their beautiful photographs.

Finally—and even if some of them don't want my gratitude—I offer my eternal thanks to the many San who have not only tolerated my presence and nagging questions over the past twenty-five years, but who also embraced me as a friend and welcomed me as a neighbor.

Notes

Chapter 1: The Rewards of Hard Work

1 All quotes by Keynes in this chapter are from his essay "The Economic Possibilities for Our Grandchildren" published in J. M. Keynes, *Essays in Persuasion* (New York: W. W. Norton, 1963), 358–73.
2 Richard B. Lee and Irven DeVore, *Man the Hunter* (Chicago: Aldine, 1968).
3 Richard B. Lee, *The !Kung San: Men, Women and Work in a Foraging Society* (Cambridge, UK: Cambridge University Press, 1979).
4 Sherwood Washburn, foreword to Richard B. Lee and Irven DeVore, eds., *Kalahari Hunter-Gatherers: Studies of the !Kung San and Their Neighbors* (Cambridge, MA: Harvard University Press, 1978).

Chapter 2: The Mother Hill

1 Joseph K. Pickrell, Nick Patterson, Chiara Barbieri, Falko Berthold, Linda Gerlach, Tom Güldemann, Blesswell Kure, Sununguko Wata Mpoloka, Hirosi Nakagawa, Christfried Naumann, Mark Lipson, Po-Ru Loh, Joseph Lachance, Joanna Mountain, Carlos D. Bustamante, Bonnie Berger, Sarah A. Tishkoff, Brenna M. Henn, Mark Stoneking, David Reich, and Brigitte Pakendorf, "The Genetic Prehistory of Southern Africa." *Nature Communications* 3, article no. 1143 (October 16, 2012): 114; doi:10.1038/ncomms2140.
2 Hie Lim Kim, Aakrosh Ratan, George H. Perry, Alvaro Montenegro, Webb Miller, and Stephan C. Schuster, "Khoisan Hunter-Gatherers Have Been the Largest Population Throughout Most of Modern-Human Demographic History." *Nature Communications* 5, article no. 5692 (December 4, 2014).

Chapter 3: A Beachside Brawl

1 E. G. Ravenstein, trans., *A Journal of the First Voyage of Vasco da Gama* (Cambridge, MA: Cambridge University Press, 2010), 1497–99.
2 Adam Smith, *An Inquiry into the Nature and Causes of the Wealth of Nations*, vol. 1 (London: W. Strahan, 1776).

Chapter 4: The Settlers

1 Noel Mostert, *Frontiers* (London: Jonathan Cape, 1992), 110.
2 R. Raven-Hart, *The Cape of Good Hope, 1652–1702: The First Fifty Years of Dutch Colonisation as Seen by Callers* (Cape Town: A. A. Balkema, 1971), 205.
3 Mostert, *Frontiers*, 115.
4 Ibid., 117.
5 Ibid., 118.
6 Robert Moffat, *Missionary Labours and Scenes in Southern Africa* (New York: Robert Carter, 1843), 54, 59.
7 Thomas Smith and John O. Choules, *The Origin and History of Missions: A Record of the Voyages, Travels, Labors, and Successes of the Various Missionaries Who Have Been Sent Forth by Protestant Societies and Churches to Evangelize the Heathen* (New York: Robert Carter, 1846).
8 James Chapman, *Travels in the Interior of South Africa Comprising Fifteen Years' Hunting and Trading; with Journeys Across the Continent from Natal to Walvis Bay, and Visits to Lake Ngami and the Victoria Falls* (London: Bell and Daldy, 1868).
9 *Beeld* (newspaper), Johannesburg, March 27, 1994.

Chapter 5: Living in the Moment

1 James Woodburn, "Egalitarian Societies." *Man, the Journal of the Royal Anthropological Institute* 17, no. 3 (1982): 431–51.

Chapter 6: Tsumkwe Road

1 Schoeman, undated memorandum, Namibian National Archives.

Chapter 8: Strong Food

1 Also known as the mongongo tree, the manketti (*Schinziophyton rautanenii*) grows well in semiarid temperate areas across central southern Africa. It is unusually prolific in the northern Kalahari.
2 According to a study conducted by Imperial College London in 2015, obesity rates worldwide tripled between 1975 and 2014 and the total number of obese people worldwide rose more than sixfold, from 105 million in 1975 to 641 million in 2014. The study also found that obesity has a correspondence with wealth. Obesity rates are highest in the world's richest country, the United States, where more people are clinically obese than are of a healthy weight and over two-thirds of the population (68.6 percent in 2011, according to the World Health Organization) are overweight. The World Health Organization also notes that even though Europeans are less likely to be obese than their friends on the other side of the Atlantic, obesity levels have grown at a similarly gut-busting rate there: around half of all Europeans are now overweight and around one in five are clinically obese. See M. di Cesare, J. Bentham, G. H. Stevens, B. Zhou, G. Danaei et al., "Trends in Adult Body-Mass Index in 200

Countries from 1975 to 2014: A Pooled Analysis of 1698 Population-Based Measurement Studies with 19.2 Million Participants." *Lancet* 387, no. 10026 (April 2, 2016): 1377–96.

3   Herman Pontzer, David A. Raichlen, Brian M. Wood, Audax Z. P. Mabulla, Susan B. Racette, and Frank W. Marlowe, "Hunter-Gatherer Energetics and Human Obesity." *PLOS ONE* 7 (July 2012): e40503; doi:10.1371/journal .pone.0040503.

4   Polly Wiessner, *Population, Subsistence and Social Networks Among the Ju/'hoansi (!Kung) Bushman: A Twenty-Five-Year Perspective.* Unpublished manuscript, Windhoek, June 1998.

Chapter 9: An Elephant Hunt

1   Galton and Andersson's African adventures are described in Galton's *Narrative of an Explorer in Tropical South Africa* (London: John Murray, 1853), which is freely available online, as well as Andersson's "Explorations in South Africa, with Route from Walfisch Bay to Lake Ngami," published in *Journal of the Royal Geographical Society of London* 25, no. 25 (1855): 79–107, and in Andersson's book *Lake Ngami: or, Explorations and Discoveries, During Four Years' Wanderings in the Wilds of South Western Africa* (New York: Harper & Brothers, 1856).

2   David S. G. Thomas and Paul A. Shaw, *The Kalahari Environment* (Cambridge, UK: Cambridge University Press, 2010), 214.

3   Noel Mostert, *Frontiers* (London: Jonathan Cape, 1992), 113.

4   David Livingstone, *Missionary Travels and Researches in South Africa* (London: John Murray, 1912), chapter 8.

Chapter 10: Pinnacle Point

1   Kyle S. Brown, Curtis W. Marean, Zenobia Jacobs, Benjamin J. Schoville, Simen Oestmo, Erich C. Fisher, Jocelyn Bernatchez, Panagiotis Karkanas, and Thalassa Matthews, "An Early and Enduring Advanced Technology Originating 71,000 Years Ago in South Africa." *Nature* 491 (November 22, 2012): 590–93; doi:10 .1038/nature11660.

2   Ibid.

3   Lucinda Backwell, Francesco d'Errico, and Lyn Wadley, "Middle Stone Age Bone Tools from the Howiesons Poort Layers, Sibudu Cave, South Africa," *Journal of Archaeological Science* 35, no. 6 (June 2008): 1566–80. Marlize Lombard, "Quartz-Tipped Arrows Older than 60 ka: Further Use-Trace Evidence from Sibudu, KwaZulu-Natal, South Africa." *Journal of Archaeological Science* 38, no. 8 (August 2011): 1918–30.

4   Peter Mitchell, "San Origins and Transition to the Later Stone Age: New Research from Border Cave, South Africa." *Southern African Journal of Science* 108, nos. 11–12 (December 2011): 5–7.

5   C. S. Chaboo, M. Biesele, R. K. Hitchcock, and A. Weeks, "Beetle and Plant Arrow Poisons of the Ju/'hoan and Hai//om San Peoples of Namibia (Insecta, Coleoptera, Chrysomelidae; Plantae, Anacardiaceae, Apocynaceae, Burseraceae)." *ZooKeys* 558 (February 1, 2016): 9–54.

Chapter 11: A Gift from God

1 Juli G. Pausas and Jon E. Keeley, "A Burning Story: The Role of Fire in the History of Life." *BioScience* 59, no. 7 (July 2009): 593–601; doi:10.1525/bio .2009.59.7.10.

2 Herman Pontzer, "Ecological Energetics in Early *Homo*." *Current Anthropology* 53, no. S6, Human Biology and the Origins of Homo (December 2012): S346–58.

3 As with so many other areas of human evolutionary research, genetic studies now offer new insights into the role of meat eating and cooking on human evolution. A recent study in comparative primate genomics shows that consumption of cooked food influences gene expression and that affected genes "bear signals of positive selection in the human lineage." This work suggests that the evolution of cooking-related genes was prevalent in early hominids, that it long predates the earliest clear archaeological evidence of cooking, and that it was likely to have played a significant role in the evolution of modern Homo sapiens. See Rachel N. Carmody, Michael Dannemann, Adrian W. Briggs, Birgit Nickel, Emily E. Groopman, Richard W. Wrangham, and Janet Kelso, "Genetic Evidence of Human Adaptation to a Cooked Diet." *Genome Biology and Evolution* 8, no. 4 (April 13, 2016): 1091–1103; doi:10.1093/gbe/evw059.

4 The Food and Agriculture Organization of the United Nations estimates that the meat industry generates nearly one-fifth of global greenhouse gas production and that around 40 percent of global grain production is used as livestock feed. It also points out that livestock and livestock feed occupy around one-third of the earth's ice-free land, transforming habitats and denying other species space to live. At the time of the Neolithic Revolution, the total biomass of all of the humans on the earth was 0.1 percent of 1 percent of all land-based mammalian biomass. Then, around two hundred years ago, humans and domestic livestock increased to between 10 and 12 percent of the total terrestrial mammalian biomass. Now it constitutes between 96 and 98 percent. See http://www.wwf .org.uk/what_we_do/changing_the_way_we_live/food/livestock_impacts.cfm.

5 L. Cordain, S. B. Eaton, J. Brand Miller, N. Mann, and K. Hill, "The Paradoxical Nature of Hunter-Gatherer Diets: Meat-Based, yet Non-Atherogenic." *European Journal of Clinical Nutrition* 56 (March 2002), Suppl. 1: S42–52.

Chapter 13: Insulting the Meat

1 Richard B. Lee, *The Dobe Ju/'hoansi*, 4th ed. (Belmont, CA: Wadsworth, 2013), 57.

2 In the UK household, poverty is officially defined as having an income of only 60 percent of the median income. Around the time of the Occupy protests, that was £14,000 ($23,000 USD) per annum. In Namibia that income would place a household comfortably in the emergent middle class. In the Central African Republic it would entitle you to be part of a small moneyed elite. So, while an income of £14,000 per year entails some hardship in the developed world, these hardships are relative rather than absolute.

Chapter 15: Fear and Farming

1   J. C. Berbesque, F. W. Marlowe, P. Shaw, and P. Thompson, "Hunter-Gatherers Have Less Famine than Agriculturalists." *Biology Letters* 10 (January 8, 2014); doi:10.1098/rsbl.2013.0853.

2   S. A. Elias and D. Schreve, "Late Pleistocene Megafaunal Extinctions." (Royal Holloway, University of London, Egham, UK, 2013). Elsevier B.V. All rights reserved.

3   Even low-grade agricultural land can now generate yields farmers would have considered inconceivable a century ago. The U.S. Department of Agriculture reports that by the turn of the new millennium the average milk cow in the United States produced almost two and a half times as much milk as the average milk cow did in 1950. They also report that over the same time period, corn yields per acre tripled. Even in the developing world, where there is a much higher proportion of subsistence farmers, crop yields have risen dramatically over the last three decades thanks to a range of technological developments. See the USDA website: http://www.ers.usda.gov/data-products/agricul tural-productivity-in-the-us/agricultural-productivity-in-the-us/#National %20Tables,%201948-2013.

4   J. C. Berbesque, F. M. Marlowe, P. Shaw, and P. Thompson, "Hunter-Gatherers Have Less Famine than Agriculturalists."

5   Stephen Shennan, Sean S. Downey, Adrian Timpson, Kevan Edinborough, Sue Colledge, Tim Kerig, Katie Manning, and Mark G. Thomas, "Regional Population Collapse Followed Initial Agriculture Booms in Mid-Holocene Europe." *Nature Communications* 4, article no. 2486 (2013); doi:10.1038/ncomms3486.

Chapter 16: Cattle Country

1   O. Mwai, O. Hanotte, Y-J. Kwon, and S. Cho, "African Indigenous Cattle: Unique Genetic Resources in a Rapidly Changing World." *Asian-Australasian Journal of Animal Sciences* 28, no. 7 (July 2015): 911–21.

2   E. Fernández, A. Pérez-Pérez, C. Gamba, E. Prats, P. Cuesta, J. Anfruns et al., "Ancient DNA Analysis of 8000 B.C. Near Eastern Farmers Supports an Early Neolithic Pioneer Maritime Colonization of Mainland Europe Through Cyprus and the Aegean Islands." *PLOS Genetics* 10, no. 6 (June 5, 2014): e1004401. H. Malmström, A. Linderholm, P. Skoglund, J. Storå, P. Sjödin, M. T. P. Gilbert, G. Holmlund, E. Willerslev, M. Jakobsson, K. Lidén, and A. Götherström, "Ancient Mitochondrial DNA from the Northern Fringe of the Neolithic Farming Expansion in Europe Sheds Light on the Dispersion Process." *Philosophical Transactions of the Royal Society B: Biological Sciences* 370, no. 1660 (January 19, 2015).

3   Per Sjödin, Himla Soodyall, and Mattias Jakobsson et al., "Lactase Persistence Alleles Reveal Partial East African Ancestry of Southern African Khoe Pastoralists." *Current Biology* 24, no. 8 (April 2014): 852–58.

4   J. Pickrell, N. Patterson, C. Barbieri, F. Berthold, L. Gerlach, T. Güldemann, B. Kure, S. W. Mpoloka, H. Nakagawa, C. Naumann et al., "The Genetic Prehistory of Southern Africa." *Nature Communications* 3, article no. 1143 (October 16, 2012): 114; doi:10.1038/ncomms2140.

5 Alberto Alesina, Paola Giuliano, and Nathan Nunn, "On the Origins of Gender Roles: Women and the Plough." *Quarterly Journal of Economics*, first published online February 19, 2013; doi:10.1093/qje/qjt005.

Chapter 17: Crazy Gods

1 In a reflection of the little care the filmmakers took with their star, he not only acted under a fictitious name but was credited as an actor under a name made up by Mimosa Films, "N!xau." In other published pieces he was sometimes referred to as Gcau Coma, (incorrectly) using the Zulu click orthography.
2 Richard B. Lee, "The Gods Must Be Crazy but the Producers Know Exactly What They Are Doing." *Southern Africa Report* (June 1985): 19–20.

Chapter 18: The Promised Land

1 Carl Benedikt Frey and Michael A. Osborne, "The Future of Employment: How Susceptible Are Jobs to Computerisation?" Oxford Martin Programme on the Impacts of Future Technology, September 17, 2013. http://www.oxford martin.ox.ac.uk/downloads/academic/The_Future_of_Employment.pdf.

Index

Note: Italic page numbers refer to maps.